how do I Look?

The Year I Stopped Shopping

by Inger D. Kenobi

First published in Great Britain 2016

Lion's Mane Publishing Ltd

www.lionsmanepublishing.com

A CIP catalogue record for this book

is available from the British Library

ISBN 978-0-9935744-0-5 Paperback

ISBN 978-0-9935744-2-9 eBook

Lion's Mane Publishing is proud to support The Woodland Trust,

the UK's leading woodland conservation charity

This book is dedicated to

Anna,

who encouraged me to
write it.

Introduction

or
How it all started

I was about to go to bed when the phone rang. I looked at the display; it was Amy. Amy and I have been best friends since, well - since forever.

'Hey Amy, what's up?'

'Listen, what do you say to a twelve-month shop-stop?'

Shop-stop? What was she talking about?

'OK, let me ask you this,' she continued. 'Do you know where your clothes are made?'

'Eh, no. Not really. Do you mean which country? India? No, wait! China!'

Was this a quiz?

'What if they're made in Bangladesh, in that factory that just burned to the ground?' she asked. 'I mean, what if your clothes were made by the people who died?'

I had read about the factory fire in the papers. Horrible as it was, I had written it off as something that had little or nothing to do with me.

'I guess it's possible,' I said. 'But how would I know for sure? It's not like it's printed on the label or anything.'

'That is precisely my point!'

'What is? I'm not following.'

'I'm saying that we have to stop buying clothes!' Amy continued. 'Since we don't know where our clothes are made, let's boycott them. I can't in good conscience keep supporting this industry, not until they clean up their act, whoever *they* turn out to be. Can you?'

'Well of course not...' I trailed off, digesting what she was saying. 'But a full on shop-stop? What would that even look like?'

She assured me that we could still buy food, books, plants, jewellery – anything at all really, just not clothes. Not new, not used, not even on sale. (Gulp!)

'Come on! It'll be fun! We'll be doing it together, our very own silent protest. And it's only for twelve months. What do you say?'

'If you put it like that...I mean...oh, what the heck! OK, I'm in! Let's do this!'

Hanging up the phone, I felt energised and excited.

First of all, this was for a good cause. Second of all, I had plenty of great clothes. I could easily go one lousy year without adding to the pile. And lastly, I do like a good challenge. Could this be any easier?

Except...I had a wedding coming up. Come to think of it, there were also vacations, birthday celebrations, maybe even a funeral. Could I really survive these events without buying anything new?

And then there was my job. I was working at the Norwegian Embassy in London. I was the personal secretary to the Ambassador; I was basically working at the White House. Could I really go a whole year without upgrading my work wardrobe?

A friend of mine followed a strict Weight Watchers regime. Her mantra was, 'If you bite it, your write it.' Keeping a food journal helped her stay focused and on track.

I decided to keep a journal too: 'If you don't buy it, you write it.' It sort of works, and what you are about to read are stories based on the written accounts of these twelve non-shopping months. The book is divided into twelve chapters, one for each month of the shop-stop.

I'm aware that many people will strongly disagree with the premise of this book. For them shopping is non-negotiable, like breathing. 'Why does it matter how or where our clothes are made?'

they might argue. 'It's a dress for Christ's sake, not a political prisoner. Get a life.'

All I can say is that my relationship with clothes profoundly changed once I stopped buying them. The shop-stop challenge became a mirror in which my vanity, insecurity, and ignorance were reflected back at me. It also highlighted how far off-base I was in regards to my own style and shopping habits. At times it felt as if I was fighting an invisible, yet powerful, opponent. Should I 'armour up' or surrender?

My strategy became to investigate everything, and to ask questions. Questions about myself, about the fast-fashion industry, and about the consumer culture we live in.

It is with this backdrop that I wrote this book. It captures a brief period of my life where even the smallest assumptions were turned upside down, and where the bigger pieces finally fell into place.

The most surprising outcome of this challenge was that the fewer clothes I had, the better I looked.

Go figure.

Chapter One
November, 2012

❝ The quickest way to get to know a woman is to go shopping with her. ❞
- Marcelene Cox

Here we go. This is my first month of not shopping. For the next twelve months I will not buy a single new outfit. I am not allowed to shop at a single store. I can't get any new clothes until next November. Wow! When you put it like that, it feels like a real David against Goliath scenario.

Actually, it doesn't feel like that at all. If anything, not shopping for a year feels totally normal. I'm still me, minus the ability to buy new clothes. How hard can it be? It's not like I've taken a vow of chastity or promised not to gossip. I don't know what I was so nervous about. Was I nervous? I can't remember.

I should introduce myself, but right now I just want you to know that I'm really thrilled you picked up this book and decided to go on this journey with me. I also want you to know that many of the topics in this book will be universal, but many of them will be specific to me and my own life. In fact, even when I *do* bring up universal topics, I'll be addressing them through the lens of my own observations and experiences. I'm not a scientist or a researcher, so that's the only way I feel comfortable writing about this stuff. With that in mind, I guess you could describe this book as part memoir, part unscientific observations, and part looking at the bigger picture. If you're thinking, 'That sounds confusing,' I don't blame you. Just keep reading.

Let's begin by looking at the fast-fashion industry.

The Fast-Fashion Industry

Fast. Fashion. Industry. What exactly does that mean? What does it stand for? That's not a simple question to answer, because it means many conflicting things, and it stands for many different issues, good and bad, all at once. What's more, these conflicting issues happen to be inseparable, like conjoined twins. One twin is all about style, clothes, fashion, and trends. It's into fun things like catwalks, dressing up, sexy underwear, and finding the perfect pair of jeans. The other twin is like a screwed up daredevil. It's responsible for pollution, child labour, and unsafe working conditions, and it wants everyone to be a reckless big spender.

The fun twin, the good twin, wins the Best Dressed award, goes to parties, and becomes friends with everyone. The evil twin lurks in the shadows, ends up on Most Wanted posters, and is banned from every respectable school, job, and institution.

What can I say? It wouldn't be life if it wasn't full of contradictions. I can only encourage you to keep these conflicting truths in your head as we make our way through the many fashion related topics in this book.

So where do *I* fit into all of this? Everywhere, I think. My own relationship to fashion is as complicated as the industry itself. On the one hand, I love clothes and I'm not afraid of dressing up. On the other hand, I also know that supporting this industry makes me feel out of integrity. There is no defending pollution, child labour, and reckless waste. However, when we go shopping, when *I* go shopping, I don't think about any of these things. I just look at the dress in front of me and think, 'I should get that!' And I know I'm not alone in doing so. It's only recently, culturally speaking, that we're starting to scratch the surface of what the fast-fashion industry truly stands for, what it's responsible for.

With that in mind, now that I think about it, supporting the fast-fashion industry not only seems selfish, it seems borderline cruel, and I'm not a cruel person.

But what does *not* supporting this industry look like? That all of these bad things go away? That I can't shop at H&M anymore? That I have to mend and make do? That I can only shop at thrift stores? That I shouldn't care about what I look like? Because I can tell you right now, that will never happen.

So where does that leave me? I have no idea, but not shopping for a year seems like a great place to start. This is my opportunity to think about, to talk about, and to delve into the bizarre world of fast-fashion. My goal is to get a better understanding of the industry itself, and also to understand my own role as a consumer.

Actually, I want to know about *everything*. About shopping behaviour. About trends. About outsourcing. About pollution. How advertising works. What sales do to us. Those kinds of things. I'm less after the *how*, how all of these things fit together, even though I'm interested in that too, but I'm more after the *why*.

More than anything I want to peek behind the curtain, ask questions, observe, and be open-minded and curious.

On a personal level, what I'm most curious about is if I'll be able to make the journey from being a mindless shopper to becoming a mindful consumer who acts according to her values. Time will tell, but one thing is for sure: this will be a year of learning. I'm excited about that.

So far I've realised three things:

1. By not shopping, Amy and I will take a moral stance and side with the factory workers. We're basically protesting slavery.

2. By not shopping, Amy and I will hand Mother Earth a sorely needed olive branch. Our carbon footprint will be reduced by an insane amount, and so by default we'll become green consumers. This is good!

3. By not shopping, Amy and I will save a lot of money. I have no idea how much money I spend on clothes every year, but whatever it is, I'll be spending it on something else from now on. Or better yet, put the money aside. My savings account will welcome the extra cash.

As you can see, this shop-stop challenge is rapidly turning into a Fast Track toward a better me. And this is only the first month! By next year I might be asked to give a TED Talk or something. All bets are off.

Looking the Part: An Overview

In the history of my life, clothes have always been about looking the part. To put it another way, clothes have always been about belonging and connection. By looking the part, I felt like I belonged to something bigger and better than myself. Even though I didn't necessarily think about it in those terms, connection was what I was after.

For instance, when I first moved to London, three years ago now, I'd just been offered the position of Private Secretary to the Ambassador of Norway. I celebrated this fantastic piece of news with a pitcher of White Russian and by going shopping. *Will you look at that suit? Check out those coats! You can never have too many office skirts. Hurry!* I shopped at any store that would have me, and I loved the rush of finding just the perfect outfit. A great sale was life-affirming, and getting something I wouldn't normally buy felt powerful and adventurous. *I can so pull this off! Talk about looking like a classy secretary!*

Because I had spent the previous decade living at a remote Tibetan Buddhist centre in California, I didn't know how to pace myself. Out shopping I acted like a starving child at a Halloween party. I didn't think about, or care about, where my clothes came from. I didn't think about, or care about, who made them. *Fast-fashion industry? Please! Don't interrupt me. I have some serious shopping to do!*

My only concern was to dress like I belonged in Belgravia, one of the grandest neighbourhoods in the world. *Me! Working in Belgrave Square. Working at an Embassy!* I couldn't believe how perfect my life was, and I was ready to look the part.

But my story of looking the part begins almost thirty years earlier. When Amy and I were little girls, looking the part meant dressing like identical twins. This was firmly rooted in the conviction that we were twins separated at birth. Just like the twins in the play *Blood Brothers*, one baby ended up with a rich family (Amy), and one ended up with a poor family (me). Sometimes I wished it was the other way around, but I had cooler uncles, plus my mom was less strict.

Amy and I took the role as twins very seriously, and so every evening we called each other on the phone and planned our matching outfits.

ME: Are you going to wear your Diana blouse tomorrow?

AMY: Yes! It's just been cleaned.

ME: Good, me too then. Skirt or trousers?

AMY: Let's wear skirts. How about the poofy ones? You can wear the purple one, and I'll wear my pink one.

ME: Perfect! Pigtails?

AMY: Of course! What else?

In our teenage years we dropped the twin act, but our friendship grew even stronger. It was like an unbreakable spell, and underneath this spell, protected by it, comforted by it, we spent hours talking about our complicated feelings and laughing at our own private jokes.

We developed a secret blinking language. No one could get a word in edgewise. We were told off for laughing too much. We lived in a very private universe.

Boys were still an enigma to us, so we played it safe and took comfort under the wings of movie star crushes. There we kept a rotating list of 'Who's Hot and Who's Not'. River Phoenix, Christian Bale, and Kenneth Branagh were definitely 'hot'. Charlie Sheen and Don Johnson were 'not'. Wil Wheaton would make the occasional guest appearances on both lists, depending on his latest movie. Harrison Ford, however, was granted immunity from such arbitrary rating systems. He was above all that, like a diplomat being whisked through border control.

During these formative years I began to take fashion cues from books and movies. *A Room with a View* spurred on a short-lived but intense Lucy Honeychurch phase. That look included long skirts, Victorian blouses, and a hairdo reminiscent of an exploded wasp's nest. After seeing *The Breakfast Club* for the 100 millionth time, I copied Judd Nelson's look to a tee: oversized grey men's coat, red plaid shirts, loose-fitted trousers, and a worn-out denim jacket. The *Princess Bride* convinced me to grow my hair even longer, and after seeing *The Horseman on the Roof*, I dyed all my clothes blue. *Danny, the Champion of the World* steered me toward tweed, corduroy, and wool.

By dressing like these fictional characters, I truly felt that I became more like them. Dressed like Lucy Honeychurch, for instance, I felt demure and charming, but with a quiet storm brewing just below the surface. Dressed like Judd Nelson I felt like a real badass, but deep down I felt vulnerable, just like I knew he did too.

Observing these different styles, I also drank in details like texture, fabric, colour combinations, and patterns. Was the coat fitted or two sizes too big? The knitted jacket: was it decorative or for warmth? What role did gloves play, if any? Like a crime scene investigator, nothing escaped my watchful eye.

And it wasn't just while watching movies that I soaked up all this information. Books were equally important. Lying in bed at night, under the covers, alone and away from the rest of the world, I read detective stories by Agatha Christie, historical novels by Richard Hermann, plays by William Shakespeare, and romantic fiction by the Brontë sisters. I pored over the characters and extracted their outfits from the pages like gold from a river bed.

In high school I went through a wonderful interlude of dressing like the *intelligentsia*. This was mainly inspired by reading the works of Milan Kundera, and by watching French-Polish movies like *The Double Life of Véronique* and *Three Colors: Blue*. In terms of style, according to me at least, this meant zero make-up, long hair, and wearing sensible leather shoes. Nothing says, 'I think, therefore I am,' like wearing sensible leather shoes.

When I grew tired of that look, just like I knew I would, I tried out the Jackie Kennedy look, the heiress look, the English boarding school look, the girl-next-door look, the *Jane Eyre* look, and the *Out of Africa* look. Nothing held my attention. Nothing stuck. My personal style moved like the wind and left a mountain of clothes in its wake.

Then *Twin Peaks* came along. I'd never been more intrigued in my entire life. But who to start dressing like first, Donna Hayward or Audrey Horne? Had I grown up with the Harry Potter books instead, I could probably have saved myself all this trouble and just put on a cloak and called it a day.

Looking back, I can see that my style-confusion (for lack of a better word) was a clear reflection of my flimsy sense of self. Who I was, my values, my direction, and what I wanted to be in this world, was all over the map.

What was that all about?

Some people would slap on a scatterbrain label. Other people would see it as being curious and adventurous. *Thank you!* You could also argue that I was just being a regular teenager.

Even so, one thing remained remarkably constant: I never followed trends. I never *ever* dressed to be stylish. Fads did absolutely nothing for me. Seeing the sea of newly permed hair, glossy lips, and

Poco Loco sweaters parading before me, I wanted to scream: *Just find your own style!* Leaning against the wall in my *Pretty in Pink* inspired costume (a pink curtain wrapped around me like a skirt and a cropped suede jacket), I felt deliciously unique.

After high school I moved to England to study archeology at the University of York. One week in I learnt two important lessons.

Lesson number one: archaeology was boring and lame.

Lesson number two: dressing like a female Indiana Jones (and thinking about changing my name to Inger Anna Jones) didn't make archaeology any less boring and lame.

I quit after four months.

Like all respectable dropouts, I set out to *find* myself. I thought I would find myself by travelling, and by trying out life-enriching but low-paying jobs, and I just assumed that at some point I'd start studying again.

That never happened. After a sequence of random events, I moved to a Tibetan Buddhist Centre in California. There I discovered a new side of myself. No, I don't mean my spiritual side; this is not a spiritual memoir, so I'll just stick to the clothes for now, if that's all right with you. The side I discovered (from a style perspective) was how much I belonged in a Buddhist community. You see, years before moving there I'd bought a lovely blue wrap-around dress. It looked exactly like the Tibetan *chuba,* the dress Buddhist women wear to religious ceremonies. And the important thing about my dress looking like a chuba, was that it made me feel like I belonged. The dress was a sign. And when someone pointed out that my burgundy French Connection trousers had the Eight Auspicious Symbols on them, everything fell into place.

Over the next ten years I wore a lot of maroon. Red too. Warm colours and floral patterns. Most of my clothes were loose-fitted and stretchy, even the mini skirts and cropped tops. I basically only wore clothes I could sit and meditate in.

Personal Style

But that was a long time ago. I'm now in my late thirties and I have finally developed my own personal style. On a good day that would be *Parisian Chic Meets Fun-seeking Vintage Girl*. It's a youthful and versatile look, kept under control by a commitment to feeling and looking awesome. (On a bad day all my clothes are wrong and I look fat.)

This means I'm in a good place to take a break from it all. Now that I no longer dabble in a new style every five minutes, and since I only have clothes that are quintessentially *me*, I can jump off the shopping carousel and walk away happy and stylish.

The Closet Clear-Out

But *how* does one walk away? When Amy approached me about not shopping for a year, I instantly knew I needed a ritual. I couldn't just stop shopping; I had to mark the occasion with a ceremony of some kind. Ceremonies are like a line in the sand marking *before* and *after*, something to navigate by. And they're fun.

Here is what I'm thinking: what better way to commemorate this event than by having a closet clear-out? This will achieve two things:

1. I'll take stock of all the clothes I have.

2. I'll move forward with a clean slate.

For those of you unfamiliar with closet clear-outs, let me explain how it works. A closet clear-out is the simple act of getting rid of all the clothes you never wear. Sounds easy? Well, it gets trickier. You see, I have found that what we actually wear, and what we *want* to wear, are often two very different things.

'Never wear' includes all the clothes we *think* we should like, but don't, so we never wear them. It also includes all the clothes we *sort of* like, all the clothes we *used* to like, and all the clothes we *think* we like, and the only reason we hang on to them is because we once bought them.

'Never wear' also includes all the clothes we *almost* sort of hate, but just in case our taste changes, we don't throw them out. This sounds insane, I know, but for unknown reasons we are strangely attached to our clothes.

Finally, 'never wear' also includes all the clothes we want to fit into, the clothes that need mending, and the all the clothes that, despite our best efforts, we never get around to ironing.

Based on all this, it's not surprising that most of us have way too many clothes, yet we feel like we have nothing to wear. This is because we actually don't *want* to wear what we have. I know you know what I mean.

I for one want to wear all my clothes, and I only want to own clothes that I want to wear, and a closet clear-out will reveal if that's the case or not.

In order to decide what to keep and what to throw out, I only have to ask myself two simple questions:

1.   Would I have bought this today?

2.   Does this represent who I am today?

If the answer is 'yes' to one or both of these questions, it's a keeper. If the answer is 'no', bye-bye baby. It makes sense, doesn't it?

If you're no longer a Michael Jackson fan, why hold on to that sequin-studded glove? Learn to let go. Or maybe you've just been promoted to junior partner at a prestigious law firm. If so, the 'Question Authority' t-shirt should be passed on to someone more worthy.

Whatever you do, and I say this from the bottom of my heart, don't EVER hold on to any of your clothes just because you once bought them. That is not a thing. If you haven't worn them in a while, there is a reason for that. Pay attention to that reason. That reason is your friend.

But, you might ask, 'What about the clothes we no longer wear, but that are filled with wonderful memories?'

You are of course talking about outfits like the first date dress, the comfy college sweater, and the killer tube top you rocked at the Madonna concert all those years ago. When it comes to 'memory lane clothes', follow Karl Lagerfeld's advice: 'Keep the best, forget the rest.' Personally I don't think it's healthy to hold on to *any* of these outfits, unless they used to belong to Marilyn Monroe or have diamonds sewn into the hem.

Enough talk. Let's begin.

Down in my bedroom it only takes me five minutes to feel like I'm drowning in clothes. You see, I stupidly threw them all on the bed. And I mean ALL of them. In good faith I emptied every drawer, closet, and storage space, thinking this was the best way to dive right in. But now I don't know where to start. There are so many clothes. Why are there so many clothes?! The pile before me is huge and mysterious.

OK, so maybe I have a more clothes than I thought I had. And maybe I don't wear all of them. Maybe I can stand to get rid of a few. That's not a bad thing. In fact, that's a good thing! Now this ritual will become more real. Great!

I start with the obvious bad boys: the brown skirt, the vagina pants, and the Bank of Scotland blazer. Too frumpy, too tight, too boring, in that order. *Gone!*

The Grace Kelly dress? Love it! A keeper, obviously.

Faded blue top? Nope. Plus, it has sweat stains under the arms. *Yuck.*

Itchy cardigan? I think not.

The Hello Kitty sweater? What possessed me to buy that one? No grown-up should ever buy something a small child or a Japanese teenager would wear. I work at an Embassy; I have a professional image to uphold. What if David Cameron drops by again?

Hmm. I guess I could wear it on weekends maybe, if I ever got into gardening or something...

Stop! Red flag! Red flag! Big fat red flag!

I throw the Hello Kitty sweater in the reject pile and remind myself that I'm not allowed to keep clothes based on 'if', 'when', or 'in the event of'. I am only dressing for the present, not the past or the future. Are we clear? Good.

This is so powerful. I am positively lighter. I am removing toxic waste from my surroundings and creating a peaceful space for myself and all my clothes.

In feng shui there's a saying, 'Clutter attracts clutter.' The opposite is also true. 'Harmony attracts harmony.' A harmonious closet is a happy closet.

Maybe I should become a decluttering Guru? I'm really getting good at this. Look at me go!

When I'm almost done with the clear-out, I can't help but notice that the reject pile is considerably larger than the keeper pile. I look at the mountain of clothes on the floor, then I glance back at the closet...so many empty hangers. Then it hits me: I HAVE NOTHING TO WEAR!

This was meant to be a symbolic exercise. It never occurred to me that I would be left with almost nothing.

This is so not happening.

I reach for the phone and call Amy.

While I wait for her to pick up, I lie down on the floor in the recovery position. I need to preserve my strength. I honestly feel faint. The whole room is spinning.

As I lie there, I can't help but wonder if everything I have told myself about my clothes, my style, and my shopping habits is maybe not what I thought it was. Could it be that I am...what's the word I'm looking for...*clueless*? I want to scream *Inconceivable!* But there is no denying it.

I thought I had good taste. Debatable.

I thought I only bought what I really liked. Wrong.

I thought I had a great selection of clothes. Wrong again.

This insight is a huge shock to me; it's a punch in the face. I mean, I don't shop *that* much. I only buy what I *truly* like, and all my clothes are really, really cool.

Right?

Wrong.

All of a sudden I'm overcome by a deep sense of failure. My shop-stop year was meant to be fun, but here I am hitting rock bottom before I've even started.

As much as I hate to admit this, it dawns on me that maybe I don't need to hop off the shopping carousel on account of the environment and human rights issues alone, but maybe I need to take a break from shopping because I'm a hopeless shopper.

A hopeless shopper with bad taste.

A hopeless shopper with nothing to wear.

The mountain of rejected clothes speaks volumes.

I recently read a fascinating book about how French women approach fashion and shopping. According to the author, French women never go berserk on sales. They never get tricked into buying a blouse two sizes too small just because it's half price. There is no 'better safe than sorry' mentality. There is no desperate justification for shopping like, 'This might look good on me one day, if I lose ten pounds and were auditioning for the remake of *The Great Gatsby*.' French women stick to a style that complements them, they wear clothes that enhance their beauty, and they shop at a handful of shops that carry clothes that suit and improve their unique style.

When I read that book, I felt an instant kinship with my gorgeous French sisters. That's how I shopped as well! Ha. Talk about being in denial. What a load of crap.

To be fair, it wasn't so much that I'd gone berserk on sales and blindly brought home a bunch of fashion mistakes. I had indeed bought clothes that I liked, I had just failed to consider if I'd ever wear them, or — and how could I have missed this? — if they would look good on me. How short-sighted is that?

I should have my brain scanned. Shops must have a moronic effect on us, because I'm telling you, something happens to our minds when out shopping. I should investigate that.

How else would you explain the number of times I've talked myself into buying clothes that should never have been made in the first place? *The waist is a bit high, but the colour is amazing! I just need to spruce it up a bit. A belt would totally do it. Problem solved! Or, OK, so maybe the sleeves are a bit weird, but look at the fabric! Since when did sleeves matter?*

That is the wrong approach to shopping; I see that now. Buying clothes shouldn't be like a parliamentary debate; it's not about compromise and presenting the case from all angles. Either we like the clothes or we don't. Either we will wear them or we won't.

I thought I knew this already, but clearly not. What else don't I know about myself? Perhaps I'm also a raving alcoholic or a talented ventriloquist; there is really no way of telling.

Amy finally picks up the phone.

> ME: I have nothing to wear! (There is no time for hello. This is a 999 call.)
>
> AMY: Ridiculous, I love all your clothes. What are you on about?
>
> ME: I have absolutely nothing to wear!
>
> AMY: You're sounding a bit hysterical.
>
> ME: You think!

I tell her about my disastrous closet clear-out, and because of our stupid, stupid pact, I can't replace all my bad clothes with good clothes for *another twelve months!* Not that I would trust myself to go shopping right now, but still, it would be nice to have the option.

> ME: Oh, what the hell. I should just figure this out in therapy like a normal person.
>
> AMY: I honestly don't understand what you're so worked up about. I'm sure you have plenty of great clothes left. Also, have you forgotten that you can sew? Just fix some of them.

Ha! That's easy for her to say; she's the one with a closet full of pretty clothes. And didn't I hear her say something about a new Boden dress? This is so unfair!

How do I look?

Perspective and Guidlines

After our talk I scrape myself off the floor and sit down on the bed. I try to think.

Amy's right. Perhaps I had gotten a bit more upset than the occasion called for. Perspective. I need to put this in perspective. So what if I have fewer clothes than Imelda Marcos? I have not been fired and will be forced to sell my kidneys on the black market. Hitler has not invaded Poland, and I'm not the last engineer left at Fukushima. My very small crisis consists of the fact that I only have two pairs of jeans left. But so what? I have plenty of other clothes.

...No I don't!

I want to tear my hair out.

I want to unplug and detox.

I need a twelve-step program.

I need a break from shopping.

My only consolation is that I'm not alone in this predicament; plenty of shoppers go astray. Why do you think thrift shops get so many donations?

But *why* do we go astray? And how did I manage to go astray without even being aware of it? I should definitely investigate *that*. A more pressing question: how can I avoid going astray in the future, once the shop-stop is over?

Maybe I need to take matters into my own hands and develop a set of shopping guidelines. Of course! That's it! I should develop shopping guidelines! I'm not talking about banal fashion style guides like, 'Ten Ways to Wear a Denim Jacket.' Or, 'Bathing Suits for the Fuller Figure.' I'm talking about an Emergency Response Guide for shopping. A set of rules that will guarantee that we only buy the loveliest of clothes — a list of rules that will prevent us from making the same stupid shopping mistakes again, and again, and again.

Based on my closet clear-out, I already know what the first guideline must be:

Don't buy anything you can't wear tomorrow.

This kind of wisdom should be passed down from generation to generation, together with the family silver and the rest of the heirlooms. How irritating that I didn't think of this two decades ago. But even if I had, I would still be faced with one big problem: what I feel like wearing tomorrow remains a moving target.

As much as I had cherished the idea of having a signature look, my taste is still all over the place. One day I want to dress like a young Mia Farrow, the next day I want to look like a James Bond girl. I love the old-money look, but I also want to wear my hair like a Geisha. Hopeless! My personal style is that of a schizophrenic time traveller. While working toward the *Parisian Chic* image, I've let myself get distracted and disoriented, and I've contributed to pollution, child labour, and toxic waste.

Fan-*fucking*-tastic.

I walk upstairs to the kitchen. My teacup needs refilling.

Fortunately, I can go from hopeless to hopeful within a matter of minutes. My little ritual didn't exactly go according to plan, but it forced me to open my eyes. I learnt something about myself, and that is never a bad thing.

With newfound insight and optimism, I'm more determined than ever to go through with this shop-stop challenge. From here on out I will blaze through this consumer culture of ours like a fearless gladiator.

Just you wait and see.

Chapter Two
December

> 6 *Happy girls are the prettiest.* 9
> *-Audrey Hepburn*

A my and I didn't flaunt our shop-stop pact, but if it happened to come up in conversations, many of the people we talked to acted flustered and offended, giving us many reasons for why they could *never* stop buying clothes.

Here are some of those reasons:

1.   I attend so many meetings.

2.   I live in London.

3.   If I don't go shopping every week I get depressed.

4.   I rarely find clothes that I like, so when I do I have no choice but to buy them.

5.   I've lost weight.

6. I'm going on vacation.

7. I'm on a diet.

8. I have a new job.

9. My favourite store has a sale coming up.

Fear

Behind these reasons, as far a I could tell, was a healthy dose of fear. Fear of missing out on the next great outfit, fear of finally finding the perfect jacket without being able to buy it, and fear of lagging behind, style-wise. There was also the fear of being stuck with nothing but old clothes, and the fear of being perceived as boring. The last two fears seemed to go hand in hand.

These were legitimate fears all right, but they were peanuts compared to the main fear, the number one fear, the fear that outweighs all the others. I'm talking about the kind of fear that is like the creepiest part of the basement, like the darkest part of the forest, and the ice-cold feeling that crawls up your spine when you think you're being followed. This fear makes you scared and small and freaked out, all at the same time. I'm talking about the fear of having nothing to wear.

'I have nothing to wear!' sets off a low-level rumble that quickly becomes a full-scale emergency. We think we're in danger. We get tunnel vision. We start to panic. Our breathing turns shallow. Time slows down. Time speeds up. We make up stories about everything that will go wrong unless we solve this Code Red clothing crises.

I'm of course exaggerating a bit, but not really.

But seriously, why are we so afraid of having nothing to wear? And what do we mean by 'nothing to wear'? If you live in my part of the world, everyone you know has more clothes than they can handle. This is a fact, so unless you're homeless, serving time in prison, or on the run, you will never run out of clothes. With that in mind, what are we talking about here?

As you will recall, after my decluttering session I honest-to-God believed I had no clothes left. This frightened me, but luckily I quickly realised how unfounded my fear was. (Theodore Roosevelt was right, we have nothing to fear but fear itself.) I had *plenty* of clothes left, but I *felt* that I didn't. I think this is a common mistake, mistaking fewer clothes for no clothes.

Also, when people say 'nothing to wear', that's often euphemism for 'nothing NEW to wear'. And when we stop shopping, new disappears from our lives, and so we panic.

But before we begin to look at the allure of NEW, let me address the peculiar statement from just a few minutes ago, the one that went, 'I can't stop shopping because I attend so many meetings.'

That's a really strange statement. It's not even true. But what this statement so clearly illustrates, and why I find it so fascinating, is that the stories we tell ourselves of why and how we shop can lead us to a crazy corner of the consumer world that is a bit like *Alice In Wonderland*. '"We're all mad here," said the Cat to Alice.'

The stories themselves are harmless; it's only when we believe in them that we limit our options. And so our world becomes microscopic, and a bit mad.

In order to move *past* the stories, we must be willing to ask ourselves questions like, 'Is this really true? Where did I learn this? Who did I learn this from? Why do I take refuge in this particular statement?'

Instead of believing that 'I attend so many meetings' is a valid reason for going shopping, let's turn our attention to one of the world's greatest style icons: Jackie Kennedy. When Jackie Kennedy worked for Viking Press, she only had two suits she wore to meetings. Why? Because she didn't want her clothes to take any attention away from her work. I don't know about you, but to me that feels a lot healthier. In terms of my own professional life, during my four years at the Embassy, no one was ever denied access to meetings based on the newness of their clothes.

The Seductive Power of New

Let's look at NEW. What does NEW mean?

When I was a little girl, the difference between my new clothes and my old ones was like night and day. The new clothes were not faded, worn out, or mended. They were in pristine condition and had that wonderful smell of something that hadn't been worn yet.

Today the line between old and new is blurred. That's because old is not old anymore, it's just *less* new. The new blouse is newer than the blouse bought last Wednesday, but neither of them can accurately be labeled *old*.

With our disposable attitude toward clothes, we're quick to buy anything we fancy, often overlooking the fact that our new clothes are not necessarily *better* than our 'old' ones, but because they are brand *new*, we attach all kinds of wonderful qualities to them.

I do this all the time.

But as I began to learn more about how my mind behaves around clothes and shopping, I began to poke big holes in the myth of NEW. I began to see that the power we invest in our new clothes is a bit like Jesus' face on a cheese sandwich: it's an illusion.

To give you an example, what do you say if someone compliments you on a new dress? You say, 'Thank you! I just got it! I'm so glad you like it!'

Right?

But what do you say if someone compliments you on an *old* dress? My guess would be, 'Oh, this old thing...'

When I got called in for a job interview at the Norwegian Embassy, my first instinct was to run (yes, run!) to town and buy new clothes. Black trousers. Crisp blue shirt. I even bought a new handbag. There was no way I was going to show up at the Embassy wearing something as grotesque as an *old* outfit. I nailed the interview, but I no longer think it had anything to do with the newness of my clothes.

I do recognise that wearing the right type of clothes can give us an extra boost of self-confidence and make us feel secure and lovely in our own skin, but all I'm asking is this: do the clothes have to be new?

Back in December 2012, the answer to that question was a big resounding YES! It was only my second month of not shopping, and I was battling four major shop-stop challenges:

1. I was desperate for a new winter coat.

2. I was going to a summer wedding in Australia.

3. I found the most amazing vintage store.

4. The sale season was about to kick off.

Challenge Number One: The Hunt for the Perfect Winter Coat

As a child I grew up with the motto: 'There is no such thing as bad weather, only bad clothes!' Dressed in multiple layers of wool, sealskin shoes, and a practical windbreaker, I was propelled out of the house with a cheerful 'Have fun!'

How had I managed to stay so warm back then, and why in God's name was it so impossible to keep the chill out now? Had London been moved to the North Pole? Had living in California made me extra sensitive to the winter months? Or could it be as simple as not having the right winter coat? It certainly wasn't for lack of trying.

When I first moved to London, I fantasized about finding the Perfect Winter Coat. I longed for the kind of coat that Lara from *Dr. Zhivago* would wear. It should make me look like I owned a horse, or that my father did. I tried to sniff out this coat, like a hog hunting for truffles, and I followed the scent trail all over London.

This is how it played out:

I go to town, I hit a few stores, but none of them carry my *Dr. Zhivago* coat. However, at this early stage in the game I'm still optimistic. *Maybe they will look different once I try them on,* I tell myself, dragging a handful of coats into the changing room with me. This illusion quickly fades. The mirrors don't lie. I look ridiculous. The coats are all wrong. I'm getting grumpy.

What am I supposed to do with this weird belt? And what is up with this oversized collar? Does it double up as a hijab? Don't get me started on this miniature jacket, it looks like it needs growth hormones. Who in their right mind would ever buy a SHORT *winter coat?*

Back home, exhausted and miserable, I resort to online shopping. The internet is bigger than all of New York, London, and Paris combined, so there is still hope. I open up my laptop and type, click, and browse. Not a single coat jumps out at me. *What is wrong with this place?! Do I have to go back in time and stock up on vintage Laura Ashley and Jaeger coats?* Apparently so, judging by their current winter collection. *Why do they want us to look like we're dead inside? Answer me!*

I'm about to give up when it hits me, *Since I'm already on the computer, why not look for new work clothes? Who said I could only shop for coats? Not that I need a new skirt or anything, but it would be interesting to see what is out there, keep my finger on the fashion pulse, so to speak.*

I sit up straighter and begin searching for pussy bow blouses, stretchy pencil skirts, cashmere cardigans, and other secretarial basics. I might not want to be a personal secretary forever, but for as long as I have that role, I'm committed to looking the part.

Oh, look at that blouse! Didn't Keira Knightley have one of those? What movie was she in again? The football one. Ah, Bend It Like Beckham, that was it. Great movie! Wasn't she also in Anna Karenina?

I go to YouTube and watch three versions of the trailer before I determine that the movie looks dreadful, but now I want to read the book again. This leads me to Amazon. *Should I buy the book used or new? While I'm at it, I might as well get another Margaret Atwood book. I wonder if she ever did a TED Talk...*

And so it continues. In a maze of searches and myriad websites, I lose my way and end up reading about Gwyneth Paltrow's daily exercise regime. 'Everyone has time to exercise two hours a day, it's a matter of prioritising,' she informs us. *Dear mother of God.*

Last winter I got *this* close to owning The Perfect Winter Coat. In Hampstead, at a wonderful second hand store, I found a gorgeous

NOA NOA coat. I paid for it, got on the tube, and rushed home to show it off to Ben.

Ben is my husband, and we have been married since 2010. He's English and I'm Norwegian. I come from good, solid farmer's stock, while Ben's family belongs to the ancient Clan Gunn. Despite our different backgrounds, Ben and I are crazy similar. It's almost spooky. We even share the same taste in clothes, so I just *knew* he would love my new NOA NOA coat.

'Look! Isn't it fantastic?' I said, smiling and parading in front of him in our living room. 'Finally a super long coat! It's almost down to my ankles! See? And it's SO comfortable. Don't you think I look like a Russian Tsarina?!'

Something about his blank stare and arched eyebrows told me he was unimpressed.

'What? What don't you like about it?' I asked, feeling panicky. 'Do I look FAT?' I twisted my head around like an owl, trying to get a better look of my behind. 'Is that it? You think the coat accentuates my chubbiness?'

Ben rolled his eyes and said in his mock calm voice, 'No, darling, you don't look fat. I just don't like the coat. It makes you look like the village spinster, the one that no one wants to talk to.'

Spinster! How rude! I hissed at him and slumped down on the sofa. But he was right. Since the coat had lived up to *some* of my requirements, I had willingly blocked out its more glaring defects, like the colour and the fabric. The pale brown colouring had a turd-like quality, and the fabric resembled old man slippers. *How frustrating!* Could a coat not be beautiful *and* warm? Was I forever doomed to pick between pretty and practical?

Even though I still needed a new winter coat, I was relieved I wouldn't be hunting for one this winter. It was too stressful. Besides, I lived in London. London! Why on earth would I go shopping when I could do things like visit the National Portrait Gallery, hang out at Gordon's Wine Bar, and go on the London Ghost Walk with my sister Elise?

Better let the coat come to me. From now on I would be like Pablo Picasso and murmur under my breath, 'I don't search, I find.'

I prayed the coat wouldn't find *me* until the shop-stop was over.

Challenge Number Two: The Wedding

At the end of December, Ben and I were going to a summer wedding in Australia. A summer wedding! In the dead of winter! I couldn't wait to get away from the cold, but then I remembered the dress code. I looked at the invitation again, cursing myself for not dealing with this any sooner. The dress code read: English Garden Party.

When it comes to weddings, it's an unspoken rule that you have to wear something new. Especially if you're a girl, which I am. And especially if it's a theme wedding, which this was. So what were my options? I had nothing to wear! (See how quickly we jump to that conclusion?)

Could I make a dress out of drapes, like Scarlett O'Hara did in *Gone with the Wind*? No, I could not. Our drapes were made from thick blue velvet.

Could Ben go by himself? That was a great idea! He could go to the wedding, and I could stay put and catch up on paperwork and organise my inbox. Or...maybe not.

How about ignoring the dress code? No, no, no! No way. I could *never* show up at a wedding wearing the wrong outfit. Not in a million years did I want to be the kind of guest who says, 'I'm really sorry I'm not following the dress code, but you see, I'm on a shop-stop. It's good for the environment!'

Wrong!

You don't arrive at a wedding, or at any social setting for that matter, declaring what you're *not* doing. You don't say you're on a diet, you don't tell everyone about your gluten allergy, and you don't talk about being on a shop-stop. Those are not fun topics of conversation. Climbing Mt. Everest is, and writing a novel is, and building an orphanage in Africa is.

I'm all about making a good first impression. I needed a new dress.

Wait a minute, who said the dress had to be new? Could it not be old? Who would notice? And even if they did, so what? *But which one of my old dresses should I choose?*

I hurried downstairs to the bedroom and looked through my dresses, what was left of them. At first glance my initial suspicion was verified: all my dresses were wrong and horrible. But then I spotted it — my blue French Connection dress.

I had forgotten all about you! No wonder really, considering it's a summer dress. Here in England we are lucky if we get two days of sun during the 'warm' season. Looking at the dress with fresh eyes, it was like I'd bought it with the upcoming wedding in mind.

- It's made of cotton - Perfect for warm weather.

- It's wrinkle-free - Perfect for travelling.

- It's sleeveless with a classic wide skirt – Perfect for an English tea-party wedding.

Shout out to all of you who are still going strong in last year's party dresses: **Yes we can!**

I found a pair of matching earrings, dug out my old Burberry sandals, and dusted off my vintage clutch bag. Shopping? Who needs it?

With that taken care of, the only thing that stood between me and Australia was a twenty-hour flight.

Challenge Number Three: Sunny Sydney and the Vintage Shop

The flight to Sydney was like a Navy SEAL Hell Week. What happens on Air China stays on Air China. By the time we stopped over in Beijing, I was so delirious and deranged that I no longer remembered who I was and why I hadn't killed myself yet. I hadn't been this starved, tired, or caffeine-deprived (who knew Air China only serves jasmine tea?) since the day I was born.

As I stumbled into the vast airport, with all the fatigue and sadness of a Gulag prisoner, I spotted a Costa Coffee sign. *Salvation, at last!* I felt like dropping to my knees and praying, only there was no time. With alarmingly quick steps I hurried over to the coffee stand and flung myself on the counter and said/shouted with ill-concealed desperation, 'Your biggest latte, please!'

The alert barista was visibly thrilled to receive such an exotic order. Maybe he thought I was cute? Who was I kidding? I looked like a POW. I needed help. I should have asked for the latte intravenously.

'Here is your latte, Madam.'

I snatched the cup from him and took a big sip. The warm liquid floated past my lips and down my throat like a life raft. *Praise the Lord! I'm just so happy I'm still allowed to buy coffee.*

At this point in my shop-stop journey I often found myself starting sentences with, 'At least I can still buy...' I couldn't buy clothes, but I could still buy everything else. I was free to purchase things like theatre tickets, dried mango, and lattes. The old me would have taken all of those things for granted, but the new me was becoming a person of healthy and enviable *perspective.* I was genuinely happy for the little things in life. This made me feel wise beyond my years.

We had some time to kill before boarding the plane again, so we swung by a touristy airport shop. I steered clear of the display of silk robes — why tempt fate? — and headed over to the knick-knack section. There I found a pair of gorgeous jade earrings. It's the kind The Girl with the Pearl Earring would have worn, had she been Asian. I've always wanted to be like her. She's so feminine.

'Get them!' Ben said.

He's always so encouraging.

I ended up getting not one, but two pairs of Asian earrings. *They will look soooooo nice with my green silk blouse! I will wear them ALL the time.*

At least that's what I told myself, jet-lagged, sleep-deprived, and with a latte rush coming on.

Ten long hours later we arrived in sunny Sydney.

Hello sunshine! Hello blue sky! Hello tank top and linen trousers!

After checking in at the hotel, and slathering ourselves with sunblock lotion, we set out to 'discover' the city.

Had this holiday taken place before the shop-stop pact, I would have swept through the city guide in search of vintage shops and 'off the beaten track' shopping opportunities. Revision: before leaving London I would have memorised the names and locations of all vintage shops within a five-mile radius.

Do I love vintage clothes? Is the Pope Catholic? There is a lot of stigma attached to wearing something used, but let me explain how I see it.

Vintage Clothes

- Have survived two wold wars and a double-dip recession.

- Are mostly made from natural fabrics.

- Are timeless.

Fast-Fashion Clothes

- The buttons fall off right away.

- Are mostly made from oil-based fabrics.

- Have a two month window of being 'in'.

Then there is the vintage shopping *experience*. It's like an Audrey Hepburn movie or a treasure hunt. You have no idea what you're going to find, but you know it will be great. You also get to know the shop owner and exchange phrases like, 'I believe Jackie O had a suit just like that.' Or, 'They just don't make them like that anymore.'

But we didn't go shopping. Actually, Ben did. He needed a new summer shirt, and so while he tried on white, beige, and taupe shirts, I restricted my movements to the men's underwear section. Again, why tempt fate?

On our second day in Sydney we went to a hipster neighbourhood called Surry Hills. With its hilly streets, colourful houses, and artistic flair, it was like being in a mini-version of San Francisco. There was so much to see: art galleries, gourmet restaurants, and quirky stores. We even walked past a vintage shop.

What I meant to say is, we *almost* walked past a vintage shop.

Have you ever felt as though your feet are frozen to the ground, while your mind is stuck in a confused battle between staying and going, unable to move in any direction?

As I stood in front of the vintage shop, unable to tear myself away, I tried to talk myself out of liking the retro display window.

Tsk, a Vespa and a jukebox. Been there done that. Show me something original, I beg of you.

But despite my best efforts to act indifferent, I couldn't deny how wonderful it all looked. Hardwood floors, retro wallpaper, and huge gilded mirrors. Everything was so tasteful and inviting. *Look at the hats, and the gloves, and the sunglasses and...is that a SADDLE?!*

I should have walked away. But, on the other hand, come to think of it, wouldn't it be rude of me *not* to have a peek? Here I was, a guest in a foreign country, and it was dead obvious that the shop owner had gone through a great deal of effort to make it look this nice. Who was I to ignore such labour of love? I was raised better than that. I had to pay my respects.

My feet sprinted over the threshold and rooted themselves to the ground.

I was in.

I held my breath.

A moment of silence please.

I was like a lioness being introduced back into the savannah. I surveyed my surroundings.

My attention zoomed in on a '50s chiffon dress. It had a wide skirt decorated with black polka dots. *I love polka dots!* The dress also had a square neckline, the kind that makes your waist appear thinner.

Yes please! It was an exemplary dress, a role model for all other dresses. I liked it. I wanted to buy it.

Given that I was on a shop-stop, the story should have ended right here. I should have said 'Nice dress!' and walked away. But I didn't, because the dress was talking to me. Maybe not exactly *talking*, but it was communicating *something*. I walked over to check it out.

Standing right next to the dress now, I instinctively began to stroke it, like I was petting a kitten. I could almost hear it purring. Right there and then I knew that this dress would be absolutely perfect for the wedding. It really, really would! I couldn't understand why I thought I could get away with wearing a simple *cotton* dress. What was I *on*? *This* was a party dress, not my outdated wrinkle-free excuse of a thing. This dress and I *belonged* together; we shared the same DNA. I had to get it. I had no choice.

Then I remembered: I was on a shop-stop. I couldn't shop for another eleven months. What were the reasons again? What was the justification for this meaningless torture? *Why, world, why?*

OK, calm down. Step away from the dress, just back away. That's right. You can do it.

I was almost returning to normal when I saw the most amazing yellow dress decorated with petite daisies. *Argh! I can't take this!*

'We have to get out of here,' I told Ben.

'Can I help you find anything?' The saleswoman had materialised by my side.

'Actually not,' I said, struggling to keep my voice calm. 'I'm on a shop-stop and can't buy anything until next November.'

'What a pity!'

Tell me about it.

Ten minutes later Ben and I sat down for lunch. By the time my salad arrived, I'd already forgotten about the dresses.

Challenge Number Four: The Beginning of the Sale Season

Back in London, Ben and I had one week to get over our jet lag before heading over to Norway for Christmas.

Christmas, like weddings, is another occasion where we are conditioned into believing that a new outfit is mandatory. But can I be the first person to point out that Christmas outfits are both ugly and unflattering? There is absolutely no other time of the year where we would be caught dead in an outfit that's fifty percent Mrs Santa, twenty-five percent Sexy Elf, and twenty-five percent Chic Ice Princess. Even little children look ridiculous buried in lace, ribbons, and red velour.

Unable to shop for a new Christmas outfit, I dug up my '60s air hostess dress. I'd never thought of it as a Christmas dress before, even though it's bright red and everything.

This right here is what not shopping is all about, finding new opportunities for old clothes. It's very Zen, this whole 'looking within, not without' business. Looking at my red dress, I felt myself transforming into a gentle Zen master of not shopping. *I think shopping not need. Lots of clothes already has.*

After a full week of Norwegian Christmas festivities, the post-Christmas sale was upon us. Yellow and orange SALE signs crisscrossed the shop windows like a sealed-off crime scene, which wasn't that far from the truth. I wasn't thinking about crimes like child labour, pollution, and the moral decline of consumerism; I was thinking about the insanity of a sweater that only yesterday cost £45, would now be on sale for a mere £15.

Sale or no sale, shopping was already becoming a fading echo of the past. Selma, my youngest sister, really wanted to go shopping though, so I agreed to tag along with her. I could be her older — nay, *wiser* — sidekick. Furthermore, here was a golden opportunity to share some of my newfound wisdom with the other bargain hunters. I could walk up to them and say things like:

'Excuse me? Do you know we only end up wearing thirty percent of all the clothes we buy? Thirty percent! With that in mind, are you sure you want to get that blouse? Orange is a very difficult colour, you know.'

'You! Wait up! Credit card debt is soaring. Are you shopping on credit today, sir? You better not be. Don't look so alarmed, I'm not the crazy one here!'

'Listen! Did you know that the average American throw away about sixty-five pounds of clothing each year? Sixty-five pounds! Straight into the trash! Hey! Where do you think you're going? Come back here! This is for your own good! YOUR FUTURE CHILDREN WILL THANK ME!'

Our first stop was H&M. 'Further reductions inside!' the window signs promised. Once inside the store I noticed an abundance of great clothes, all marked down and tastefully displayed. I saw stacks of trousers, rows of shirts, and big red SALE signs hanging over designated areas. Over in the corner there was an entire section dedicated to the clothes that were fifty percent off half price. All I had to do was buy them, and they would be mine.

Not that I wanted anything, or...did I? I couldn't tell. I wasn't thinking clearly. The voices in my head went back and forth. *Leave the store!* Don't be silly! *Buy something.* NO! *But look at these clothes!* Leave me be!

These voices caught me off-guard. I thought I was over shopping. So where did this simmering yearning come from? What did it mean? Would I get trapped in a battle of wills *every* single time I walked into a store? Was that how this year would play out for me? How embarrassing!

In all fairness, maybe it wasn't so surprising that I wasn't quite where I wanted to be with all of this. On the one side of the scale were almost three decades of mindless shopping, weighing about three thousand pounds. On the other side of the scale were two meagre months of not shopping, weighing less than one pound. Come to think of it, it was actually a bit weird I hadn't given in yet.

I knew I couldn't artificially stop myself from wanting all these clothes, but I *could* stop myself from acting on my impulses, just like

I had done at the Australian vintage store. The seductive voice in my head that kept whispering: *It's on sale! What are you waiting for? Buy something!* was not in charge, it was just one of the many voices in my head fighting for my attention.

Intrigued by this situation, I decided to stay put and observe all of my inner voices, just to see what they were capable of. That, plus I had to wait for Selma.

First out were the needy toddler voices. They were in excellent form.

Will you look at that jacket? You have to buy that jacket! It has the power to change your life IN SO MANY WAYS. And look at that blue skirt over there. We like blue. Blue is good. Blue goes with everything; everybody knows that. Flannel shirt! Soft, cuddly flannel shirt! Gimme gimme! WE WANT A FLANNEL SHIRT. Hey?! Why aren't you moving? Didn't you hear us? Go over there and grab it! Give it to us! Give it to us now!

When the toddler voices understood I wasn't going to budge, they sent in the big guns. In entered the crazy inner voice equivalent of Lady Macbeth. Let me tell you, she was not in the mood for excuses.

Look at all these lovely clothes. I know you want them. You're lusting after them. So why don't you buy them? Didn't Amy say you could buy underwear? A top resembles a bra. A skirt resembles panties. Don't be so bloody weak and narrow-minded. It's all just clothes. What exactly is your problem?

Observing these voices was a lot more fun than giving into them, but after a while they ran out of steam and faded away. That allowed for a more loving voice to emerge, the generous voice.

Someone once told me, 'You get what you want by giving it.'

Standing in the aisles at H&M I decided to take that advice to heart and buy some clothes for my lovely little sister. Being on a shop-stop might be absurdly difficult, but being a generous person who buys beautiful clothes for others felt right and rewarding.

There is actually a study on how buying stuff for others makes us happier than when we buy things for ourselves. It's counterintuitive, I know, but it also makes sense. I mean, what could be better than making other people happy?

Selma picked out a stretchy lace top and some hair accessories. Afterwards we went to our favourite coffee bar and ordered cinnamon buns and tea. Life was good again, even though I could still feel Lady Macbeth brewing in the background.

Developing Non-Shopping Strategies

Based on my December shop-stop challenges, I saw that not shopping is less about 'staying away from shops' and more about developing non-shopping strategies and flexing the mind muscles. So far I'd learnt four valuable strategies.

1. The coat dilemma reminded me to cultivate patience. Let the coat come to me.

2. The dress dilemma reminded med to think outside the box. Does the dress have to be new? Can I make it myself?

3. The vintage store dilemma reminded me that I have the option to walk away, and that out of sight is out of mind.

4. And finally, the sale incident reminded me that I'm the one in charge (not my crazy inner voices), and that generosity beats selfish spending.

Mixing all these insights together, I came up with the second Emergency Shopping Guideline:

Don't buy anything you don't need.

Shop owners will hate this guideline, but I'm willing to live with that.

But wait! Hold on just a minute! Did this new guideline mean I would never go shopping again? Had I just dug my own shopping grave? This freaked me out a bit, but I also knew I didn't have to worry about that for another ten months.

Amy

But how was Amy doing, my partner in crime? For starters, she was beginning to take better care of the clothes she already had. Brilliant. Secondly, she found herself buying fewer clothes for her little girls. *Does this party dress still fit? Can this coat last another season? Can I fix this sweater?* Yes, yes, and yes! Wonderful. Also, just like me, she was getting better at creating new outfits by simply trying out new combinations.

I don't know about you, but I definitely tend to pair up the same clothes in the same old ways, over and over again. But now, with fewer clothes to choose from, Amy and I were forced to mix and match in new ways. We also began to use the clothes we were 'saving' for later. Saving for what, we didn't know, but we didn't feel we could wear them on a regular Wednesday. With those outfits added to the main bulk, our possibilities were suddenly endless.

But of course, just like me, Amy had a few near misses. Like when the Hobbs sales catalogue appeared in her mailbox. She flicked through it, saw a lot of beautiful clothes she liked (at half price!), and thought to herself, 'Maybe I can relax my rules a little bit? After all, if I got this cardigan, I would strictly use it for work. We all know that work clothes don't count. They are office necessities, like printers and laptops.'

Realising she was heading into dangerous territory, she threw the catalogue in the recycling bin where it got buried under a stack of newspapers.

A few days later, after dinner, she could feel the catalogue calling her. She grabbed her flashlight and hurried to the garage to steal another look. As she kneeled down on the cold cement floor, flashlight in one hand and the catalogue in the other, she thought to herself, 'What the hell am I doing?' She ran back inside, locked the door, and rang me.

I was beginning to understand why Alcoholics Anonymous has a buddy system. You need someone to keep it real. Amy and I were in this together.

Now that we knew what to avoid (shops, catalogues, and listening to our crazy inner voices), moving forward would be dead easy. Our new plan was to keep it real and stay focused.

That plan worked brilliantly, until the sale season came to London and hit the city like a hurricane.

Chapter Three

January

> **6** *Fashion is a form of ugliness so intolerable that we have to alter it every six months.* **9**
> *- Oscar Wilde*

I'm back in London, it's January, and the sale madness is spreading through the city like wildfire. We're talking big league sale-a-thon, a consumer fest, a national spending-palooza. The little sale spree I witnessed in Norway was a tiny discount fart compared to this production. January in London is shopping at its loudest. In other words: this just got real.

Sale Season. Or, Crazy Town

Even on a regular Thursday in March, London is a Holy Grail for shoppers. On a yearly basis, in Oxford Street alone, we're talking over 200 million shoppers. Tourists shop, locals shop, and people on business trips shop.

To give you a visual, last spring I witnessed a room full of foreign bankers break out in a sweat as they fled the lecture hall early. They were dying to hit Harrods before catching the plane back home. Watching them scramble into the row of taxis waiting outside, you'd think they were boarding the last train out of East Berlin.

I'd forgotten how all-consuming the London shopping vibe gets. This January it's following me around like a drug-filled cloud.

Opening my email, sale ads are spilling into my inbox. Collecting my mail, sale catalogues are spilling out of my mailbox. Looking through the newspaper, ad campaigns are jumping out at me. Walking down the street, every shop window is emblazoned with high-pitched trigger words like SALE, DISCOUNT, REDUCED PRICES, and HALF OFF.

The message is urgent, like a warning, or a 'Wanted' poster. Hurry! Let the shopping begin!

The message is also upbeat. We can look like the photoshopped people, wearing what they're wearing! 'Now at a reduced cost!'

Finally, the message is clear and simple: *Buy, buy, buy!* Shop! Shop! Shop!

At work my colleagues are showing off all the sale items they've snapped up. 'Look what I got!' is the phrase they use. No one likes to use the word 'bought'. 'Look how much I saved!' is also thrown around.

But I don't want to hear about your shopping spree. You found clothes. In a store. That you paid for. Good for you! Congratulations! Now leave me alone.

When will this madness end? I'm no expert on brainwashing, but I'm starting to get the gist of it. The human mind is rendered helpless against such blatant attacks. Only blind and deaf people, and those in solitary confinement, can escape this nationwide shopping propaganda.

What I need is a safe house, or a shopping-protection program. I'm sorry, but where are my Greenpeace comrades-in-arms? Where is the counterattack? Where are the billboards promoting being happier with less? Where are the ads about saving instead of spending?

You know what? As much as I hate to tell you this, it's working. I'm getting pulled in. This speaks to the power of suggestion. A small part of me knows that I don't want to go shopping, but another part of me, a bigger part, is positively itching to hit the sales. I'm so ashamed to admit this, you have no idea. I fancied myself being so much better than this. I thought I could just surf through this year on a wave of calm. I thought it would be fun. I didn't expect to *struggle*. I didn't expect to feel so many conflicting feelings. What is happening to me?

But seriously. Did I really think I would be able to withstand the pressure of the city? Did I actually think I would be able to go against the natural flow of things and reduce myself to an outcast, a *freak*?

I feel lonely. Not shopping in January feels surprisingly lonely. I'm outnumbered. I'm excluded from all the hoopla. I don't get to sit at the table with the cool girls. I can't join the other shoppers, and I can't show off my new outfits — because I don't have any. I have *nothing*. The way I see it, I'm left with only one choice: I have to go shopping.

You know what they say: if you can't beat them, join them.

Shopping Spy

Don't worry, I'm not *really* going shopping. I'm not going to break my pact with Amy. I'll be doing research. My plan is simple: I will infiltrate the shops like a spy and observe the other shoppers up close.

I have to do this. I need to understand what is going on with me. I need to dissect if it's the clothes, the shops, or the collective act of shopping that is tugging at me. It's a risky move, but what's the worst that can happen? Either I'll have a total meltdown and have to be airlifted to a secure location, or I'll learn something.

After work I get off the bus by Marble Arch and head toward Oxford Street. Behind the enemy lines I instantly blend in with the other shoppers.

First stop is Topshop. Thanks to Kate Moss, Topshop is like a magnet for all fashion enthusiasts. Wearing something designed by her is the next best thing to *being* her, or at least being as thin as her.

The second I'm inside the store I feel hot and uncomfortable. The store is like an anthill on acid. It's so crowded that the only way I'm able to move is by walking sideways, mimicking the gait of a beach crab. I try to make myself as small as humanly possible, but somehow that only makes it worse. I have no choice but to thrust out my elbows and step on people's toes. *That's it, just push your way through.* I'm channelling Darwin. This is survival of the fittest.

When I reach the sale racks at the back of the store, I've already lost the will to live. I look around. Where are all the beautiful clothes? Everything is higgledy-piggledy, chaotic and messy. Some of the clothes are even crumpled up on the floor like yesterday's laundry. It's like being at a frat party. The staff must be on an extended tea-break or something, or in hiding. (Not that I blame them.)

As I crane my neck to see what's going on at the other end of the store, I wonder if the deafening music is intentional. You know, to quickly repel less serious shoppers. If so, it's working like a charm. I untangle myself from the other shoppers and head straight for the exit door.

Out on the street I immediately feel better. *That was dreadful.* In all fairness, I did see a nice handbag, a vintage-y looking one, but getting it would have required techniques normally reserved for hostage negotiation situations.

Next stop is Monsoon. I've always liked Monsoon. They sell clothes you want to wear if your Grammy-winning cousin is hosting a garden party, or if you want to look professional without being mistaken for an auditor.

At Monsoon the music is just right. *That's more like it!* But then I notice all the people. This place is as packed as a United Nations refugee camp. *Doesn't anyone have a date, or a movie to go to? Doesn't anyone have a hobby? A life?* Apparently not. Not only that, but the percentage of amateur shoppers is staggering.

Clue number one: they have unwisely brought their children. While the little ones scream and run around threatening to smear jam all over the half-priced party dresses and needing to go pee-pee, mommy is conveniently blocking out the sounds of her own offspring.

'Not now, Sarah! Can't you see mommy is busy? Go and find your brother.'

Clue number two: they are wearing way too many clothes and carrying heavy bags. They will never make it. They are exhausted before they even begin. One of them looks like she's about to faint. There should be an Emergency Station in here. Why didn't anyone think of that?

Overall impression about Monsoon: too many children and way too packed. But what about the clothes? Were they nice? Did they come in my size? I couldn't tell you. All the clothes were so squashed together that only Jaws of Life would have been able to pry them apart.

I know I said I wanted to go shopping, but that urge is quickly fading. If I could bypass the shops, this street, the other people, and somehow end up with a pile of lovely new clothes...then *maybe*. But to put up with all of this just to get another pair of jeans? You've got to be kidding me.

I make my way over to Primark.

On a good day Primark is a multicoloured eyesore, an in-your-face kaleidoscope of outfits representing every style, size, and colour. It's a big, loud, and shambolic shopping experience. People love it. On a bad day Primark feels like a scene from *Mad Max*.

When I walk into Primark this cold January evening, I see a crowd gone wild. Scanning the store, I instantly conclude that the sale madness has pushed this discount dominion into a state of anarchy. Every shopper is moving fast and mechanically, and they're all dragging Primark shopping baskets behind them.

What kind of shopping weirdness is going on in here? I see people literally *grabbing* clothes off the sale racks and catapulting them into their baskets. From where I'm standing, the 'should I or should I not buy this?' screening process takes three seconds or less.

Am I missing something? What's the rush? Is the rapture upon us? Will these clothes be what we wear in the underground bunkers hiding from the aliens? Your guess is as good as mine; I just know it's not natural to stock up on so many clothes. It's not shopping. It's hoarding. It's frankly a bit sickening.

The posh voice in my head thinks, 'Shoppers at Selfridges or Harrods would never behave in such a beastly manner.' There I picture an elegant lady in her sixties picking out a casual black cashmere cardigan (the kind I'll always wear when I retire), which she pays for with her late husband's platinum card. Then she boards her private jet and takes off to Martha's Vineyard where she spends the weekend musing about the Kennedys and sipping Long Island Iced Tea.

Snapping out of this vision, I leave Primark and walk outside. It's getting dark, but the shoppers are still going strong. Not me. I need an ejection seat, or a self-destruct button. What part of me thought this would be fun? I'm done playing secret agent. I give up. I want to go home. But I have one more stop to make. For the sake of research I'll go to Selfridges, and *then* I'll call it a night.

Selfridges is a bit like a Tibetan mastiff, freakishly big and overpriced. I track down the main entrance and walk through the imposing doors.

What fresh hell is this?

Shoppers at Selfridges, contrary to what I had imagined, are just as manic as all the other shoppers I've encountered this evening. Sure, the lighting is sort of pleasant, and the customers carry very expensive handbags, but their behaviour is just as deranged. Grabbing. Touching. Pushing. Bulldozing. Their faces are alert but expressionless (Botox?), and there is a joyless vibe in the air. I feel so sad. I want to send these people off to a happiness seminar or something. Anything but this.

I'm about to leave when I remember that Selfridges is the only place in the world that sells my perfume. A perfume so expensive that I had to forget about it the second I smelled it. *What's it called again? Betty wants an Abortion...? No, that can't be right.*

I make my way over to the perfume section and look around. I used to like scents like *Paris, Volupté,* and *Lou Lou,* but that was decades ago. I don't want to smell like 1992. I want a signature scent. Perfume is not clothing, so technically I'm not breaking any rules here. And you know what they say — it's better to smell good than not.

Juliette Has A Gun! That's the name of the perfume! I grab a small Selfridges man and ask where I might find it. He guides me over to the Juliette counter and leaves me to it.

Juliette counter? What is all this? In my mind there was only one Juliette perfume, but in front of me are eight different Juliette bottles. Now I have to spray and sniff tiny strips of white paper and compare the scents. This is silly. I hate this shit. When did I hang out at Selfridges anyway? Never, that's when.

But, since I'm now a mindful shopper, shouldn't I cultivate the finer things in life? What woman doesn't own an expensive perfume? Perfume is a staple, the platform which everything else is built upon. Is it not? To quote Coco Chanel: 'A woman who doesn't wear perfume has no future.'

Who can tell anymore, but here I am, so I might as well make the most of it. After a few rounds of sniffing and spraying, I decide which Juliette scent I like the most. *Miss Charming* is definitely my new scent. I pay for it and head outside carrying the bright yellow Selfridges bag that signals, 'I just spent way too much money!'

Debriefing

Arriving home that evening, I dropped my Selfridges bag in the hallway, made a strong cup of milky tea, and began to sort through my impressions.

Before conducting this experiment, I was convinced that by not shopping during the sale season I was missing out on a spectacular social fun-fest. But then, curiously enough, after only half an hour on Oxford Street I was ready to smash my head in.

Fascinating. Why such a big gap between my expectations and my experiences?

Was I was bothered by all the people? Or maybe I hadn't eaten enough beforehand? Or could it be that I no longer knew how to be a shopper? Had the shop-stop pact made me out of sync with consumer culture? Perhaps...? That would at least explain why this evening felt so alienating to me.

As much as I liked this theory, I knew it wasn't the full explanation. I had to dig deeper.

Before conducting this experiment, I had wanted to know if it was the clothes, the shops, or the collective act of shopping that was tugging at me.

I decided to go through these points one by one, hoping it would bring me closer to the truth.

a) **Clothes -** Had I wanted new clothes? No, I didn't want any new clothes, yet I felt compelled to go shopping. Weird.

b) **Shops -** Did I miss being inside shops? No, that wasn't it either. I was certain of it.

c) **The collective act of shopping -** Did I miss the *idea* of being a shopper? Yes! That's it! I had missed being a carefree shopper! I had missed the *experience* of shopping.

Even though this felt true, it made no sense. If I had missed being a carefree shopper, why had only five minutes inside Topshop put me off shopping for life? Had I missed something I didn't even like? Was that even possible?

I had to dig even deeper.

I asked myself, in the past when I'd gone shopping, had it been as fun as I thought it was, or had the thrill of getting new clothes erased all the bad memories related to shopping. *Plausible.*

Or, had I bought into the idea of shopping being the ultimate fun-fest?

Popular Culture and Shopping

According to movies like *Confessions of a Shopaholic, Pretty Woman, The Devil Wears Prada,* and *Clueless,* not to mention TV series like *Sex and the City* and *Friends,* being pretty, finding love, and having profound (yet humorous) moments of self-discovery seem to go hand in hand with shopping and fashion. The message is:

- You have to be original, but you have to look exactly like this.

- You have to be smart and cool, but make sure you spend most of your time, energy, and money on clothes.

- You have to lead a rich and interesting life, but stick to topics like boyfriends, sex, and shopping.

Shopping montages in movies, in case you haven't noticed, have a triumphant edge to them. Watching the heroine strut out of the store, carrying her own body weight in shopping bags and smiling from ear to ear, we're left feeling like we've just witnessed a small, but significant, miracle. 'She found the right dress! Now he will finally propose!'

This threadbare cliché, oversimplified as it might seem, is undoubtedly responsible for many a misguided shopping trip.

In contrast, according to Hollywood's portrayal of women, women who have turned their back on consumer culture, or women who don't give a hoot about clothes and fashion, are often cast in roles such as:

- Woo-woo women with names like Rainbow and Butterfly. These kindly lady-folks talk to spirits, raise bees, and sleep on a futon mattress on the floor.

- Judgmental women with frugal personalities and pursed lips.

- Meek spinsters.

- Cult members.

In conclusion: taking clues from popular culture, you're either a frivolous and fabulous shopper, or you're some peculiar thrifty person who doesn't want to have fun.

This made me wonder, have female characters always been stuck in such extreme and closed-minded views?

Let's have a look.

Once upon a time, in a magical place called Hollywood, they used to make movies featuring inspiring and intelligent leading ladies. I'm talking about movies from the '30s, '40s, and '50s. These movies might be old, but who can forget the riveting storyline of *His Girl Friday*? Or the brilliant dialogue and characters in movies like *Bringing up Baby, It Happened One Night,* and *My Favourite Wife*?

If you haven't seen these movies, go and find them right now. I'm telling you, close this book, make some popcorn, and prepare yourself for some serious movie fun. Go ahead. I'm not going anywhere.

Now, where were we?

One interesting thing about these movies, and many other movies from this era, is that the clothes were remarkable. They were stunning, in fact. But as gorgeous as these clothes were, the clothes were never the story. That's the point I'm trying to make.

What Greta Garbo, Irene Dunne, Katharine Hepburn, or Bette Davis wore on the silver screen didn't make their characters more or less likeable. A walk-in closet was not an indicator of a rich inner life, or lack thereof. If the leading lady happened to wear a fabulous dress in one of the scenes, so be it. Big deal. Who cares? Claudette Colbert was adored for her gumption, not her gowns.

So what happened? What happened to the strong female leads? Curious to find out, I Googled 'modern movies with strong female leads'. The following movies made the list: *Pretty Woman, Legally Blonde, Bridget Jones's Diary, Clueless,* and *Basic Instinct.*

As much as I wanted to laugh at this list and dismiss it as superficial drivel, it made my insides curdle. This was a recent list. This was not some old scroll representing outdated thinking patterns of the past. This list made it painfully obvious that we have a long way to go. Actually, it made it obvious that we haven't come very far at all. According to this list, should we choose to believe it, women have become *more* image-obsessed over the past sixty years, not less.

Just *how* image-obsessed we all are, and how it plays out in our daily lives, will of course vary from person to person, and from situation to situation. Nevertheless, I don't think it's a coincidence that we live in a world where every female public figure is ruthlessly judged by her looks. She's not only judged by *what* she is wearing, but also by *who* she is wearing, and *where* she wore it. When Sharon Stone wore a charcoal turtleneck from Gap to the Oscars, she made fashion history. The next day women all over the world went bananas trying to copy her style. However, if a female public figure wears the 'wrong' outfit — or God forbid, leaves the house without makeup — there is no stopping the shitstorm coming her way.

Clothes, shopping, and fashion — the whole shebang — are stuck in such extreme views. I'm calling out for some grey zones, or at least a legitimate representation of the complexities of the issues. Because the truth of the matter is that clothes are neither good nor bad, they are both. Fashion and shopping is not reserved for shallow people with only two brain cells, nor is it anywhere *near* as important as some people make it out to be. I agree with Margaret Atwood when she says, 'I wouldn't want to live in a world where people didn't dress up from time to time. It would be very boring.' And I applaud Joan Rivers for saying, 'People who take fashion seriously are idiots.'

More statements like that, please. And how about some new role models?

Shopping and Role Models

Dream with me. How helpful would it be if someone like Meryl Streep or Amy Poehler fronted an anti-consumerism campaign? What if Jennifer Aniston spoke out against fast-fashion and shopping? Can you feel how powerful that would be? In the same way that Ricky Gervais is a brilliant advocate for animal rights, and how Linda McCartney was stellar ambassador for vegetarians, the 'Shop Less Live More' movement (or 'Less Shopping More Gumption' movement) needs a face.

And you know what, let's retire the 'Best Dressed' and 'Worst Dressed' lists. We can do so much better than that, don't you think?

I'm not suggesting that we have change everything right away. After all, I can't *force* popular culture and Hollywood to come up with new role models for us. I'm just playing around with the idea of scrutinising the existing ones and holding them up against who I am and who I want to be.

Buyer's Remorse (and how to avoid it)

I'm going to take a sharp right turn here and talk about buyer's remorse.

I'm sure buyer's remorse happens all year round, but it's never more present than during the sale season.

Casting my mind back to last year's sale, I remembered going shopping. I remembered buying all kinds of new clothes. Had it been fun? What did I buy?

Out shopping I was having the time of my life. *Will you look at these beauties?! Look at that dress! This is FANTASTIC!*

The very next day I felt like one of characters in the *Hangover* movies. *What happened yesterday? What did I buy? Where did I go? Was I DRUGGED?*

Shopping mistake number one was the blue shift dress. Buying it I thought, 'This dress will be my new everything dress! I will wear it all the time!' Only I didn't, because even with a slip underneath, this dress suffered from an unmistakable case of VPL (visible panty line). It also made my stomach look kind of wobbly, so then I tried to wear it with a big sweater over it, which predictably made everything worse.

Shopping mistake number two was the grey winter coat. I told myself how soft and lush it was, not noticing how it was that annoying length that makes it impossible to walk in. I tried to wear it without buttoning it, but that defeated the whole purpose of staying warm. Wearing it with a sweater underneath made me look like a bag lady. (Why do I always try to fix fashion emergencies with a sweater?)

Shopping mistake number three was the light blue cocktail dress. The Embassy hosts lots of fancy events, so I figured I could splurge on a new evening outfit. This dress, however, would only work on someone built a la Dolly Parton...that wouldn't be me. I don't know why I didn't notice that; I just know I *loved* the fabric.

Not willing to admit defeat, my buyer's remorse was quickly swept under the rug with an upbeat, 'It's only clothes! And they were dead cheap! It would have been stupid *not* to get them. If they don't work out, I can always get more stuff!'

From the planet's perspective, this is plain suicide.

From the perspective of the fifteen million textile workers worldwide, it must be disheartening to know that they're risking their lives making clothes we don't even wear (or like).

From a financial perspective...*well*. It's ridiculous.

Fortunately my failed shopping trips can be fuel for my brand new Emergency Shopping Guidelines. Like Jennifer Aniston so beautifully put it, 'There are no regrets in life, just lessons.'

If you follow my new guidelines, you'll never buy a single bad outfit ever again. That's a promise.

And listen, I want you to know that I don't care what you look like or what kind of clothes you buy; that's entirely up to you. I just want to come up with guidelines that will reduce our collective carbon footprint. In order for that to happen, there needs to be a more vigorous screening process in place. In my opinion, buying clothes should ideally be as difficult as getting into the Freemasons.

Here are my new guidelines:

1. **If you don't like it, don't buy it.** 'Ooh, half price! It's not exactly my style, but I should give it a try! Who knows? Maybe snakeskin print will be my new thing!' Sounds

familiar? Two weeks later you won't remember how little you paid for whatever you thought you liked, you just know you hate it and will never wear it. So here's the deal: if what you like happens to be on sale, hurrah for you. If you're drawn to the orange price tag alone, snap out of it.

2. **If it's uncomfortable, don't buy it.** It's one thing to look fabulous standing still in a changing room, but real life requires manoeuvring around. It's only when we get back home that we discover how the shirt feels like a straightjacket, how the dress creeps up when we walk, and how the jumper pinches in all the wrong places. Let comfort be your guide. Don't buy clothes you can't stand wearing.

3. **If it doesn't go with any of your other clothes, don't buy it.** This is an important guideline. Not so much from a style or comfort perspective, but from a 'don't drain the earth's natural resources for clothes you never wear' point of view. Having a lot of clothes that only work on their own is like having a kitchen full of ingredients you can't cook with. *Hm, what can I make with olives, liquorice, and oat-bran?* In contrast, when your new clothes complement your existing outfits, the possibilities are endless. I want my wardrobe to be like a friendly neighbourhood, everyone getting along and living in harmony. Even new clothes will be old one day, so let's make sure we build long-lasting and meaningful alliances.

Shoes

So far I haven't mentioned shoes. That's because unlike most women, I would rather eat my own vomit than go shoe shopping. Amy knows this about me, so when we went over the rules for our shop-stop pact, shoes never came up.

So why do I hate buying shoes? Well, my feet are so small that the only shoes that fit me come from the children's shoes department. And believe me, nothing takes the joy out of shoe shopping like being perched on a low chair built for little people under a poster of Spongebob Squarepants. Also, it's just not the same when you have to fight off angry mothers who think I'm in the wrong store. 'That's clearly not your size!' one mother snarled at me. 'I need that shoe for my daughter! Give it to me before I get the shop manager.' (OK, that only happened once, but it was pretty scary.)

Having small feet is like having an embarrassing relative. You try not to cringe, but you catch yourself wishing for an invisibility cloak. Like the time when the airport security guard told me, 'I need your shoes too, madam, not just your son's.' (I don't have a son.) Or the time I'd kicked off my shoes by my desk, and upon seeing these shoes one of my colleagues thought I'd brought my daughter to work with me. (I don't have a daughter.) Then there are all those people who point at my feet and exclaim, 'Look at those tiny feet! I don't know how you're able to stand! Oh my God! It looks like you're about to fall over any minute now!' (I like to think of my feet as Cinderella-ish. But whatever.)

So yeah, I hate shoe shopping.

But as January was drawing to a close, I noticed that one of my colleagues was wearing really great shoes. Great as in tiny. Tiny like my feet. So I asked this colleague, let's call her Gigi, 'Where did you get those shoes?'

'From the Little Shoe Shop by Baker Street.'

She said it so matter-of-factly, like finding great shoes for small feet is the most natural thing in the world. I had expected her to say that she had bribed one of Santa's elves, that her father was a shoemaker, or how there was this special place on the other side of the moon.

The Little Shoe Shop?

I immediately Googled it, just to make sure it was a real place. It was. Now what? Did the shop-stop pact prevent me from buying shoes? I called Amy for guidance.

ME: I have found a shoe store that sells shoes in my size.

(*Silence...*)

ME: Amy?

AMY: Not a children's store?

ME: Not a children's store.

AMY: Where?

ME: Near Baker Street.

AMY: And they sell nice shoes? Not just for old people?

Years earlier, Amy had accompanied me to a shoe shop for problem feet. (Why do they call them 'problem feet'? It makes it sound like they are juvenile delinquents.) As I sighed and slumped, looking at rows and rows of sensible shoes, the sales guy with the protruding Adam's apple said in a nasal voice, 'This is not a fashion store, you know.'

Duh.

> ME: No, I'm telling you. They sell normal shoes, pretty shoes, shoes *you* can buy, only they come in MY size!
>
> AMY: What are you waiting for? Don't go crazy, but buy some shoes for Christ's sake. God knows you've been waiting long enough.

And this, ladies and gentlemen, is why Amy is my best friend. She gets me. She knew this had nothing to do with being a mini Carrie Bradshaw, but all about finally being able to buy shoes free from Velcro straps and Disney motifs.

The very next day I went to The Little Shoe Shop. I'd never been so jazzed up over shoes before! *So this is what the hype is all about?* There were no mocking large sizes, only petite wonders. Some shoes were even too small for me! Can you believe it?

I worked my way through the shop systematically, not rushing, but savouring every moment. After careful examination, I landed on three pairs. A scarlet red pair with a suede heel and a cute bow, a sexy pair of black pumps, and a pair of beige Mary Janes.

I can't tell you how grateful I was to discover this shoe shop just as I was weaning myself off clothes shopping. Or maybe it was the other way around? Maybe I discovered the shoe shop *because* I wasn't so preoccupied with clothes for a change?

Later that evening I walked around the living room wearing my new red shoes. I couldn't believe how great they were. I posted a picture of them on Twitter. I felt like I'd just won an award, but I also felt a bit insecure. So I asked Ben, 'What do you think? Do my feet look like Minnie Mouse in these shoes?'

'I'm not following.'

'My shoes? Do they look like something Minnie Mouse would wear? I just don't want to walk around looking like a cartoon character.'

'There is nothing wrong with Minnie Mouse's feet, dear,' Ben said. 'It's her ears that are a bit funny.'

Shopping as the Ultimate Female Bonding Experience

Did you notice that I went shoe shopping all by myself? That I didn't bring a girlfriend with me? That's because I'm a lone shopper.

One of the many myths orbiting shopping is that shopping is the ultimate female bonding experience. It's our own fault. Women go on shopping sprees, shopping outings, boast about what they buy, and proudly share shopping secrets. Women even go on shopping *vacations* together. *Oh, we've just been on a short trip to Prague. Have you been there? The stores are to die for!*

Being a practical person, I find the whole routine of shopping with another person quite tedious. In fact, I find the whole routine of waiting to see what the other person wants to buy quite boring. What role does the other person play? What could they possibly bring to the equation that I can't provide for myself? Unless they are paying for my purchases, I would rather shop alone.

Alone, I can browse without having to constantly approve or

disapprove of the other person's finds. Alone, I can try on clothes in peace and quiet. Alone, I can leave whenever I want to.

The times I *have* gone shopping with someone else, it was never to have a *bonding experience*. The people I've gone shopping with are people I love spending time with anyway.

I know I'm not alone in feeling this way. I know plenty of people who prefer solo shopping trips, so where does this myth come from? Is this another thing we can blame popular culture for? I want to say yes, but since I don't know I'll have to say *maybe*.

What I *do* know is that shopping malls are often accredited with being an integral part of the women's liberation movement.

To understand why, we have to travel back in time to Victorian England. And the store I've chosen to illustrate this point is none other than Selfridges.

Before the arrival of department stores, or shopping malls, no respectable lady would ever leave the house without a suitable chaperone, and that same lady would never go shopping unless she knew exactly what she was buying. Browsing was considered vulgar, and back in Victorian England shopping was a necessity, not a hobby.

Mr Selfridge changed all that. He had a radical new vision for shopping. He wanted shopping to be less about the goods you bought, and more about the lifestyle, the beauty, and the glamour the products represented. He backed up this vision by filling his new department store with gorgeous flower arrangements, art installations, and amazing products. All the products were beautifully displayed, not frugally kept behind glass cabinet doors (which had been the custom at the time), and every customer was free to touch, look, and smell as much as she or he pleased. Browsing was encouraged, and Mr Selfridge made all his customers feel appreciated by inventing slogans like, 'The customer is always right', and 'Give the lady what she wants'. The people of London had never experienced anything like it. Virtually everything about this new department store was mind-blowingly novel and unconventional. This was not shopping. This was like going to the theatre, or to an art gallery. But more importantly — and this is the part that ties in with the women's liberation movement — since Selfridges was a highly respectable place, fine ladies could meet up there unaccompanied by chaperons. They could spend a whole day there just shopping and browsing, turning shopping into a hobby and a pastime, much like it is today.

I get how liberating this must have been, but I also know that the world has changed a lot since 1909. The reality of the situation is that women nowadays can meet up wherever they want. They can meet up at the cinema, art galleries, jungle safaris, writer's workshops, cigar bars, the beach, or just hang out at home with a bottle of wine and giggle the night away. Just to name a few. I'm not saying we *don't* do any of these things, because we do, but for unknown reasons the myth that shopping is the ultimate female bonding experience is still going strong.

Not Shopping is Female Bonding at its Loudest

To prove that myth wrong, I've now arrived at the part of the story where my friend Sarah came to visit.

Sarah is a gem. Having her as a friend means laughing a lot and having both insightful and silly conversations. She is someone I can lean on, trust my secrets with, and expect total honesty from. She's like ten people in one, and she's the only person I know who is just as comfortable carving a canoe as she is mixing cocktails. She also speaks four languages.

Normally when friends visit me in London they're dying to go shopping, so you can imagine my joy when Sarah announced she was on a shop-stop. Now I could look forward to a shopping-free weekend filled with art, food, and friendship.

Sarah and I visited Tate Modern, we went on walks on Hampstead Heath, and we ate breakfast at Harrods. We ate dinner at the local pub, laughed our heads off, and drank endless cups of tea. We also drank wine. We talked. I don't think we slept much.

When the weekend was over, I couldn't help but wonder, 'With

so much fun going on, how did we ever have time for shopping?'
    NOT shopping is female bonding at its loudest.

Chapter Four

February

> **6** *Buy less, choose well, make it last.* **9**
> *- Vivienne Westwood*

So far we've talked a little bit about consumer culture, role models, shopping behaviour, Emergency Shopping Guidelines, and looked at developing non-shopping strategies. Now it's time to get down to brass tacks. It's time to take a closer look at the people who make our clothes: the textile workers.

Who Makes Our Clothes?

Before this shop-stop challenge, I'm afraid I didn't really think about the textile workers. As in, I didn't think about them at all. Why get depressed? It was much more pleasant to imagine that our clothes were born out of thin air, floating through the sky like little fashion angels.

Even so, as much as I hated to admit it, in the back of my mind I knew that the average textile worker was underpaid, overworked, and lived an anonymous existence somewhere in Asia. I also knew that this was a fairly new workforce. You only have to go back a few generations before you find people who used to make all their own clothes, or had them made by a local seamstress or tailor. Back then, the very idea of having your clothes made at the other side of the world, and not even measured to fit your own specific size and needs, would have been absurd.

To make this point more personal, it's my pleasure to introduce you to a few wonderful women in my own family.

First out is great-great-grandma Inger. In the few pictures I've seen of her, she is either knitting or spinning wool. She's making clothes. This was considered normal.

Her daughter, great-grandmother Anna, lived on a small farm and raised eleven children. Because she was such a great seamstress, each one of those kids had remarkably nice clothes: pleated skirts, ruffled blouses, vests, and suits. There was never a button out of place or a stain in sight. Living on a pig farm was no excuse to get sloppy with appearances. Looking at childhood pictures of my grandmother, you would think she grew up in Paris, not in Nazi-occupied Norway.

My grandmother, Grandma Inger, moved away from the farm and became a teacher. She got married and went on to have four children: one girl and three boys. My earliest memory of my grandmother is watching her busy, busy hands. They were always immersed in sewing, knitting, embroidering, or crocheting. In her house there was never an inch of fabric, yarn, or thread that didn't get put to good use. She once made handles for a tote bag out of an old pair of leather boots. She made necklaces out of copper plates. She also made most of her own clothes, claiming that ready-made ones were overpriced and poorly made.

My grandmother's oldest child (that would be my mother) got married when she was sixteen, and by the time she was nineteen she was the only student at her high school raising two kids. We didn't have a lot of money — as in none — but you'd never guess that by looking at us. I had ironed ribbons in my hair and the most adorable outfits.

Mom was a ferocious knitter, and my wardrobe was filled with cute little sweaters, skirts, hats, and dresses with the most intricate patterns. My favourite outfit was my knitted trousers, my Happy Trousers. I was a very gullible child, so when mom told me that these trousers had the power to make me insanely happy, I believed her. Wearing those colourful, clown-like, larger-than-life trousers, I made Pollyanna look like the Angel of Death.

Take a moment now and think about your own parents. Can they knit, sew, weave, embroider, or crochet? One of them? None of them? So go back a generation or two, and don't only focus on the women. My grandfather was a great weaver, and many of the Tibetan lamas I've met took great pride in knowing how to sew.

Think about your friends. Do they know how to sew? What about yourself? Do you know how an outfit is put together?

Let me guess. That would be a 'no'?

How do I know that? Because we, as in you and me, belong to the first generation in human history that doesn't know a sewing machine from a hole in the ground.

Actually, I *do* know how to sew, but that's not the point. The point is that over a relatively short period of time, we, as a people, have become clothing illiterate.

How did that happen? How did we lose those skills? And how can we get them back?

I know sewing is making a comeback, but for the most part we think of sewing as something retired spinsters do. Craftsmanship is lame (even using the word craftsmanship in a sentence is totally lame-o), and who wants to think about how our clothes are made? It's *wearing* them that matters.

I do acknowledge that if we went back to making all our own clothes, there wouldn't be time for much else, and that would be a shame. But I also know that leaving it all up to the textile industry, is like handing over power of attorney to a crazy gang member.

Knowledge is power, and I think it's time we took some of that power back.

Quality

But how do we begin to take that power back? I'm glad you asked. Part of the answer lies with learning about quality.

When Great-grandma Anna was a young girl, families in Norway spent maybe thirteen percent of their income on clothes. In the U.S. they spent a bit more, sometimes up to twenty percent. Today an average family spends only three percent of their income on clothes, even though the amount of clothes they buy has quadrupled. As a result, the women in the UK have *four times* as many clothes as they did in the 1980s.

The truly wild thing about having this abundance of cheap and disposable clothes is (according to Vivienne Westwood, and I happen to agree with her) that we have 'never looked worse.' We buy clothes based on price and volume, and we pay zero attention to putting together a good look. Not because we don't want to, but because in the midst of the avalanche that is the fast-fashion industry, we got so excited by the cheap prices that we forgot to ask about quality. No one seemed to notice that it got left behind, trampled to death under the weight of mass production.

But how did this happen? And why?

In the 1960s, the majority of the clothes for sale in the U.S. were made in the U.S. In the decades that followed, more and more businesses began to operate on an international scale, and a slew of textile factories opened up in countries like China, Bangladesh, and India. Soon over eighty percent of all clothes were imported from Asia, and people in the West welcomed these cheap clothes with wide open arms.

We thought the clothes were just that: *cheaper*. We didn't notice that the workers who used to specialise in certain hems, who knew the difference between a French seam and a chain stitch, and who knew just how to make that little dart in the sleeve lining so the coat would fit better, got tossed out with the polluted bath water. In the name of profit margins and efficiency, the new factories 'invested' in cheap labour, crammed production lines, simple design, and basic equipment. Well-made clothes were out. Mass production was in. Investing in clothes was out. Disposable clothes were in. Taking care of our clothes was out. Buying new stuff was the new way forward.

Despite all these changes, we still, bafflingly, expect our clothes to make us look and feel good. Given the decline in standards and erosion of quality, that's like expecting junk food to be nutritious and wholesome.

I have to admit, part of me is impressed with how the outsourcing evolved. Building all the factories, moving businesses overseas, working out trade agreements, tax issues, the whole financial side, all of it must have taken a lot of planning, capital, and foresight. Not to mention a blatant disregard for human rights issues. I mean, who in this day and age employs children? What is this, a Charles Dickens novel?

Another part of me is annoyed that they managed to pull this stunt off. I feel like we've been tricked by a magician using clever distraction techniques. Because it can't be denied, to the untrained eye the clothes produced today look similar to the clothes produced before the outsourcing began. Blinded by how much fun it is to buy a blouse that costs only £2.99, we don't see the disaster staring back at us.

This is where learning about quality becomes important. Let's say you tried on a jacket made in 1950 (pre mass-production era), followed by a jacket made in 2013 (the height of the fast-fashion period). What would you notice, what would you learn? I can promise you right now, the difference in quality would shock and alarm you.

If you then proceeded study the design and compared how the jackets were made, how they were put together, you would see the gaping gulf between them.

Inspired by this, let's pretend that you asked someone to show you a few basic sewing tricks. And let's pretend that you bought a coat from the Salvation Army, ripped it apart and spent about twenty minutes examining it inside out. What would you learn?

By learning a little bit about how our clothes are put together, you will (hopefully) start to buy better clothes. You will develop an eye for quality. At the very least, you will no longer be distracted by the cheap prices and flashy fabrics. 'Sewn together with only two seams? No wonder it doesn't fit right.' Or, 'That hem is a joke. It will never stand the test of time.' Like a trained sorceress, you will become a smart and sophisticated shopper.

I'm not suggesting you have to spend a lot of time on this. You don't even have to learn how to sew. I'm only encouraging you to be curious and ask questions about the products you buy.

In the meantime, please keep in mind that quality doesn't always have to do with price or brands. Cheap clothes can be of excellent quality, and expensive ones can be hyped up and overpriced. More on that later, but here is a little trick to get you started down the path of quality: clothes made from natural fabrics are superior to those made from synthetic ones. If you focus on fabrics alone, you'll be miles ahead of the other clueless shoppers.

Look at the Label

A study conducted by Hoechst Fibers Industries in the early 1980s found that eighty-nine percent of the population couldn't tell the difference between polyester and natural fibers like cotton, wool, and silk. More alarmingly, people didn't even *care* about the difference.

You *should* care, and I'll tell you why: synthetic fabrics don't breathe. Meaning, you might as well be wearing a plastic bag. No air gets in, no air gets out. This is why a breezy-looking summer dress made of viscose will leave you sweating like a pig, and an acrylic shirt will leave you feeling wooden and restricted. Don't be fooled. Look at the label.

I don't want to get into a lengthy comparison between all the different fabrics out there, but I will introduce you to the differences between silk and polyester. (Just to be clear, silk is a natural fabric and polyester is a synthetic one.)

Silk or Polyester?

Silk was discovered by a Chinese empress. Polyester was invented in a laboratory. The shiny silk thread comes from the cocoon of the precious silkworm, and each cocoon contains a single silk thread that measures up to 900 meters, more than three times the length of London Bridge. The polyester thread, in comparison, is manufactured from industrial ingredients like coal, water, and petroleum. This new fabric was introduced to the world in the 1950s under slogans like, 'Scrunch it! Pull it!' It became famous for being the fabric you could wear for *sixty-eight days* straight without having to wash or iron it. Silk, on the other hand, is revered for being luxurious, mysterious, and exotic. In addition to being shiny and beautiful, silk keeps you warm in the winter and cool in the summer.

If silk is the Paris of the fabric world, polyester is Detroit, after all the manufacturing plants shut down and the banks repossessed most of the houses.

Do you still want to buy that polyester dress?

Natural fabrics can be more expensive than synthetic ones, but personally I would rather have one cashmere sweater than eight acrylic ones. And if it's warmth you're after, stick with natural fabrics like wool, cashmere, and silk. Acrylic and polyester don't stand a chance against the winter cold.

Based on all this, the Emergency Shopping Guideline for February has to be:

Quality over quantity.

The Mind and Shopping

It's confession time. Even though I know about sewing, fabrics, quality control, and all the rest of it, it didn't prevent me from buying the worst kinds of clothes. How many times have I looked through my wardrobe and asked: *I bought THIS? I wanted to wear THAT?* How many clothes did I get rid of during the closet clear-out?

How do I look?

To me this illustrates how complicated the realm of shopping is. Even with the best intentions, and even when we're armed with knowledge and understanding, we go astray. I know I said jokingly, 'Something happens to my mind when out shopping,' but it's actually true.

Curious to find out *what* exactly, I did some research and came across three illuminating explanations.

1. **The psychological explanation.** Have you heard about the mere-exposure-effect? It means that the more we see something, the more we think we like it. Get exposed to a thing, an idea, a product, or an outfit often enough, and your mind will begin to develop a preference for it.

   I can attest to that. This happens to me all the time. For instance, for the entire month of January I caught myself checking out studs. Yes, studs! I'm talking about those shiny metal spikes often found on clothes worn by cowboys, punkers, and strippers. Everywhere I looked, people wore studded shoes, studded jackets, studded hair clips, studded trousers, studded handbags, you name it. It was like watching barnacles on a pirate ship. As a result I said to myself, 'I might look good in that!'

   Thank goodness I was on a shop-stop, otherwise I might be sitting here decked out like Johnny Rotten's grandchild. Which would be perfectly fine, mind you, it just wouldn't be *me*. But show me something often enough, and my mind will start to wonder if it *should* be me.

2. **The religious explanation.** According to Buddhist scriptures, our human existence is often referred to as the Desire Realm. One of the many characteristics of the Desire Realm is our meaningless, but ambitious, pursuit of material things. We crave and we crave, and we buy and we buy. The things we acquire are not the problem;

that's not why this pursuit is considered meaningless. It's meaningless because we're never satisfied. Regardless of how much we have, how much we own, or how often we go shopping, it's never enough. We can always think of one more thing to get. There is always a newer version. An upgrade. Something fancier. Something different. Something new! So we keep on shopping, keep on wanting, lusting, craving more and more things, and then one day we die.

The end.

3. **The scientific explanation.** This explanation addresses the fact that our brains were developed for a very different world than the one we now live in. As hunter-gatherers we used to live shorter lives, we had fewer choices, and we met fewer people. It was also a life filled with many uncertainties; we had no idea where our next meal would come from or what dangers lurked around the next corner. In order to survive we had to act on our impulses and chase after what we needed. If we didn't bring home the bacon, pun intended, we would die. You snooze, you lose, so you better get out there and hunt, gather, and hoard as much as you can. If you replace those words with browse, shop, and binge, we're back to the present time. What we *need* and what we *want* is no longer in short supply, but our brain doesn't know that. It's still in survival mode. When it comes to shopping, we're still hunter-gatherers, hardwired to grab everything we can get our hands on. We are not trained to think, 'Wait a minute, there will be another sale next year, I should just skip this one. And besides, I already have enough clothes to keep me safe and warm, so I'm good.'

That's not how it works.

However, given that this is how we survived for ninety percent of our human history, is it any wonder that we still haven't registered that we already have enough? The same behaviour that laid the foundation for our very existence is now leaving us sick, unsatisfied, in debt, confused, and hungry for more — and to repeat Vivienne Westwood's statement, we've 'never looked worse.'

This is just a quick and superficial overview of the brain on shopping, but I believe these explanations drive home the point that shopping can't be dismissed as 'just' shopping. In order to fully understand what we're dealing with, we have to zoom *way* in, focus on just one person, ourselves, and then we have to zoom *way* out, get a bird's-eye view, and learn about things like culture, evolution, neuroscience, and habits. Even religion.

Vacation Wardrobe

February is the month of Valentines and romance, and Ben and I celebrated this with a mini-break in Bath. We normally go to the Cotswolds for Valentine's weekend, but this year we thought we'd mix it up a bit.

We stayed at a nice hotel, and over breakfast I keenly observed all the other guests, looking at what they were wearing. Since I was writing about clothes and fashion, I felt it gave me a free pass to play Fashion Police. I was ruthless.

These people are so poorly dressed that I almost feel embarrassed for them. I thought this was a sophisticated place, and yet every single person has unwisely chosen to bring their most unflattering outfits. The girl with the overflowing muffin top should never wear such a boxy cardigan. The woman in the corner looks like she is going for the 'estate agent slash stripper' combo. And what possessed that flat-chested woman to wear a top with a plunging neckline? It's like a roadmap to nowhere.

None of these women were unattractive, quite the contrary, they just didn't know how to dress. Or maybe they did.

I think I know what's going on here, I thought to myself. *This is all about the vacation wardrobe.*

Since we buy way too many clothes, we end up with an abundance of outfits that we never wear. Yes? These outfits are either too small, too uncomfortable, too bold or...too something else. Basically, they are the result of shopping in hunter-gatherer mode. My new theory, based on what I was seeing, was that these mishaps come with us on vacation. We believe that once we are removed from everyday life, we become different people — more bold, more adventurous, thinner obviously — and ergo, should wear different clothes.

I'm as guilty of this as the next person. Abroad I always fancy myself transforming into the very essence of elegance. I picture myself stepping off the Orient Express in a crisp linen suit. Or biking through Tuscany wearing a red cotton dress. In my fantasy world, all holiday pictures of me are amazing. So why in God's name did I bring my yellow flabby shorts to China? Why did I wear that unshapely blue skirt in Spain? And why did I stroll through Paris in faux leather leggings? I looked like an idiot.

You'd think I should know that if my clothes don't work at home, they sure as hell don't work on vacation. I mean, *now* I know, but back then I felt that all my clothes deserved to be used, like they have feelings or something. *No clothes left behind. Come on you guys! This way!*

The packing process leading up to these trips were just as nuts. I always felt I was just one wrong outfit away from ruining the entire vacation wardrobe. (But seriously, clothes are so tricky. Put on the wrong long-sleeved jersey and you look like you're on your way to a grunge gathering in Seattle.) This made me quibble over questions like:

Should I bring my Kate Moss hat? What about jewellery? And how many sweaters do I need? And what kind of underwear should I bring? The everyday stuff, or the fancy selection that lives at the back of my drawer? Does this dress make me look like a porcelain doll? Maybe if I removed the bow...

That's the rambling of a crazy person. But now, with less stuff to choose from, I felt like I'd been saved from myself. Packing for my holiday in Bath was a breeze, and the few clothes I brought with me were all gorgeous.

I took another bite of my toast and looked down at what I was wearing: cashmere cardigan, striped tank top, and skinny jeans. I poured myself another cup of tea and concluded I was the best-dressed person in the room. Objectively speaking, obviously.

Vacation Shopping

Holidays are for reading, and after breakfast Ben and I went to a tucked away coffee house called Same, Same But Different. There we made ourselves a little nest out of tea, coffee, treats, and books.

Even though I was totally engrossed in my book, I couldn't help but notice that every single person walking past the windows was carrying shopping bags. Was I jealous? Not so much jealous, but now that I fancied myself to be an expert on quality shopping, I felt I should be allowed to shop a *little*, but I didn't. Besides, I knew that shopping while on vacation, even on a mini-break like this, is like playing Russian Roulette.

When on vacation we lower our shopping guard. It happens every single time. The second we arrive at a new place our taste flies out the window, and all of a sudden fridge magnets and odd trinkets seems like a perfectly reasonable idea. It's only when we get back home we realise we don't like macramé, and how the beach towel decorated with the map over the city is butt-ugly.

Shopping on vacation can also be quite stressful. A few years ago I went on a girl-trip to India. Before going, people had warned me about the plague (watch out for rats), rape (don't walk the streets alone), and the famous Delhi belly (don't drink the water). However, nobody warned me about *shopping* in India. I'm not exaggerating when I say it was the hardest part of the journey, and that includes being robbed by a Holy Man. After just twenty minutes in New Delhi,

I was ready to join an Ashram and shave my head, just to avoid all the shops.

From a quality point of view, I wish I'd bought more things in India: the silk, the cashmere, the authentic tea, and the delicious spices, but I just couldn't handle all the mayhem that went along with buying them. Also, it's hard on the soul to shop for luxury goods when everywhere you go, you bump into malnourished women, kids with polio, and toothless beggars. It's like going for a spa treatment in hell.

Grandma was always a big holiday shopper. Returning from Egypt, Thailand, and Russia, she showered us with gifts and souvenirs. She also splurged on things for herself. I distinctly remember a set of china cups from the Imperial Porcelain Factory in St. Petersburg. They were hand-painted by Russian artisans and embellished with 18-karat gold. Years later, when Mikhail Gorbachev resigned from office, in his television speech he drank from a cup with the exact same design. Grandma was so proud.

Shopping as Disguise

Back at work, after the weekend in Bath, I found an official-looking envelope in my cubbyhole. *What's this?* I tore it open and gasped in surprise. *I've been given a raise! A ten percent raise! I know I asked for one, but I do that every year. Maybe all the nagging finally wore them down?*

Not to sound ungrateful, but I was a bit annoyed that this raise was given to me during a shop-stop year. I was so proud to leave Bath empty-handed, but now I felt I should celebrate my raise with a new dress or something. I deserved it.

Goodness, when will this waxing and waning stop already? When will I stop making such a big deal out of not shopping and just move on with my life?

But *why* did I feel compelled to celebrate my raise by going shopping? I didn't want to go shopping, yet I wanted to. Could both of these thoughts be true at the same time? Possibly. They both *felt* true. But how could that be?

Confusing as this was, I had to accept the fact that I was in the process of unlearning everything I thought I knew about clothes, shopping, and myself. What happened inside my head was a massive colliding of concepts, ideas, and beliefs. Mental Big Bang.

Part of the problem, I realised, is that buying something new is just a small, and often an insignificant, aspect of shopping. I now saw that shopping also serves as a reward, as an emotional crutch, and sometimes like a therapy session. Yes, all of those things.

When one of my friends, let's call her Marian, found out that her fiancé had cheated on her, she was outraged. 'I can't believe he had an affair with that stupid slut from the supermarket!'

Her justifiable rage was soon soothed by lots and lots of shopping. Beaming with adrenalin and glee, and a hint of revenge, she showed me all the things she'd bought: new boots, dresses, sweaters, and accessories. None of these items took away the disappointment and hurt, but at least she sailed through her breakup in fabulous new outfits.

My point is this: shopping is great at disguising itself. Shopping shows up as insecurity. Shopping shows up as addiction. Shopping shows up as boredom. Shopping shows up as attention-craving. Shopping shows up as revenge. Shopping shows up as partying. Shopping shows up as grief. Shopping shows up as triumph.

Shopping embodies all our emotions.

What a trickster.

Here are some of my own emotionally-induced shopping trips:

My-boyfriend-doesn't-get-me shopping trip
He has been such a douche bag lately. I just need a new sweater and then everything will go back to normal. Just seeing me in this adorable angora sweater will make him realise how much he loves me and he'll start doing twice as much housework!

I'm-bored-out-of-my-mind shopping trip
My life is a wasteland; I'm stuck in a rut; I need some excitement, something to shake things up a bit. I don't really want to go paragliding,

but how about a new skirt? By getting a new look I will attract new opportunities. Everybody knows that's how it works. 'Be the change you wish to see in the world.' Something like that.

I'm-such-a-good-person shopping trip

I'm a good person. I recycle. I don't steal. I don't Facebook at work. I'm punctual. I often give my spare change to beggars, especially those with pets. It's only right that I treat myself to something new, something really nice. I've earned it. I'm totally worth it.

I wonder what hunter-gatherers did when they needed to vent or celebrate. Did they kill an extra bison? Did they dig up a tree and thrash the branches around? Who knows? I just knew I wouldn't be celebrating my raise by doing any of that, and I didn't go shopping either. But I did buy a train ticket to Glasgow. That's where Amy lives, and I hadn't seen her in ages.

Decluttering with Amy

And so it happened that I went on my second weekend trip this February. On the train to Glasgow I had plenty of time to observe the other passengers. I couldn't help but wonder what mixed bag of emotions inspired *their* shopping sprees. Based on what they were wearing, I'd say crushing boredom. And they all looked so similar, like they'd just been to the same dull office party.

This made me even more pleased with my own outfit: cashmere cardigan, striped tank top, and skinny jeans.

That's right, the same outfit I wore in Bath. Classic, casual, yet stylish. This time I'd paired it with a bright red handbag. I'm in love with this outfit. If I had to commit to a single outfit for the rest of my life, this would be it. Once you've found your signature look, you can take your foot off the shopping pedal and enjoy the ride.

Amy meets me at the train station, and the moment I see her I feel bubbly and excited. *Anything can happen!* She is the funniest person I know, and smart too. I am so proud of our friendship.

Glasgow is cold and grey, but we light candles, put on music, and make cocktails: Rhubarb Bellinis. *To us!* We have not shopped since the beginning of November, and if this was a religion we would be enlightened by now.

After the second drink — OK, fifth drink — we decide to look through Amy's clothes. Unlike me, she has not had a closet clear-out. She needs my help. She tells me this. 'I can't do this by myself, I need your help,' is how she puts it. And boy, is she right. Where to even begin?

For instance, there is this peculiar obsession with jersey turtlenecks. Worn with jeans, maybe. But worn underneath a dress? A travesty. Unless you plan to join a cult, there is no excuse for dressing like a brainwashed freak. Amy sees my point and reluctantly throws them away. All of them.

'But what do I wear when I'm cold?' she says.

What stone has she been living under? Do like Michelle Obama, of course. Wear a nice cardigan on *top* of the dresses, not underneath them.

Amy unearths a beautiful navy cardigan and tries it on over a selection of previously drab-looking dresses. Now she looks ten years younger, and more fun. We experiment with belts and shoes too, and we agree that this wardrobe has untapped resources.

Wardrobe mistake number two is all the ultra-trendy stuff. The green dress looks like something the loser on *The Apprentice* would wear. It has too many pleats, and what's up with the asymmetrical fabric configurations? Thumbs down. We also throw out the grey trousers, the prison guard suit, and the shapeless denim skirt.

My educated guess would be that all of these clothes were bought in a state of sleep-deprived confusion, the result of shopping online while the kids were bathing, or bought in a hurry before picking them up from school.

Wardrobe mistake number three, which is not entirely Amy's fault, is the poor quality of the clothes. My vintage coats and jackets still look as good as new, while Amy's new-ish winter coat looks like it's been through a hijacking. *Adios!*

As predicted, based on my own decluttering exercise, the size of the reject pile is shockingly huge. Amy is upset. She can't believe a pile *this* big represents nothing but shopping mistakes. 'Surely I can wear that blouse with something!'

The whole evening has been like that, like a tug of war. Me pointing out how unattractive something is, and her trying to justify why she should keep it.

I steer Amy toward her closet and show her what she's left with: a closet full of nothing but beautiful clothes.

Imagining loving all your clothes. Imagine adoring all your outfits. No, seriously. Stop for a minute and pretend that's the case. This means you no longer have to wonder about what to wear. There will be no more excuses, weird compromises, or half measures. All your clothes fill you with happiness, confidence, and serenity. Close your eyes. What does that feel like? Isn't it magical?

Amy lets me pack up all the horrible clothes, and the next day we bring them to a local charity shop. Interestingly enough, she can't quite remember what she's gotten rid of. The alcohol might have something to do with that, but still. 'Maybe I should have another look, just to be sure,' she says.

I refuse, and she gives in.

I couldn't help but think, *It's odd how good I'm getting at this. Getting rid of things I mean.*

Anyone who knew me growing up will tell you that I used to collect everything from old socks to used movie tickets. My room was a living museum to all my interests and activities, and I kept it freakishly neat and clean. In case I went missing (kidnapped, murdered, my body buried in the forest, the usual stuff), I didn't want the detectives going through my things to say, 'Can you believe this mess? We'll never catch the killer.'

Then one day I came across the Chinese proverb, 'If you own more than ten things, the things own you,' and something inside me shifted. I saw that I wasn't so much collecting treasures as I was morbidly attached to every single object floating around in my universe. So I loosened my grip, but I was still holding on for dear life. It wasn't until I moved to the Buddhist centre I discovered the joy of less, and I've been scaling back ever since.

All I'm saying is that I recognised what Amy was going through; it's called separation anxiety. I just no longer thought it should apply to clothes, or other inanimate objects, for that matter.

With the closet clear-out over and done with, Amy brings me to all of Glasgow's finest bakeries and cafés. We have so much to talk about, and we are eager to get through all of our pressing topics and personal revelations. We constantly interrupt each other and finish each other's sentences. It's always been that way with us. Dying to share. Committed to listening. Laughing so much that we fall over sideways.

The Wedding Dress

Three days later I'm let in on a little secret. One of my colleagues, let's call her Tina, is getting married. *Congratulations!* She and her boyfriend will elope to Las Vegas and exchange vows in a chapel. *Love it! What fun!* Then she tells me, 'I don't think I'll be wearing a wedding dress.'

Excuse me?

Repeat that, please. I don't think I head you correctly.

The idea of not dressing up for the most romantic day of your life, the one and only day you can get away with wearing a veil, is horrifying to me. I can't believe she's even considering this. On the other hand, I get why she doesn't want to spend thousands of pounds on a dress she'll only wear once.

While 'normal' clothes are getting cheaper and cheaper, wedding dresses are getting more and more expensive. Considering that the average wedding dress costs close to £2000, what exactly are we paying for?

Are wedding dresses made with special techniques and sewn with stitches reserved for bridal-wear production? Sadly, no. Unless you are Kate Middleton, where the maidens working on her dress washed their hands every half hour and changed their needles just as often, your wedding dress will be machine-sewn in China.

Are wedding dresses made from special fabrics? Not so much. Most wedding dresses are made from polyester.

So why the steep price tag? Because we totally suck at buying wedding dresses, that's why. Wedding boutiques are posh money traps, like airports and Selfridges, and wedding dresses are marked up because brides are willing to pay the inflated price.

Fortunately there are many other alternatives. You can have your wedding dress made by a seamstress (like grandma did), borrow it (like mom did), buy a party dress at a regular store (like my sister did), or you can buy it from a thrift store (like I did).

When Ben and I got married, I wore a gorgeous pure silk, cream-coloured designer dress. I looked like a 1940s movie star, and I felt like a million bucks. The dress set me back £25.

I'm telling all of this to Tina, and she finally agrees to go wedding dress shopping with me. 'Just to see!' I encourage her. I brief her about a small cluster of vintage shops right by Waterloo station, and judging by the smile on her face, I can tell she is really looking forward to going there, and so am I.

By the time we get off the tube, the dying day is rapidly fading into fifty shades of grey. We cross under a cheerless steel bridge and enter the abandoned street. Seen from the outside, our wedding dress hunt looks more like a tribute to *Bleak House* than a colourful Hollywood movie montage. But who cares, it's the inside that counts.

Entering Radio Days, a vintage shop like no other, I take great pleasure in noticing that I feel fine. Nothing is tempting me. None of the clothes are talking to me. This makes sense. This is not my first rodeo. By now I know what I'm dealing with. I take a deep breath and congratulate myself. I'm finally over shopping.

But as my eyes adjust to the inside light, and as I take in each and every detail — the horn buttons, the fine fabrics, the stacks of Frank Sinatra hats in the corner, the richness of the display — my calm begins to waver.

'Not this again!' I whisper to no one in particular, sending the mannequin wearing the vintage safari suit an angry look.

Even though I haven't seen anything in particular that I like, there is this deep fundamental sensation that something is being kept from me. Now I wish I'd left my wallet at home. Having money is too dangerous. It's too tempting. *I shouldn't even be here.*

The last statement is in fact true. I am supposed to patch a phone call through from the Norwegian Prime Minister to Number 10 Downing Street. It could happen anytime from now until midnight. What if there is no cell phone signal in the store? I should never have left the office. *What have I done?*

The bridal section is disappointingly slim, but there are plenty of other gowns that could easily pass as a wedding dress. Tina disappears into the changing room to try on a few promising pieces.

I scan the store for somewhere to sit, and that's when I notice a flask-green dress displayed on the opposite wall.

Hold on. Flask-Green? *Seriously? Aiaiai!* It's only my favourite colour in the whole wide world. Considering how difficult it is to come across anything flask-green, and considering how hard it is to find a great dress, finding a flask-green dress is a miracle equal to when Lazarus returned from the dead. *Look at it! How could I not want that dress? It's spread out like a dancing angel; it is positively alive with charm and happiness.* I soak up all the details: full skirt, cinched-in waist, and a teardrop neckline. I feel like crying. I want to scream.

I'm sad.

I'm happy.

I'm confused.

I'm hyperventilating.

I walk toward it, as if in a trance, and I know with every cell in my body that this dress represents everything I've ever dreamed of. The urge to buy, to own, to take home, is suddenly overwhelming.

Shit! What do I do? I HAVE to get it. It's not like I have a choice. There must be a way. I look around for clues. I try to come up with a plan.

First: I check out the size of my handbag. Would the dress fit inside it? Amy and I never said anything about stealing. I crane my neck to see what the clerk is doing. Maybe I could distract him?

Then: what if I can get Tina to buy it for me? As a thank-you gesture for going wedding dress shopping with her? Scratch that.

Then: buy it for someone else and then borrow it all the time? *That could work...*

Tina emerges from the changing room. She looks stunning, but sadly the dress is baby blue. We try to make it work, but we both agree that she doesn't want the dress to be the 'something blue' on her wedding day. She returns to the changing room.

In the back of my head I am still trying to figure out how to get the dress.

What if I tell the clerk I have cancer?

As my thoughts are spinning out of control, Tina announces that she is done looking. We can leave now.

Darn! I mean *good!* Leaving this place is my only hope to get the dress out of my mind and move on with my empty life. I want to hug it goodbye, but that would be weird. I hurry out of the store and don't look back. This is no time for melancholy.

Next stop is a vintage shop named What the Butler Wore. Here there are only two wedding dresses. The first one looks like an oversized tutu, something a toddler would wear in a school play. I hate it. The second dress takes my breath away. It has an understated bridal look: straight lines, embroidered neckline, and the most wonderful fabric. I touch it and realise the dress is made from baby-soft velvet. Tina tries it on. It fits her like a glove, like a gorgeous, beautiful, elegant glove. The only problem is the long sleeves. She had pictured a strapless dress, or at least one with short sleeves. She is concerned this will be too hot for Las Vegas.

I see her point, but I don't see why this should discourage her from getting the dress. Being perpetually solution-oriented, I tell her that if she really likes the dress, I will fix the sleeves for her. 'Consider it my wedding gift!' I say.

That seals the deal, and Tina goes to pay for it. The price: £60.

How do I look?

This calls for a celebration. As we walk to the nearest pub, a part of me is still sulking over the flask-green dress, but I no longer feel like I want to die. That part has passed. Besides, the joy of finding the perfect wedding dress for Tina completely overshadows any of my own petty feelings.

The bride-to-be orders wine, and just at that moment my phone rings. It's from the Norwegian Prime Minister's office. I tell them I'm ready to patch the call through.

Chapter Five

March

> **6** *Trendy is the last stage before tacky.* **9**
> *- Karl Lagerfeld*

In this chapter we'll be looking at trends. But what do we mean by trends? Is it the same as *fashionable?* And who decides what's in and what's out, and how does that process even work? And why weren't there any punkers in the Middle Ages, and how come Queen Victoria never wore mini-skirts? When it comes to clothes and fashion, is it all about timing?

Trends

Designers often say they get inspiration from watching regular people on the streets. We, the public, influence the trend-setters. But as we all know, whatever *they* design, *we* will wear. What we buy is no accident. Trend guides. Advertisements. Billboards. Fashion shows. Magazines. These kinds of things not only shape *what* we like, but *when* we're supposed to like it. In other words, trends are what happens when a small group of people decide what a larger group of people should be wearing, and for how long.

Besides the obvious weaknesses with this system, a collective following of trends is also absurd. With everyone looking like they've been dipped in the same dye, trends come across as shallow and short-sighted. Where do crucial things like body type, personality, age, and taste come into the picture?

It was by *not* following trends that Jackie Kennedy became one of the world's greatest trendsetters. When Hillary Clinton asked her for fashion advice, Jackie replied, 'You have to be you.'

That will be our Emergency Shopping Guideline for March:

You have to be you.
Figure out who you are and dress accordingly.

I remember walking around downtown after the second *Matrix* movie had been released, *The Matrix Reloaded*. How did I know that *The Matrix Reloaded* had just been released? Because everyone was dressed up as Trinity and Neo. Black leggings. Hair slicked back. Some sort of coat, black or grey. Shiny if you could find one. Long, always.

As if by an unspoken agreement, the stores and shoppers had decided this was the new trend. Shortly after, as by an unspoken agreement, the shops cleared away the leather and PVC clothing, and people stopped wearing long coats and using greasy hair products.

A new trend used to hang around for years, sometimes decades. At the very least, a new look would last a full season, and it often marked a clear break from what had come before, reflecting social, political, and economical changes.

Thanks to the fast-fashion industry, we now have a trend carousel that acts like it's on a diet of crack and Red Bull. This carousel is gathering speed as we speak, spinning faster and faster, spitting out more and more clothes. Stores like H&M and Topshop now receive new inventory every single week. Let me repeat that: *every single week!* In my opinion, to call that a trend would be like mistaking a Twitter feed for a book. Words like *burst, flick,* and *fling* feels a lot more appropriate. 'I'm wearing the latest fling.' Yes, I like the sound of that. That's what people should be saying.

Considering how short our fashion cycles have become, you can almost pinpoint the *exact* month something was bought, which will be great for future archaeologists. 'Look! An owl-print blouse! That dates this settlement back to May 2012. Quick! Get National Geographic on the phone!'

Even though new clothes can spruce up an otherwise boring week, I have to admit that when I see people wearing *nothing* but new and trendy clothes, I get both sad and suspicious. What happened to all their old clothes? What are they hiding? In my opinion, seasonally replacing all your clothes only makes sense if you're in a witness protection program.

Before this shop-stop, I kind of knew the fashion carousel was churning out more and more clothes, but I also didn't think it was true. Or possible, for that matter. How could it be? It sounded too hectic and confusing. Which it is.

Spring Trends

Sitting on the 82 bus, commuting to work, driving through Oxford Street every single day, twice a day, five days a week, I feel like I'm stuck in a *Twilight Zone* version of *Groundhog Day.* Instead of everything being the same day after day, everything is always different. I'm of course referring to the rotating shop window displays.

I've never really paid attention to them before, but now I can't help but notice how often they're changing. Not only that, judging by the signs in the windows, the new spring trends are here.

But how can that be? It's only March. March isn't a spring month. It's a winter month. Isn't it? Or did that change?

As for the new spring trends, I'm amazed at what I see. The shops are filling up with all kinds of hideous outfits my brain refuses to take in. *What the…?*

In the spirit of learning I buy a few fashion magazines. I've never done this before. Now I know why. They put me to sleep. They are all filled with mind-numbing headlines like *Top Ten Fashion Trends, How to Wear This Year's Spring Fashion, Mix and Match!*, and *Do's and Don'ts* lists.

The only quibble I have with these headlines is that they leave no room for personal expression. What happened to Yves Saint Laurent's statement: 'Fashion fade, style is eternal'?

According to these magazines, we're all supposed to wear *this* kind of sweater, buy *this* kind of trousers, and wear pricey designer belts over *these* fashion 'must-haves'. (Must-haves, what a funny phrase. Especially considering how the very same objects will probably end up on the *Don'ts* list within two months. Max.)

Since I'm not shopping this season, here are some of the trends I will miss out on this spring. Miss out on, saved from…you be the judge.

- Leather

- Floral prints

- Ethnic prints

- Stripes

- Flamenco ruffles

- '90s throwbacks

Is this what fashion has been reduced to? Or returned to, I should say? None of the items on this list can qualify as a new trend; this is a regurgitated mixture of everything we've seen a million times before. I'm not surprised. Given that our current trend cycles have the lifespan of a mayfly, who has the time to come up with something new?

Oscar de la Renta once said: 'My role as a designer is to make a woman feel her very best.'

I know for a fact that I can't feel my very best in flamenco ruffles and '90s throwbacks, so I'm glad I'm forced to sit this one out. Thank goodness I'm on a shop-stop.

Personal Style. Or, Clothes as Storytellers

Personal style, unlike short-lived trends, is all about wearing clothes that reflect our identity and interests. So when people say that clothes are mini-biographies, scripts, and a plot made from fabric and thread, that's what they mean. They mean that our clothes say something about who we are, without having to use words. Or as Orson Welles so well put it: 'Style is knowing who you are, what you want to say, and not giving a damn.'

When I lived at the Buddhist centre, one of the older students once told me in a husky Mother Superior voice, 'I won't buy another outfit for as long as I live. A new dress won't help me when I die.' She also said stuff like, 'Religion is all about *surrender.*'

I wanted to point out that clothes are fun, and part of what makes them fun is playing with new looks and creating your own style. Creating a style based on the fact that we one day will die... well, that's not fun.

Personal style also ties in with social status and group mentality, and what we wear becomes the distilled visual aid of what our group and social status stands for. In that regard, clothes become clues, like in a mystery novel.

'The crucifix necklace suggests the girl is a Christian.' Or, 'The red glasses, spiky hair, and trendy t-shirt suggest the man reads *The New Yorker.*'

That doesn't mean these 'clues' are intentional. Far from it. Body language, for the most part, isn't intentional either. Neither are facial expressions. It doesn't matter; they still speak louder than words. It's just a fact of life that regardless of who we are (a widow, a diplomat, an enlightened being, a prostitute), and regardless of what we put on in the mornings (or wake up in, depending on the circumstances), we are all — literally — wrapped up in our own private story.

The first time I became aware of clothes as storytellers was in 1983. That was the summer my mom bought an old Ford and drove south. We were moving to Spain.

I was only eight years old, and after three long days of driving and listening to Steely Dan, we finally crossed the Spanish border. We rented a house, settled in, and spent the next twelve months living in a rural village.

A peculiar aspect of village life was that most of the women who lived there wore black clothes. Women of all ages. Every single day, black clothes only. This piqued my curiosity. Didn't they get hot? *Why* didn't they get hot? And why didn't they want to wear cute summer dresses? Didn't they like them?

When I asked my mom about this, she said, 'Black is the colour of mourning.'

'But why do all of them wear black, all the time?' I asked, looking at a leathery old woman sitting outside her house, knitting and wearing black from top to toe.

Mom explained that Spain had been through a Civil War, followed by a dictatorship under Francisco Franco, and during that long dark period, lots of people, especially men, had died, leaving a nation of widows behind. And in Spain widows always wear black.

'All these women are widows?' I asked. This put everything in a new light. I couldn't help but wonder how their husbands had died, if they still missed them, and if they missed wearing regular clothes. I remember thinking that wearing black was almost like wearing an armour of grief.

Inspired by this discovery, I began to notice how the same type of people gravitate toward the same type of clothes. I was not the first person on earth to ever notice this, but I found it extremely fascinating.

At the hospital I observed that the nurses wearing blue uniforms were much kinder than the nurses wearing white uniforms. Coincidence? Was blue a *kinder* colour?

I noticed that the moms with perms and tucked-in blouses were much stricter than the moms wearing shawls and flowy tops. Did the perm make them stricter, or was it the other way around? What came first, the shawls or the laid-back attitude?

As a high school student at the local Waldorf school (or Steiner school as some people call it), I noticed a definite 'Waldorf' uniform amongst the teachers. They were all a bit blurry around the edges, and you could never really tell where one piece of clothing began and where the other one ended. Shoes were of the sensible, chunky variety. Years later, when I visited Waldorf schools in Napa Valley and Pennsylvania, I observed the very same fashion code, down to the knitted scarves and the semi-precious stone earrings. What came first, the layered look or the love for anthroposophy?

Right after high school I landed a job as a dishwasher (landed is maybe a strong word), and I was appalled to learn that I had to wear a uniform. Even thought this uniform was my hippest outfit to date (jeans and a black t-shirt), it wasn't *me*. I missed wearing *my* clothes. That's when I knew I could never become a nurse or a police officer. All jobs requiring uniforms were forever off the table.

However, uniforms, just like personal style, are also great storytellers. The same goes for religious wear. They say something about what you do, who you answer to, and what you believe in.

Religious Wear

When I boarded the plane to San Francisco and moved to the Tibetan Buddhist centre, I knew my searching days were over. I had found my tribe. I had found my true calling.

For those of you who have never lived at a Tibetan Buddhist centre, you'd be interested to know that a centre is not the same as a monastery. So if you're looking through my Facebook page in search of pictures of me with a shaved head and wearing saffron-coloured robes, I'm sorry to disappoint you.

Also, if it had been a monastery, I don't think I could have moved there. As much as a small part of me will always dream of becoming a Julie Andrews-type nun, Buddhist nuns have a huge disadvantage: they look like men. While the bald head and mid-calf-length robes is a great look for a tall, skinny man, it does nothing for the ladies.

At any rate, the centre, *my* centre, consisted of what you would call lay practitioners, or householders. This meant we could have relationships, kids even, keep our hair, and drink alcohol. The only unusual thing about us what that we lived together in a commune, at a *gonpa* (remote place), in search of a higher truth and enlightenment. And as I mentioned in chapter one, I already had a *chuba*, so I fit right in.

At the same time, perhaps for the first time in my life, I found myself in a situation where style and looks scurried away and took a modest backseat. As Buddhists, we were all about cultivating *inner* beauty, not outer. But even in this rustic, reflective, and remote environment, and even when I attended retreats in the forest, in the deepest dark of winter, where sleep was reduced to four hours per night, where every meal was taken standing up, and doing the dishes meant rinsing your plastic cup in a bathtub converted into an industrial-size sink, my standards didn't drop. I still cared about what I looked like. I didn't expect that to be the case, but for some reason it didn't bother me. I decided I'd rather be an authentic vain person than act like I was 'over' clothes. Besides, I wasn't the only one. Each and every one of us had our own unique style. And even though none of us were stylish in the traditional sense of the word, of all the spiritual groups out there, I felt I'd hit the jackpot. Our clothes said: we're spiritual *and* beautiful.

To paint a picture of what we looked like, let me break our styles into five main categories for you:

1. **The laid-back look.** The people belonging to this group had more important things to think about than their clothes. They wouldn't know a fashionable outfit if it stared them in the face, so naturally I thought these people

were nuts. At the same time I admired their 'I couldn't care less about what I look like' stance. Somehow I found it reassuring.

2.   **The fabulous look.** This group claimed their appearance was an offering to all sentient beings. Count me in! I wanted to make an offering too! I didn't go as far as to take up yoga and stop eating sugar, but I did join in on the cascading long hair, fine outfits in vivid colours, and the appropriate amount of jewellery. We looked like we were straight out of an Indian scroll painting. I also added a dash of lipstick and mascara, which was a break from the norm, but I didn't care. Without lipstick and mascara I look like a pug. I have no recognisable facial features.

3.   **The normal look.** These people wore the same type of clothes as they had worn before moving there, and they didn't see what meditating and having a guru had anything to do with how they dressed. That I got. We lived in California, 1998, not Tibet, two thousand years ago. There is no time like the present.

4.   **The hippie look.** This was California, after all, so of course we had our fair share of hippies. Hippies love community living. They are great at it. Even though I've never understood the love for tie-dye, free love, and not shaving your armpits, the part I'm drawn to are the flowy dresses and the long skirts. There is something so gentle about that look. It makes me feel like I'm in the presence of kindness itself.

5.   **The Tibetan Yogi look.** A small number of the students couldn't wait to shed their Western identity, and so they embarked on the quest to become a Tibetan yogi. This look starts with growing your hair long, and when it's even longer you wear it in a knot on the top of your head (this

part takes the longest, and we call this hairstyle a top-knot), followed by wearing loose-fitted clothes in muted colours, followed by adorning yourself with conch earrings and other religious jewellery, and finally by walking around barefoot and peppering your speech with Tibetan words and phrases. Congratulations! You're a yogi.

I'm fully aware that when people write or talk about religious living, they often skip over topics regarding clothes and style. Is this because these people will have you believe that once they found God or whatever, they stopped caring about what they looked like? I can only speak for myself, but in my experience even the people who make a point about *not* caring about their looks and clothes, still care, just in a different way. It's also worth mentioning that making a big deal about not caring is just the flip side of caring, so it all evens out in the end.

As for the people who *do* care, who *do* make an effort, they are mostly too modest to admit this. They will have you believe that their stunning beauty and amazing outfits are the results of prayers and incense.

But listen, part of that is actually true. Take my own lama for instance. He could have been a model. He was as charismatic as ten rock stars combined. He looked like Brad Pitt's older brother. To this day he's the most perfect and beautiful human being I have ever had the good fortune to meet. Did he care about any of that? Nope. Had he perfected some elaborate beauty regime? Not to my knowledge. All I ever saw in his bathroom was a bar of Ayurvedic soap and a tube of herbal toothpaste. As far as I could tell, he didn't care about outer stuff, which was probably why he felt so beautiful to me. Or maybe he just was authentic. Authenticity is a powerful form of enchantment.

Even so, to this day I think there must have been something magical about the land. How else would you explain that everyone who ever lived there hasn't really aged? I mean, we have *aged*, but not like normal people do. Even the people who are now in their seventies have something unmistakably youthful about them. I feel like we're the youthful equivalent of that tribe that can't get HIV. We really *did* hit the jackpot.

But just so you don't think I'm a totally shallow person with really screwed up priorities, I would like pause here and briefly explain that it was the teacher, the teachings, the community itself, living with like-minded people, the sense of collective purpose, the whole package, even how the land was permeated with a scent of dry earth, forest, and Tibetan incense, that led to the jackpot feeling. However, since this is not a book about my wild years as a spiritual seeker, I'm focusing in on the clothes. But first, a little more background information.

There were thirty to forty of us in total, living on two hundred acres and studying with the same teacher. We ran a publishing company, a store, a communal kitchen, and an office. In addition, we worked construction, had a mechanic's bay, and a shop dedicated to woodwork and maintenance projects. We were very busy.

On top of all that, there were endless Buddhist projects. Building and painting of statues. Translating and publishing of books. Organising of events and hosting elaborate ceremonies.

It was during these ceremonies that we all dressed up in those gorgeous clothes I'd been so drawn to from the beginning. Chubas. Zens. Brocade tops with princess sleeves. These Oriental-inspired outfits were a rich display of bright colours and beautiful patterns. We looked so pretty, which was not important, but we still did.

The important thing, and this is really neat, was that every colour, shape, and object had multiple layers of meaning. Outer, inner, and secret, to be exact. I was now part of a world where everything was a mark of something else. The colour red was not just a colour, it symbolised magnetising powers and life-force. The lotus flower represented purity of body, speech, and mind. The peacock feather represented transforming poison into nectar of wisdom and accomplishment. And so on and so forth.

We also gravitated toward feng shui, astrology and I Ching. Everything was done with purpose, like we were following an ancient protocol guide.

Little did I know that when I started to work at the Norwegian Embassy, I would encounter many of the same tendencies. Only there I didn't consult the stars or sacred scriptures; instead I had to navigate through the bewilderment we call British etiquette. Let me tell you, it's just as complicated.

At any rate, for those of you who didn't drop out of college and spend your twenties living in spiritual community, your relationship with clothes would have been very different than mine. Instead of developing an irrational fondness for the colour maroon, you would have learned to power dress. Instead of letting your hair grow super long, you would have tried out at least five or six different hairstyles. Instead of finding clothes that were comfortable to meditate in, you figured out what to wear for Casual Fridays.

Personal style and clothes as storytellers will always be shaped by the setting we belong to. But what came first, the setting or the style?

Again, I'm just asking questions, pondering the many ways our clothes shape our lives and values. And how our lives and values shape our clothes.

Consumers

Let's forget about clothes for a second. What I'm interested in when moving forward — not just with this book, but also with my life — is what kind of stories do we tell as consumers? What are we communicating?

Are we mindless consumers?

Kind?

Ethical?

Selfish?

Sustainable?

Can we tick more than one box? To tell you the truth, that question has never come up for me before.

Consumer.

What kind of word is that? The image that comes to mind is that of a snake eating a rabbit. 'The snake consumed the rabbit.' It sounds evil, like someone with really bad intentions. *Customer* is more elegant. That I like. *Shopper* sounds frivolous. *Purchaser* is too formal, like you're ordering drilling gear for an oil rig.

But the question still remains, what do our shopping habits reveal about us as consumers? Or to put it another way: what does our consumer culture say about us as a people?

Speaking for myself, as a non-shopper, I'm clearly a 'conscious consumer with a big heart'. Straight to the point. No grey zones. Friend of the earth. Supporter of the underdog.

But what happens when I start shopping again? How can I make sure I stay on the right side of the tracks? And at what point do I cross over from being a 'normal' consumer to becoming a selfish, petty shopaholic that destroys the earth? Is it when I buy two blouses instead of one? Or when I buy an extra pair of trousers, eve though I don't really need them?

We don't live in a world where we're handed a personal shopping quota, or a yearly t-shirt allowance. Not yet at least. No external forces will monitor any of my purchases, so I don't think there is a real way of telling.

Also, shopping habits vary from person to person, and from year to year. While one shopper will seek out the Fair Trade brands and ethical stores, another shopper will shop for the sake of shopping. Is that how we can tell the 'good' shoppers from the 'bad' ones? Whether or not they shop at ethical stores?

When thinking about this stuff, my thoughts take off in three different directions.

The first thing that hits me is that the average shopper is not an evil monster. He or she is a functional member of our society. She (or he) is not a drunk, or a dangerous criminal. She can walk, she can talk, she can make dinner and hold down a job. She does charity work, she raises children, and she can arrange birthday parties for her best friend.

The second thing that hits me is that most of us might never experience the devastating effect of drought, food shortage, and rising sea levels, so it's hard for us to connect the dots between a sale over here and a polluting factory over there. I think we're stuck in this weird place where we look around to see how other people are handling it. (I know I am.) We think that if only those people over *there* stopped shopping, or if that country over *there* began cleaning up its act, we would be fine again.

But is that what being a mindful consumer means, someone who looks to others for guidance? (As you might have noticed, I'm using the phrases *mindful consumer* and *conscious consumer* interchangeably.)

The third thing that hits me is that even though we're good people doing the best we can, every single shopping trip has unintended consequences. It all boils down to simple math. Once the rainforest has been cut down, it will take forever to grow back again, if at all. Once the rivers have been polluted with factory chemicals, it's near impossible to get them clean again. Once endangered species have lost their natural habitats, they can't just pack up and leave. Where would they go? And so the solution is...what?

When reading about things like segregation, discrimination, shipping criminals overseas to Australia, or child labour during the industrial revolution, we shake our well-educated heads in disbelief. Those were some really questionable decision. We can admit that now. But what will future generations think about *us*?

Maybe our future grandchildren will look at CCTV footage of today's shoppers milling up and down the streets of New York, London, Paris, and Tokyo, wondering what on earth motivated them. *They're behaving like sheep. Who is giving them orders? Is this part of a religious ritual? Does anyone understand what is happening here?*

On another screen there might be footage of factories in China, India, and Cambodia, depicting people sewing nonstop, like slaves working in the cotton fields. *Who did they make all these clothes for? Didn't they know that this mass-production destroyed our rivers and forests? Who was in charge? Were people OK with this?*

I'm the first person to admit that in the past my good intentions never stretched as far as shopping. Amnesty membership, yes. Giving money to charity, absolutely. Thinking about how my shopping habits destroys the earth? Never.

Just like most of the population, I was disconnected from the shadow sides of shopping, and I couldn't begin to imagine how polarising the fast-fashion industry truly is.

Part of it has to do with the fact that I'm entrenched in a consumer culture that thinks nothing of hanging out at the mall all day. Another part of it has to do with lack of information. Clothes are still associated with fun and fashion. We're not trained to look behind the glossy façade.

Now, after five months of not shopping, I've come to understand that if the fast-fashion industry was a party, it would be the hangover part. Which brings me to my next question: when will we sober up?

The Perfect Winter Coat

As I'm writing this, I feel superior in every way. I'm taking a stand and speaking up about important issues. I'm glowing from the inside out, and part of me is a bit amazed that not more people are following in my footsteps. I feel like Greenpeace should be asking me to head up a sustainable-fashion campaign. Or better yet, through osmosis everyone should stop shopping and together we would save the planet and free all the textile workers, just like in the last scene of *Indiana Jones and the Temple of Doom*.

Whenever I'm feeling this great about myself, I know my downfall is right around the corner. Just look at these examples from the past.

When I felt that my meditation practice was only minutes away from turning me into the next Buddha, I slumped into a mega-annoying depression.

The time I felt I was the best personal secretary since Ms Moneypenny, I mixed up the dates in the Ambassador's calendar and sent him to the wrong gallery opening.

Hubris is a dangerous thing. It throws all kinds of shit your way, and in this instant it was The Perfect Winter Coat. This is what happened:

My mother-in-law lives in Belsize Park, in a great garden flat with her two cats. She used to be John Major's spin doctor, so everywhere I go I meet people who know her, or know *of* her. 'You're related to Sheila Gunn!' they say with astonishment and admiration. I nod, totally aware that their esteem of me just shot up a few notches. She and I get along like a house on fire, and from day one she's been like a second mother to me.

One day after work, on our way to see her, Ben and I discovered a new charity shop, right by the tube station. Ben suggested we should go inside and have a look. I followed him on reflex, thinking I could politely browse. What could be the harm?

I casually looked through the clothes, aware that I was starting to feel hungry, and also a bit bored. I was about to tell Ben we should leave when something caught my eyes. Something white. Something long. Something that looked like The Perfect Winter Coat. *Could it really be?*

It was. It truly was. Within seconds I knew it ticked all the right boxes.

-It was one hundred percent wool.

-It was off-white.

-It was in the shape of a timeless princess coat.

Oh, and one more. It was only £12.

No! No! No! A good coat can scramble anyone's brain, but a great coat will instantly somersault my mind into fight or flight mode. I wanted to fight, which meant I had to come up with a plan. A good one.

Hold it! Time out! Why was I thinking about buying a coat? I knew I couldn't buy it, but my brain refused to accept that fact. And that's when it hit me: not shopping was not for me.

Forget about the shop-stop and being the bigger person. Just get the coat. Go ahead. Let's call this challenge for what it really is, a meaningless exercise in misery and fake charity. What are you trying to prove? Who are you trying to impress? Throw in the towel. No one will blame you. Besides, didn't Amy promise you that not shopping would be fun? Unless I've totally misunderstood what fun means, I don't see what's so fun about not getting The Perfect Winter Coat.

These thoughts were dangerously convincing. They had my full attention. I was ready to accept any reason, listen to any voice, and grasp at any straw that would allow me to get the coat.

It reminded me of the time I tried to give up chocolate. Foolishly thinking I could just will myself to not crave chocolate anymore, the following inner monologue took me by surprise:

Good God, of course I can eat chocolate! I don't want to be like those boring bitches who only eat salad and look to Thinspiration for life-advice. Honestly, who is more fun-loving, Nigella Lawson or some loser who thinks that food is the enemy? After all, life is to be ENJOYED, not an exercise in sensory deprivation. Where is the fun in THAT?

I like to use this example because it perfectly illustrates that even when we're dealing with something as innocent as chocolate, it brings up all kinds of conflicting voices and feelings. So the question for me became: how do I deal with this?

Fact number one: I had waited my whole life for this coat.

Fact number two: I was on a shop-stop.

Questions number one: why would the coat find me if I wasn't supposed to buy it?

Questions number two: was this some sort of prank?

Solution: put up a Chinese wall between my mind and the coat.

That didn't work. There was no wall, only despair

Five months into the shop-stop, and I was still losing my mind over clothes? *Are you freaking kidding me?* This made me feel frozen and resentful, and frankly a bit angry. But who was I angry at? Myself? The coat? The store? I couldn't tell. It was like I had a PhD in brain dysfunction.

I blamed hunger. One should never go shopping while hungry.

Hello! I shouldn't even be in a store, let alone be thinking about shopping. *Pull yourself together!*

But this coat was mine! I wanted it! Which I knew counted for nothing. I had no ownership over this coat. So why did I feel like a betrayed lover?

Ben saw me looking at the coat and suggested that I should go and try it on.

Was he mad? Didn't he know that if I tried it on, I'd never been able to take it off again?

Maybe I can just hold it up and look at it in the mirror?

Feeling suddenly curious about what it would feel like to wear it, I headed toward the changing room.

What a surprise, the coat fit perfectly. Even the buttons were gorgeous. By now I was getting a really strong 'curl up in the corner and cry' vibe. Why couldn't this be 'The year I'm allowed to shop all I want!' year? And why was the urge to buy so hard to resist? It wasn't like I like I was weaning myself off cocaine or opium here. This wasn't like *Sophie's Choice*. Also, I had twenty or so other coats at home, so what exactly was my problem?

Maybe it was time to admit that I'm really passionate about clothes, and that shopping *does* come into that equation sometimes. To be fair, my argument had never been with the clothes themselves, only with the industry that provides us with them. I didn't *hate* clothes. I hated unsafe factories and slave wages. I *loved* clothes, and not being able to buy something I liked was, well...hard. It's called being human.

'Does it fit you?' Ben's voice pierced through the changing room curtain.

What was that? Did he just ask me if it fit me? What difference did it make? The non-shopping pact didn't include a clause that said, 'If it fits you, you can buy it.'

I yanked the curtain aside.

Ben smiled. 'It looks perfect on you!'

Then he saw my unhappy face and realised what I already

knew: it wasn't meant to be.

As if encouraged by this, he took a step toward me. 'You know what?' he said. 'You and Amy have no rules against receiving gifts, do you?'

Where is he going with this? I shook my head slowly, fully aware of how volcanic this situation was. I shifted my legs a bit, attempting to appear less stiff and rigid. I couldn't let him know how much I wanted this coat, that would only make it worse.

'Hand it over,' he said, stretching out his arms.

I didn't move.

'I'm getting this for you,' he said, laughing. 'Consider it a spring gift.'

I'm not sure how it happened, but somehow the coat peeled off me, and Ben walked over to the till and paid for it.

A surge of rejuvenated love and energy bubbled up inside me. 'Oh my God! I have the best husband in the world!' I sang to myself. Wearing this coat would signal 'person with envious style and perfect spouse'. Was it really to be mine? I couldn't believe it! And what if I had found it all by myself, without Ben being there to buy it for me? Better not to think about it.

But I had to admit that the whole thing was a bit odd, and totally out of character. Ben had *never* bought me any clothes before. Not even sexy underwear, which I'm told is totally normal.

I had bought *him* a coat once; a handsome camel hair coat with a beige velvet collar. A Hugo Boss classic. I loved it. He refused to wear it.

'Why?' I asked, incredulous.

'It makes me look like an Eastern European hit man,' he replied.

I saw his point. Still, that deed must have planted a strong seed for some serious coat karma, because all I knew was that on the brink of spring, the manic manhunt for the Perfect Winter Coat was finally over.

Curtains

Amy has never shared my obsession with coats, but now she was developing a peculiar obsession with curtains. I say peculiar, because home improvements and interior decorating have never been on her radar. I'm not saying she is not any good at it; I'm just saying she has never showed the slightest interest in it before. In fact, the selling point of her new house was that they could move straight in without having to 'lift a single paint brush!'

So you can understand my confusion when lunch break after lunch break was spent listening to Amy go on and on about the new curtains she wanted to buy. These curtains were for the master bedroom, so they would have to match the bedding. Also, she informed me, they should double up as living room curtains, just in case they ended up remodelling the house.

'Uh...You're remodelling the house?' I asked.

'No, but I'm just saying, if we *were*, in the future sometime, the curtains will have to be moved downstairs to the living room.'

Go on...

'The most important things about these new curtains is that they have to block out ALL traces of light,' she said.

Amy is a very light sleeper, and she doesn't want to be woken up by any kind of sunshine, or street light, or car light, or...I got her point.

'What about two layers of curtains?' she said. 'You know, a decorative set that you can see from the inside, and the light-blocking ones behind them?' she mused. 'And what length do you think? All the way to the floor, or just underneath the window ledge?'

The questions seemed to multiply.

'How would lace look, both from a bedroom and a living room perspective? What if they decide to knock down a wall and move the master bedroom downstairs? Is maroon too 1998? What do you think about blinds? Would suede look cool? What about tiebacks or those fancy tassels...?'

This is very typical of Amy. Both the obsessive part and the indecision, as well as the bit where everything must have multiple uses. Crazy as this makes me, I also find it adorable. Her back-and-forth mindset makes it near impossible to reach a final conclusion, but it's also highly entertaining. The whole thing reminded me of Nadine from *Twin Peaks*. Who else fusses this much over curtains?

In the end Amy went with her old curtains. I was not surprised.

The Office Sale

One quiet afternoon, while sitting at my desk and doing paperwork, I received an email from Gigi, my colleague with the small feet. She was selling some of her designer handbags and clothes. 'First serves first! Really great prices!' her email informed me.

The prices *were* crazy good, only £50 for a Louis Vuitton bag is a steal. Not that I was the least bit tempted. I don't 'get' designer handbags, but I felt curious about the clothes. Besides, ignoring the email felt rude.

In Gigi's office, rummaging through her clothes, a pair of tweed trousers snatched my attention. They looked like they belonged to a dressage heiress; they were precisely the kind of trousers I would wear if I'd ever gone horseback riding with Lady Di. I just *knew* they would look amazing on me. For starters, my butt would look ten years younger, at least.

I grabbed them and went to the loo to try them on. Looking is free, right?

Shit! They looked better on than I had anticipated. It was like I didn't have any thighs. In these trousers I was positively super skinny. *Think...How can I swing this?* Inspired by my winter coat success I thought, *I'm pretty sure I can find a way to buy them, without actually buying them...I'm not buying them from a store, so clearly it wouldn't count as shopping. Or would it? I don't see how. This is a grey area. What if these trousers are just considered part of a makeover session? Like in The Breakfast Club, or Clueless? Makeovers happen all the time, and the vital ingredient is — voila! — new clothes.*

How do I look?

Good grief. Enough already. If this was a makeover session, David Cameron is the Queen of Sheba. I couldn't fake my way into owning these trousers. I even thought about phoning Ben to see if he wanted to buy them for me, but that felt icky, like accepting a bribe, or Nazi gold. Buying the coat for me was an act of genuine generosity, a totally different scenario. Now I just felt stupid.

I brought the trousers back to Gigi.

'No good?' she asked.

'Yeah, no,' I said and shrugged. 'They just didn't fit right.'

Learning Curve

The tweed trouser incident made me think about how easy it was to get sucked back into consumer mode. Or as Al Pacino put it, 'Just when you think you're out, they pull you back in.'

I didn't know what to do with that.

I couldn't reconcile the fact that one moment my mind was spinning with glittering insights about decluttering, new role models, and how *not* shopping is female bonding at its loudest, and the next moment I was loosing my mind over a coat and lusting after a pair of tweed trousers. Hit repeat.

Starting out, I had told myself, 'Just stay away from shops and you'll be fine.' But as it turned out, I wasn't even safe in my own office building. I had totally underestimated this challenge.

Above my desk was a red panic button. If I pressed it, Diplomatic Protection officers would arrive within four minutes. After trying on the tweed trousers, *another* pair of clothing I wasn't allowed to buy, I was gripped with an overpowering urge to press the button. I could use the distraction.

Instead, I called Amy.

'I almost bought a pair of trousers today,' I told her. 'I told myself that if I didn't wear them until November, it wouldn't count as shopping.'

Amy admitted she'd had similar thoughts. *Buy now, wear later!*

sounded like the ultimate loophole, but since it involved shopping, we both agreed it very much counted as cheating.

Amy had an idea. 'How about writing things down?'

Ideally, when this challenge was over, shopping would be a thing of the past. But just in case that didn't happen, and based on how tricky this had turned out to be, Amy suggested we make a list of all the clothes we wanted to buy once the ban was lifted.

We could look. We could imagine. We just couldn't shop...yet.

What a great idea! I'm a huge fan of lists, and this one felt both creative and wholesome. Just thinking about the list made me feel less panicky about all the clothes I wasn't able to buy. Now I could keep track of them! How great was that?

As soon as I got off the phone I wrote down the following:

- Black dress

- Skinny jeans

- An off-white blouse, preferably with a pussy bow

- A comfortable blazer (why are they all so stiff?)

- A black cardigan

- Stripy sweater

- More tank tops

This list would lay the groundwork for my future self. Come November I would approach shopping with a firm and manageable strategy. More clarity, and less fast-fashion shopping victim. That was the goal.

Maybe that's what it means to be a conscious consumer, not someone who doesn't shop at all, but someone who shops with a strategy?

That felt true. It had an honest ring to it. Good!

But what would the next months bring? November 1 was still miles away. If the previous months were anything to go by, the road ahead would be rocky, unpredictable, challenging, and difficult. Which is one respect was fine, it meant it wouldn't be boring. I pictured myself growing and learning and coming up with all kinds of new insights. But when would it become fun? When would this shop-stop challenge become easy?

As difficult as this had turned out to be, I could never go back to being a weak-willed and mindless shopper, that much I knew. Those days were over for good. However, I had yet to reach my goal of becoming a mindful shopper with Yoda-like impulse control. I was currently stuck in a place where I was neither mindless nor mindful. I wanted to speed up the process, but there was no getting around it, I'd reached the place of no return. I was stuck in the messy middle.

Chapter Six

April

6 *The whole thing of clothes is insane.*

You can spend a dollar on a jacket in a thrift store. And you can spend a thousand dollars on a jacket in a shop.

And if you saw those two jackets walking down the street, you probably wouldn't know which was which. **9**

- Helen Mirren

Before looking at the topics I have in mind for this chapter — dress codes, clothes and aging, sewing, and fashion role models — I have a confession to make. It's nothing major. It's just about work. I feel trapped. I don't know how else to put it.

Feeling Trapped

I'm worried that my job is a bit repetitive, or worse: that I'm dwarfing my true purpose in life. The shiny veneer attached to working at an Embassy is starting to peel off, and I find myself staring at the cracks. Suddenly I don't want a 9-to-5 existence anymore. I want to expand my options. I want to do something different. I want excitement. I'm sick of sitting at a desk all day long. I want to move around. I want to use my brain in a new way. I can do this job blindfolded. I want out.

I hate feeling this way. I should feel grateful for even having a job, but I'm now at that desperate place where I ask myself questions like: what is my true calling? What do I want to do instead? What *can* I do instead? What does my life look like in five months, five years, or fifteen years from now? The idea of staying here for the next fifteen years feels like death by a thousand cuts. But, and this is where I hit a dead end, I have nowhere else to go. I don't have a backup plan. So what do I do with these thoughts? Do I act on them, or do I ignore them?

Both options seem impossible. I just want to go back to how it was in the beginning.

When I first got this job, the escapist in me adored how the Embassy was a world clouded in rituals, status, and traditions. At what other workplace does the new boss get picked up by a horse and carriage, taken to Buckingham Palace where he (or she) presents their credentials to the Queen, followed by a champagne reception where the majority of the guests have honorific titles?

Having spent my twenties around meditation masters who not only could change the weather, bend metal, read minds, and communicate with the dead, but who could also remember all their previous lifetimes and pull scriptures out of lakes and rocks, I was drawn to (or addicted to) any kind of job that had a whiff of magic and power.

But the older I get, the less impressed I am with things like power, status, and titles. My original enthusiasm for these things has slowed to a crawl. I won't deny that working for an Ambassador with everything that entails — running errands for royalties, attending private gallery openings, meeting famous people, being invited to Embassy events — can be fun and rewarding (and it makes for great dinner conversations, like the story about when I hitchhiked through Europe with the Norwegian King during the ash-cloud), but it no longer feels important. It feels frivolous, like a masquerade. Now I would much rather have a job I'm passionate about than a prestigious one. And I would much rather hang out with like-minded people who accept me for who I am, and not based on where I work, or who I'm connected with.

This is so frustrating. It's not fair. I always thought this job would lead to something. I've always thought of this job as a stepping stone, not my final destination. However, I never made a plan B. I just assumed that something would magically happen to me.

So what's next?

Should I go back to school? Look for a new job? Move? Everything feels like way too much work. I just want to be headhunted, promoted, or win the lottery. Is that so much to ask for?

But how did I even get this job? That might be something you've been wondering about.

I've always had a natural aptitude for secretarial work, and my years at the Buddhist centre weirdly prepared me for this role. There I worked side by side with the Dalai Lama's previous right hand, I helped with event planning, I organised schedules, and I was the personal assistant to many a lama. Before moving to London I also served a short stint at a Norwegian oil company. So when applying for this job, I knew I was more than qualified for the role.

I got the job, but three years later I no longer want the job.

Still, feeling stuck at a place like the Embassy isn't all that bad. Especially not this month. Right now we're busy preparing for the seventieth anniversary of Operation Gunnerside, the sabotage of Nazi Germany's atomic bomb program. We're talking Churchill's secret army. We're talking war heroes. We're talking secret missions. Let's face it, I'm living in a spy novel.

The Gap Incident

There are two extraordinary things about this anniversary. One, the leader of the operation, Mr Joachim Rønneberg, is still alive. Two, he's coming to London as our guest of honour.

The news that this legendary war hero is coming to London is spreading like wildfire. Everyone and their uncle wants to participate in the historic festivities, and countless schedules are being synchronised and shifted around to make it happen.

From the Norwegian side we're expecting the Minister of Defence, the Chief of Defence, fellow war comrades of Mr Rønneberg, historians, and several high-ranking members of the Norwegian army.

From the British side I'm told to add the following to the guest list: Chief of Defence (and his staff), several MPs, the notorious Lord Montagu, and Lord Astor of Hever.

'Hever, as in Hever Castle, Anne Boleyn's childhood home?' I ask.

'Yes, but he doesn't like to talk about it. Wrong side of the Royal family, if you know what I mean.'

It's Monday morning, and I'm in full throttle: updating the guest-lists, sending out invitations, booking drivers, arranging airport pick-ups, scheduling meetings with the local police, seating plans, and hotel bookings. As soon as I'm done with one task, three more pop up. It's heavenly! I love being busy. It makes me feel useful.

All of sudden my phone rings. While scanning the latest version of the program and simultaneously opening my Ambassador's mail, I wedge the phone between my neck and shoulder and say, 'Hello, this is Inger.'

AMY: Hi, are you busy?

ME: Amy?

AMY: I need your help.

ME: Why are you whispering?

AMY: I'm in the changing room at Gap.

Uh-oh. This can't be good. I leave my desk and quickly walk downstairs to the big empty meeting room and close the door.

ME: Shoot. What's going on with you? Why are you at Gap?

AMY: Well, eh...you know that stripy sweater that's on both our 'things we can get in November' list?

ME: Yes...

AMY: I'm wearing it!

ME: What do you mean you're wearing it?

AMY: I was on my way to the library, and then an invisible force pulled me into the store. Before I could stop myself, I grabbed the sweater, and now somehow it's on me!

ME: Well, take it off!

AMY: I can't! It's on sale, and it's incredibly soft.

ME: You know better than going around trying on clothes. What is wrong with you?

AMY: You're right, I shouldn't even be here, but listen. What if I buy it now, but don't wear it until November? Sort of like a present for my future self? Can't I just save it for later? It's fifty percent off!

ME: Nope. We've been through this already, remember? Just take it off. This is wrong, and you know it.

AMY: Argh! You are so right. But what will I do? It's absolutely perfect, and November is really far away. By then the sweater will be gone, and then what will I wear?

ME: I don't care. Look. Just take the sweater off, give it back to the nice saleslady, and walk out of the store.

AMY: Do you really think I can do it?

ME: There is nothing to it, just stay focused and get out of there as fast as you can.

I Have Nothing to Wear

So far this month I haven't even thought about shopping. I've just been coasting along, wearing whatever I'm wearing. But Amy's Gap incident has opened my eyes to the fact that 'coasting along' is not going to cut it for the Gunnerside Anniversary week. I will be in the company of the man who singlehandedly put an end to Hitler's nuclear program. The press will follow us everywhere. I can't...I mean...I've been so busy planning and preparing for this event that I've overlooked the fact that I'll actually be *attending* all the posts on the program. In person. Wearing clothes. Only I have nothing to wear.

I could so easily freak out right now.

I grab a copy of the program and flick through it. Great! All the venues are amazing. House of Lords; Special Forces Club; the Ambassador's residence; the Norwegian Church - this is a disaster. But why do I act surprised? I wrote the damn program.

Now I know how Cinderella must have felt when she received the invitation to the ball: thrilled at the prospect of going, crushed when realising she had nothing to wear.

*I could use a Fairy Godmother...*No wait! I got a better idea. What I need is a fashion role model.

Fashion Role Models

Whenever I find myself in a clothing pickle, I ask myself questions like:

- Who would have played me in a movie, and what would they wear?

- What famous person has been in a similar situation?

- Who are my fashion role models?

The last question is easy to answer, Jackie Kennedy of course. But I'm not sure about the whole retro look. I could follow her advice,

'You have to be you.' But...I don't know who I am in this setting.

What about Lorelai Gilmore? Should I copy her style? As much as I love her knitted cardigans and whimsical dresses, that's not going to cut it for these events.

Think! Who attends lots of public events, in the company of influential people? I should dress like HER.

The only women that comes to mind are Mother Teresa, Angela Merkel, and Nancy Reagan. *Great work, brain. NOT!*

I blame the jeans. I've become so addicted to them that I've forgotten how to dress in anything else. I know it's not the most appropriate Embassy attire, but I figure as long as I pair them with really pretty tops and put my hair up in a nice 'do, I can get away with it. Also, if you think about it, most of the time I'm seated at my desk, so I'm only really visible from the waist up.

However, I can't visit the House of Lords looking like a hip barista. I need new clothes.

Interestingly enough, and to my great relief, this clothing crisis doesn't make me want to go shopping. That's because I know that going shopping when I don't even know what I'm looking for puts me in a deranged mood. So no, I don't want to go shopping. I just need to find a fashion role model.

Later that day, sitting on the bus on my way home from work, I think, *I know who can be my role model! I know whose style I can mimic! This is perfect!*

It's the Duchess of Cambridge! Kate Middleton! Who better to see me through this apparel crisis than Princess Diana's very own daughter-in-law?

When Diana married Prince Charles, I cut my hair short and dressed up in frilly white blouses. Diana became one of the world's greatest style icons, and I became slightly obsessed with her. I secretly hoped that she and I would meet one day, and we would become best friends. The newspapers would print pictures of us together, but they would never figure out who I was. 'Who's that girl? Lady Di's secret new best friend?' the headlines would read. When I got older, these daydreams faded away, but I still kept an eye on her. She was fabulous.

As soon as I get home from work I peruse the internet for Kate-inspired fashion clues. Right off the bat I notice that the young Duchess wears a lot of coats. *Excellent! A fellow coat enthusiast!* I also notice that she doesn't wear them in the same way that you and I wear them, thrown over whatever jumble we're wearing underneath. Kate wears her coats as a complete outfit. It's like she's wearing a suit or a dress, only it's vastly more elegant than an actual two-piece suit. A two-piece suit makes you look like you're about to sit down and do people's taxes, or hand them the breakdown of the funeral costs. An elegant coat, on the other hand, signals Walt Disney is my uncle, lunch with friends (or with the cast of *Friends*), or that you've just had a boat named after you. Nobody messes with a girl in a good coat.

The best thing about the coat look, in my opinion, is that once you put it on, there is nothing more to it. Pair it with a nice pair of shoes and a fun scarf, and you're dressed. That's it!

A lot of Kate's coats have three-quarter sleeves. This appeals to the Jackie Kennedy fan in me, and it makes your arms look really slender. Most of her coats come to right above the knee, which turns out to be the perfect length for a coat. *Why am I just noticing this?*

You might be thinking that it's all swell and fine that I have figured out what to wear, but so what? How does this help me? I'm not Kate. I don't have the world's best designers at my fingertips. If anything, I'm the *opposite* of all of that. More importantly, I can't even go shopping. Surely I'm getting all worked up over nothing. Right? Wrong. Let me remind you of one crucial factor: I can sew.

Sewing!

I'm delighted to notice that sewing is making a comeback. It's being rebranded as *green* and *thrifty*. This sewing revival means that I can finally talk about my love for fabrics, sewing, and textiles without worrying about sounding like an old lady. I remember thinking, 'Am I so antiquated that no other hobby will have me?' But then I also remembered how much fun it was to sew with Grandma growing up.

Observing what Grandma could do with fabric and scissors was like watching a spectacular Las Vegas show, and mastering her dingy old Husqvarna machine was like having a date with the world's most amazing robot.

My turn!

Thanks to Grandma (and her old sewing machine) my clothes don't scare me. I'm in charge. I decide. When looking at clothes through the eyes of a seamstress, no outfit is a finished product; there is always room for improvement. To quote Jackie O: 'An inch off can make all the difference.'

In addition to Grandma, I have another sewing mentor, my dear friend Helene.

I've known Helene since high school, but it wasn't until she moved to the Buddhist centre and I went to visit her, that we became close friends. I'm not sure how I discovered that she could sew, but it must have come up somehow, because all of a sudden we did all these sewing projects together. Her attention to details, and the amount of work that went into every little hem, was shocking. *Surely this can't be necessary...?*

While I was more of a 'let's throw this together and call it a day' seamstress, Helene's sewing routine involved intense measuring, a high level of ironing, and a keen interest in mastering new sewing techniques. I envied her concentration and focus, but I also knew there was no way I wanted to spend *that* much time on one lousy alteration.

Her skills must have been contagious somehow, because one day, after finishing a project, I looked at myself in the mirror and thought, 'Stand back! Did I do this? This is incredible!'

Helene taught me that it's not the size of the project that matters, but how well you do it. In her own words, 'Putting in an extra half hour can make all the difference.'

Having friends you can learn from, and who keep inspiring you to do better, is priceless.

Regardless of how you learn to sew (by yourself, take a course, or find a mentor), there are basically two approaches to sewing.

The first one is the difficult approach. Here you have to juggle sewing patterns, multiple stitches, accuracy, loose pieces of fabric, and you have to rely on a long list of sewing skills. Otherwise you're screwed. When following this approach you start with nothing, then hours, days, sometimes weeks later, you have a fully formed outfit.

The second approach is the easy one, the one I prefer. Here you take a piece of clothing that is already fully made, and all you have to do is change the buttons or fix a hem. This is called re-sewing. Or mending. Or upcycling.

If you want to get into sewing, this is where you start. Don't start with buttonholes and zippers. It will only end in tears. The few times I've made a dress from scratch following a complicated pattern, it took up so much of my time that I felt depressed for weeks afterwards. Never again.

So be kind to yourself, start with shortening the sleeves or turning a skirt into a pillowcase. These projects are so easy I'm surprised not more people do them. Or find a piece of clothing you never wear and ask yourself, 'What would I have to change in order to make it wearable?'

Is it by taking off the collar?

Is it by removing the sleeves?

Is it by turning it into a skirt?

Don't be afraid to experiment. Just play around and have fun with it. In sewing there are no mistakes, only learning.

The Re-Sewing Session

After this short sewing introduction, I'm now ready to transform some of my coats into Kate-inspired coats. Let the re-sewing session begin!

First out is my navy blue coat. It's made from a really soft fabric, almost like thin fleece, and I love the shiny military buttons. What I *don't* love about this coat is the sleeves. They come all the way down to my fingertips. Pathetic. It gives off a *Gangs of New York* vibe. No wonder I never wear it.

Next in line is my black trench coat. On this one the sleeves are just plain wrong. They are equipped with what can only be described as miniature equestrian arm belts. As a result the sleeves poof out at the bottom, like a shower cap that has lost its elasticity. In what universe has that ever been stylish? In addition, the coat is *way* too long; it makes me look like a chess piece. I put the coat aside and move on to coat number three.

This one is a real wonder, the jewel in the crown, my amazing Anthropologie spring coat. It has an understated floral pattern and a soft pink lining, and when I bought it in Berkeley all those years ago, I knew I would wear it all the time. It would go with *everything*. So why does it hang at the back of the closet collecting dust? It's those darn long sleeves again. On this coat they're both long *and* loose, and unwisely 'decorated' with a giant green button and a long buttonhole thingy. It flops around like a listless tongue.

A few hours later all three coats have been carefully altered. They have gone from being unwearable to something that inspires confidence and style. It's the ultimate makeover. I try them on in turn, and looking at my own reflection in the mirror, I can't help but congratulate myself on this stunning transformation. For people who don't know how to sew (i.e., most people), it's almost impossible to understand the joy I'm feeling right now. The fact that the coats look *this* great, is *my* doing. MINE. I did this! I feel as if I've invented chocolate, or something equally crucial for the survival of mankind.

My mind races back over other successful sewing jobs: the dress that I wore to my sister's wedding, all the cute summer outfits, the correct black dress, and that gorgeous quilt I made from all my leftover fabrics. Back then I never thought that sewing would be a lifesaver in a non-shopping year. I just assumed it would come in handy if I ever got stuck on a deserted island, or if I ended up in some kind of post-nuclear war scenario. Equipped with much-sought-after sewing skills, it's not difficult to cast myself in the role of a survivor.

If we *do* survive some crazy disaster in the future, I'll be the one sewing clothes out of repossessed palm tree leaves and milk cartons.

The Anniversary Week

With my work wardrobe taken care of, I'm more than ready for the Gunnerside anniversary week.

The Defence Attaché is in charge of the planning committee, and at the end of every meeting he asks the one question that all men and women in uniform must ask: 'What is the worst thing that can happen?' And then we prepare for that.

Military personnel are so organised, and surprisingly laid-back and funny. *Perhaps I should consider a career in the armed forces?* It would certainly be exciting. And even though I don't like uniforms per se, military uniforms are smoking hot. (Please don't tell anyone I said that.)

Mr Rønneberg, now ninety-three years of age, has arrived in London and is full of life and infectious energy. People have voiced concern that the packed schedule will be too much for him, but all the commotion and activities seem to have an invigorating effect. Mr Rønneberg darts from post to post (as fast as a man in his tenth decade can dart), gives speeches, poses for the cameras, and meets with the reporters.

I have his driver on speed dial, in case he gets tired. I'm also trained in first aid, should it come to that. And in case you were wondering, my navy blue coat looked absolutely gorgeous next to the Norwegian Royal Guards. I had my picture taken with them, which I immediately emailed to all of my girlfriends. They responded exactly as I had hoped: with envy.

Of all the events this week, the one I want to share with you is the luncheon at the House of Lords. The private dining room was potent with historical significance, and the atmosphere was intimate and luxurious. The polished chairs, monogrammed plates, printed menus, starched tablecloths, and the tasteful floral arrangements made me feel like I was travelling on the Orient Express, or dining at

The Ritz.

Not that I would know anything about what that is like. I've never done much fine dining in my life, especially not of the variety with five different forks and an assembly of crystal glasses. Habitually, I throw everything in a bowl and eat while watching TV or reading. But thanks to this job, I'm expanding my culinary repertoire. Like a native of fine dining halls, I now place my napkin in my lap (without first looking to see how others are doing 'it'), I'm an expert at small-talk, and I no longer feel compelled to jump up and offer my assistance when the servants bring in the food.

At this luncheon, the soldier seated to my right insisted that his steak tasted 'just like wolf.' I asked how he could possibly know such a thing. Then I noticed all the medals on his chest, and all of a sudden I was lost in thoughts about him being in some scary combat situation, possibly in the mountains, where killing a wolf and subsequently eating it would be his only chance of survival. I tried to put these dramatic thoughts out of my head, but the deep, long scar running down the side of his face only served to intensify them.

The only answer he offered me was a playful smirk.

Wolf or no wolf, my own vegetarian meal was excellent, and I felt honoured and proud to be in the company of so many wonderful people without spilling my wine or needing to get up in the middle of the meal to pee. (There is no good time to excuse yourself, there just isn't.)

Dress Codes

When the lunch was over, one of the other soldiers approached me and asked in a conspiratorial tone, 'What is the dress code for the dinner this evening?'

This brings me straight to an important aspect of Embassy life: the dress code.

The most important thing to keep in mind about diplomatic dress codes is that it's never about taste, it's always about rules. These dress codes are not whimsical (come as your favourite superhero!), or optional (come as you are!). When attending functions like Ascot, the Christmas ball at Buckingham Palace, and Trooping the Colour (the Queen's birthday parade), not adhering to the dress code is not only rude, it's embarrassing. No one wants to be the weirdo showing up in a Morning Coat when the invitation clearly stated *Evening* Coat. You'd be the laughing stock of the season. There's is a reason Cinderella couldn't go to the ball until she had acquired the appropriate gown.

In the beginning I didn't know what any of it meant. *Evening Wear? Business Casual? White Tie? Lounge Suit? What are these people talking about?*

I also didn't know where to wear what, and so I consulted *Debrett's,* the holy bible of form and etiquette. I read that book cover to cover, and I underlined, memorised, and took notes.

All this studying paid off. Now I know that with a short-sleeved dress you wear long gloves, and with a long-sleeved dress you wear short gloves. No, you don't have to buy the most outrageous hat to attend Ascot. A nice fascinator will do. I let the ladies know that they don't wear tiaras unless specified in the invitations, and the gentlemen don't wear their medals unless the invitation includes the line *'with decorations.'*

Within the four walls of the Embassy, on a regular Tuesday, the dress code is less formal, but what constitutes as 'less formal' in *this* setting is tailored suits, flawless make-up, and sporting designer labels. The most casual outfit I've ever seen on a diplomat is a pair of Armani jeans and a cashmere sweater that probably cost more than what I pay in rent.

At any rate, the soldier asking about the dress code was enquiring on behalf of one of the politicians. She couldn't decide if she should wear a dress or a suit.

This pleased me for two reasons. Firstly, it meant I wasn't the only person fretting over what to wear. And secondly, the fact that *I* was consulted about this important matter could only mean that I *looked* like someone who knew about important matters.

It also meant that being a successful and influential politician doesn't shield you from asking the time old question: what shall I wear? (By the way, the answer I gave was 'dress'.)

Observing a Different Fashion Sphere

A great bonus of this anniversary week, something I hadn't thought about beforehand, was that women of all ages and all walks of life would participate in the festivities. This gave me a golden opportunity to observe a completely different fashion sphere. I had so many questions. What would Mrs Rønneberg wear? What about the wives of the MPs? Would they look conservative and demure, or would they pull out all the stops?

And what about the soldiers? Would the female soldiers show up in uniform? If so, skirts or trousers?

What I learnt both impressed and surprised me.

Observing the Older Ladies

Contrary to popular beliefs, women in their seventies and eighties have far more style and personal flair than their younger sisters. Vivienne Westwood agrees with me on this. She recently said something similar.

During the dinner at the Ambassador's residence, it was truly inspiring to see how elegant and chic these old ladies looked, despite their wrinkles and grey hair. Mrs Rønneberg's emerald-green trench coat, and her blue Chanel-looking suit with white piping, had me drooling with envy. She had JE NE SAIS QUOI written all over her. She belonged on the front cover of *Vogue* magazine, and she wasn't the only one. These old ladies looked fantastic. Not just 'fantastic-for-their-age' good looking, but truly stunning. Standing next to them I felt like a grey mouse, and I was wearing pink.

What was their secret? (And where could I get my hands on an emerald-green trench coat?) Were they devotees of juice cleanses, yoga, meditation, and beauty sleep? Or did they drink a medicinal glass of red wine every evening? What? What did they know that I didn't?

I can only speculate, but I think it has something to do with coming of age back when clothes were made to last. These ladies learnt how to dress in an era of quality, not quantity. Saved from growing up with spoon-fed trends (or flicks, bursts, and flings), they invested in timeless outfits that served their personal preferences and unique sense of style. And since style is ageless, these women might as well have been drinking from the fountain of youth.

Observing the Middle Aged Women

But what did the other women wear? The younger ones? Based on what I was seeing, the women in their mid-forties and fifties, especially those belonging in a certain tax bracket, seemed to suffer from the delusion that the more money you have, the more money you should spend on clothes. As if driven by an invisible force (or fear), these ladies wore an impenetrable armour of expensive brands and designer labels. Why? Where was the panache? The zest? The flair?

These women were, after all, post-student life, post-struggling to make ends meet, post-raising toddlers, and post-finding good jobs. Possibly even post-divorce. And at the other end of all that, they all dressed the same? Most peculiar. When would personal style burst into view? If not now, when? And what was up with all the designer labels?

When it comes to clothes, I'm one hundred percent non-elitist. I can't for the life of me understand why so many women are exclusively drawn to expensive brands.

Expensive Brands

Actually, there are two things about I don't understand about designer labels and expensive brands.

1.   What's the allure?

2.   Why are these brands so expensive?

Why do people say, 'You're wearing Gucci!' with the same kind of enthusiasm normally reserved for statements like, 'You slept with Bradley Cooper!'? What's that all about?

In all honesty, I'm no stranger to inflating clothes with unrealistic hopes and expectations. Many years ago I found a Prada skirt at a thrift shop. *A Prada skirt! For only £35! Mine!*

I wrote on Facebook, 'Inger wears Prada.' For about five seconds I felt like I'd 'made' it.

But here's the thing. The skirt was uncomfortable. It didn't sit right, I didn't like wearing it, and so the shame-spiral began.

Why don't you love your Prada skirt? It's only every girl's dream! Feel how soft the fabric is! Look at the fine stitches! You HAVE to make this work! We're talking Prada here!

Had the skirt been from Primark, I wouldn't have thought twice about not liking it. *What did you expect, it's only Primark!*

We act like Gucci is the Lady of the manor, and Gap is only the footman. As much as I love Burberry and Chanel, I deeply disagree with the idea that a logo can define who I am. And even though there are many excellent reasons for buying a fine piece of clothing, attaching an inflated sense of importance to wearing certain kinds of brands goes against everything I believe in. More to the point, buying clothes based on brands alone is just as weird as being addicted to bargain shopping.

Allure aside, why the steep price tag?

After all, the textile workers making expensive clothes don't get paid more than the textile workers whipping out the weekly trends. And it's not like designer brands are hatched from an organic gilded hatchery located in the posh part of town right next to the Mayor's office, while fast-fashion factories are shunned to the slummy areas. No, that's not how it works. In fact, textile factories often receive orders from a wide range of brands, both the crazy expensive ones and the crazy cheap ones.

So remind me again, why are designer brands so expensive?

Well, supermodels cost money. Celebrity endorsements cost

money. Renting shops in high-class areas costs money. Advertisement campaigns cost money. Quality of the fabric does enter into the equation, so does craftsmanship and design, but it's the machinery *around* these labels that drives up the price, not the clothes themselves. So when you buy a super pricey handbag or a crazy expensive skirt, you're mostly paying for an image. Plain and simple. This helps explain why Armani jeans cost as much as £150 while Primark jeans only cost £10.

Look. I'm not telling you anything new here. And I'm not telling you to stop wearing luxury brands or designer labels. If that's what you like, be my guest. If that's what you can afford, congratulations. You've done well for yourself. You should feel proud. I mean it.

But I get worried. I worry that the tantalising allure of wearing expensive brands comes with financial implications we're unfit to deal with. We're the most in-debt people ever to have walked the earth. Credit card debt is soaring. So I worry when I hear about young girls feeling peer-pressured into 'investing' in luxury brands. I worry that when Carrie Bradshaw says, 'I want my money where I can see it, in my closet,' she's flirting with the idea that it's fun to be financially irresponsible, as long as you're wearing Prada.

All I'm saying is, if you can't afford to pay £80 for a pair of jeans, please don't.

Based on all this, the Emergency Shopping Guide for April will have to be:

If you can't afford it, don't buy it.

Some Thoughts on Aging

Returning from the Ambassador's dinner party I told Ben, 'The older ladies were so much fun! I simply ADORED them!'

I couldn't shut up about it. I went into a long speech about how the older guests — both the men and the women — dressed better, laugh more, and were far more interesting than the younger ones. And with the exception of the lively wife of one of the MPs, the middle-aged women didn't smile or laugh nearly as much as the women in their eighties.

I felt like I belonged to the wrong generation. I wanted to be more like *them. Why wasn't I born in the '30s!*

I told Ben how one lady, a war veteran, raised her wine glass and said, 'I love being old! You can do whatever you want, whenever you want to. It's brilliant!'

She was in her mid-eighties, and so hunched over that her body almost formed a perfect circle.

Lord Montegou was wheelchair-bound, yet his gentle round face was mesmerizing. I will never forget his piercing eyes.

'And you should have seen the tall man with the thick white hair,' I went on. 'He grabbed his blue trench coat, headed for the front door, and said in a loud clear voice, "I'm going out to experience life! See you all later!" This man was in his nineties!'

Why did the younger women, the middle-aged women, only have half the life-force of the women twice their age? Could the explanation be that the middle-aged women felt let down by their clothes, like I did with my Prada skirt? *Damn you skirt! You were supposed to make me feel amazing, so why do I feel like a mousy nanny?* Or could it be that in mid-life we're so busy trying to make a mark that we forget how to let loose and enjoy ourselves? Or is it that we know that our life is already halfway over, and the thought of more wrinkles makes us suicidal?

If you're stuck glorifying your twenties, like one of my friends who said, 'I just want to wear red-hot shorts again!' then aging will be a depressing, slow decline where death will be your only reward. Who wants to go through life trapped in thinking patterns like that? I don't, which is why at the tender age of twenty-two I devised a 'love-your-age' plan. I promised myself that if I lived past the age of thirty-six, I would treat every passing year as a bonus year. Every year passed thirty-six would be a gift. That's the age Lady Di was when she died, and for some reason that made an impression on me. I intensified my plan by promising myself that I would look for the best in every decade, not fret over days gone by.

I've stayed true to my promises, and I can honestly tell you that I love growing older. Being in the company of these incredible ladies only confirmed what I've always suspected to be true: the older you get, the more fun you have.

Rana Plaza

On April 24th, 2013, Rana Plaza, a nine-storey garment factory in Dhaka, Bangladesh, collapsed and killed 1,129 people. An additional 2,515 people were injured.

Receiving this news made me feel as if I'd been framed. *Clothes are meant to be fun!* Even as I'm writing this book and I'm *supposed* to look at the dark side of the fast-fashion industry, which is the entire premise for this shop-stop, I can't bring myself to dwell there for any great length of time. My mind wants to jump to happier topics.

But this time I can't look away. The magnitude of the disaster is too devastating to be ignored. It's staring me right in the face, and I don't know where to turn.

When I went along with this 'easy' challenge, I thought we were protesting a crappy situation. I didn't expect Rana Plaza. None of us did.

What makes something like Rana Plaza inexcusable, as far as I'm concerned, is that it could have been prevented. I don't quite understand how we can fix the ozone layer, or prevent droughts (shorter showers?), but I do know that if a nine-storey building displays huge cracks in the wall, and you still insist on cramming thousands of people inside that very same building, that strikes me as a terrible way of running a business.

Regulation and safety protocols do exist, we're told; they're just not implemented. Factory owners and middlemen are under too much pressure to keep the costs down, and no one is enforcing the rules.

As I'm following the news, I read stories about survivors who cut off their limbs in order to break free from the rubble. Another girl drank her own urine to stay hydrated. Family members are searching the morgues for their loved ones, while others are waiting for the DNA results to identify the many body parts.

I can't work out how I'm supposed to feel. Everybody wants answers. Everybody wants this day to go away.

As I struggle to take it all in - what it means, whose fault it is, the people who died, the whole mess - for reasons I can't explain, there is one picture from the Rana Plaza ruins I can't get out of my head. You've probably seen it. It's the picture of a young man and a beautiful woman, lying face to face like two adorable interlocked seahorses. It's hard to make out all the details, but it looks like they're holding hands.

The striking thing about this image is how peaceful they look. There is no blood. Every limb looks intact. If I didn't know any better, I'd say they were sleeping. I can almost hear them breathing. Not for a second do they look like two people who just had their entire world cave in on them. It's only when your eyes shift to the bricks and the rubble surrounding them that you realise they're not lying on a soft bed. For all intents and purposes, they're lying in a grave.

There is already a lot of talk about accountability and transparency, which is great. OK, it's a bit late in the game, but you have to start somewhere. People are also raising a lot of questions. Who's responsible? Who's to blame? The Western retailers? The buyers? The local factory owners? The government? The consumers?

These are complicated issues, and when life gets complicated, I'm often reminded of something the Dalai Lama once said: 'Be kind whenever possible. It's always possible.'

It's a great quote. In this particular situation it reminds me that a 'poor them' response doesn't really cut it. It's so easy to create a big gulf between them and us, observing their miserable lives from afar, thinking it has nothing to do with me. What I need to remember, what we all need to remember, is that there is no gulf between *us* and *them*, not really. In both worlds people want to be happy. In both worlds people want to have a decent salary and safe working conditions. We all want to come home in the evening and relax with our family and friends. None of us are blasé about making rent, feeding our children, or having a day off. Poverty, exploitation, hunger, and death are not more acceptable (or tolerable) in underdeveloped countries than in, say, Norway or England. Those things are bad across the board.

The bottom line is, no one should have to risk their lives so that we can buy clothes for under a fiver.

If I was a textile worker in Bangladesh, it would be nice to know that the people on the other side of the world were starting to wake up to the grim realities of my life. It would be nice to know that someone spoke up on my behalf and had my back. It would be nice to know that someone cared. That my life mattered.

Just imagine, what if it was *you* who went to work at Rana Plaza on the morning of April 24? Or your daughter?

People often ask me why I stopped shopping. I used to give a lot of different answers. Now I just say 'Rana Plaza.'

They get it. We all get it.

Chapter Seven

May

6 *Whoever does not visit Paris regularly*
will never really be elegant. **9**

- Honoré de Balzac

One of the many fast-fashion chains being scrutinised after the Rana Plaza disaster was the Swedish brand H&M.

Me and H&M, A Love Story

The story about me and H&M can be traced back to the mid-1980s. That's when I discovered their store, on a busy street, right next to the new mall and the newly renovated buildings. These developments were all indicators of a city going through rapid change and growing prosperity. The Norwegian oil adventure was in mid-flight, and over the next few decades my hometown, Stavanger, went from being a sleepy little fishing hub to becoming the oil capital of Europe.

Walking through the doors at H&M, it was love at first sight. My body hummed with excitement. *Holy crap!* I buzzed up and down the aisles, almost in a state of hysterics. *Will you look at all these outfits! This is incredible!*

These clothes were not practical clothes, or back-to-school clothes, or hand-knitted clothes, or hand-me-downs. These clothes were what I had always hoped clothes could be: an extension of the very essence of me-ness. It was really quite lovely.

Under the H&M umbrella were many different styles: sporty H&M, posh H&M, classic H&M, youthful H&M, and businesswoman H&M. The categories seemed endless. With so many categories to choose from, these clothes never felt trendy; they were just plain cool. Also, when you grew tired of one category, you could just move on to the next. The fashion fun was non-stop.

H&M also had a men's department, a children's department, a baby department, and a maternity department. It also seemed to be one of the few stores that grasped the idea of an entire line dedicated to teenagers. *Sign me up!*

I saved all my babysitting money and went shopping. Me at H&M, buying skirts. Me at H&M, looking at jackets. Me at H&M, checking out the padded bras. Me at H&M, hitting the sales.

Whenever I went abroad, I immediately sought out the local H&M store. When I moved to California, I couldn't believe nobody had heard of H&M. Whenever I was back in Stavanger, I always stopped by H&M. Always buying a new pair of Jackie Kennedy sunglasses. Always stocking up on underwear and black tights. Always checking out the hair accessory selection.

But now, with this Bangladesh disaster happening, I feel betrayed by H&M, and by the rest of the fast-fashion industry for that matter. It's like discovering that your favourite uncle is Saddam Hussein, and so everything becomes tainted. You feel disappointed and sick to your stomach, but then you secretly hope you will be allowed to keep all the gifts he's given you, which makes you feel selfish and even more sick to your stomach.

Now I ask the question: *how could I not have known?* Shouldn't I have suspected something? Back then I mean, when it all started.

Shouldn't the low prices have raised alarm? Where there any clues? Did I miss something? Was I blind?

In my defence, what you have to understand is that back in the '80s and '90s, no one spoke about the *fast*-fashion industry. There was no *fast*. It was only THE fashion industry. Period.

Besides, we were too busy dealing with the Berlin Wall, Tiananmen Square, and the first Gulf War. Greenpeace was getting some traction with the environmental types, but all I can remember from *that* crowd was massive protests against whaling, and something about an oil spill. Then Ceausescu got executed on live TV, Nelson Mandela was freed from prison, and the Soviet Union collapsed.

The only bad publicity H&M got was in regards to their yearly underwear campaign. Nobody suspected any foul play. And even if they did, it certainly wasn't newsworthy. The people who *made* the clothes didn't make the headlines. The clothes did.

But even if younger me had known that something was a bit off with the way my clothes were made, never in my wildest dreams would I have guessed the extent of the disaster. It's not how I was raised to think about clothes. It's like when people tried to tell me that Frank Sinatra was involved with the mafia. *Get out of here!* The whole thing seemed so far-fetched.

Obviously, as the years went by, I started to get a feeling for what was going on, but if you remember, the shop-stop was Amy's idea, not mine. She was the one who said enough is enough. She was the one who wanted to take a stand. She was the one who stopped pretending. I wasn't really paying attention. I thought it would work itself out somehow, similar to how we stopped believing that the earth was flat, and how we stopped burning witches.

Now I know that's not going to happen, and even if it did, I still have to take responsibility for my own actions. Right now that means not shopping, but what else can I do? What else do we need to pay attention to?

The C Words

Since we've now moved the topic of clothes and shopping away from the private sphere (shopping behaviour, dress codes, clothes as storytellers, and how the mind relates to it all), and into the public sphere (outsourcing, textile workers, Rana Plaza), this feels like a good place to bring up clothes in relationship to climate change and carbon footprints.

Climate changes are the planetary environmental changes set in motion by our consumer culture. As we all know, these changes are advancing quicker than we can manage them. Forests are disappearing. Icecaps are melting. Animal species are dying out. Sea levels are rising.

Carbon footprint is defined as the amount of carbon dioxide released into the atmosphere as a result of the activities of a particular individual, organisation, or community.

I don't know about you, but I've never associated climate change with clothes before. Child labour, yes. Pollution, no. In my mind, pollution has always been related to fracking, oil spills, regular traffic, nuclear reactors, garbage, and the Chernobyl disaster. Not once have I looked at a spring coat and thought, 'Argh! Get that polluting monster away from me!'

But textile production, each step of the way — from growing the cotton to dyeing the fabric, from creating synthetic textiles to shipping them abroad, to the plastic bag we carry our clothes home in, to when we throw our clothes in the garbage — is every bit as guilty of destroying the planet as all the other culprits out there. I'm just not used to thinking about it in that way.

I won't deny that one of the reasons I find the topic of clothes and pollution so difficult to think about, and why my mind resists going there, is how much I don't *want* to think about it. My hesitation has to do with the scale of the matter. I can't contain all the information. It's too much. It's too disturbing. And also, there is this cosy idea that once we run out of power, we'll just light more candles and gather around the fireplace and tell stories, when the truth of the matter is that the effects of climate changes will be a pain in the ass. They already are, just not in my part of the world. Which makes it easy to overlook all the scary statistics.

Looking at the statistics has a price, you see. It means I have to pay attention. It means I have to take responsibility for my own role in this mess. It means I have to think about my actions. But I'm not a climate scientist, I'm only a personal secretary. Where to even begin?

I hear murmurs about a whole new shopping subculture: Fair Trade shopping, eco shopping, green brands, and sustainable labels.

Is that the way forward?

Yes and no. No and yes.

As far as the textile industry goes, organic cotton or not, cotton still needs water to grow; fair trade or not, the clothes still need to be shipped to the stores, which causes air pollution and waste.

So where does that leave us? Where does it leave *me?*

Should we all start living like the Amish? Is that our only hope of survival?

What I find so interesting about the Amish is that they are twenty percent less depressed than the national average. In Norway, on the other hand (the distant, nouveau riche, oil relative of the Saudi states), the rate of suicide has doubled since the '70s.

But no, I'm not ready to live like the Amish. I don't want to churn my own butter, and I can't imagine a life without electricity. Plus, I've already lived in a commune, and believe me, it has its drawbacks.

Short of changing my entire lifestyle, but still wanting to reduce my carbon footprint, consuming less seems like the obvious place to start. This strategy can be summed up in three words: reduce, reuse, and recycle. Sounds simple, doesn't it? That's because it is, and that's why I love this strategy so much. If you make it too complicated, we'll all give up before we've even started. Nobody wants to give up their car, but I think we all can handle consuming less. Not off-the-grid less, just less, regular brands *and* fair trade products alike.

Now I know what the Emergency Shopping Guideline for May must be:

Reduce, reuse, recycle.

Regardless of our lifestyle and background, by following this strategy, we can all take the necessary steps toward a greener future. Steps like replacing plastic bags with tote bags. Driving less. Travel less by plane. Eating less meat. Build smaller houses. Use less electricity. Buy fewer clothes.

Start with what inspires you. For me it was this shop-stop, for you it might be taking shorter showers. Everything helps. The important thing is to break out of our collective denial and start doing *something*.

Personally I can't think of any downsides with this strategy. This is a win-win situation. Less is more.

Why Less is More

Barry Schwartz, a professor of Social Theory and Social Action, wrote an eye-opening book entitled *The Paradox of Choice: Why Less is More.*

According to Schwartz, we now have more stuff than before, we shop more than we did before, and we have more options about what to buy than we used to have.

Has this made us any happier? Most certainly not. In fact, all these options have made us *less* happy.

How can this be?

In the beginning of Schwartz's book there is an amusing anecdote about him going to Gap to buy a pair of regular jeans. As he quickly finds out, however, regular does not exist anymore. Instead, the salesperson asks if he wants, and I quote, 'Stonewashed, acid-washed, or distressed? Do you want them button-fly or zipper-fly? Do you want them faded or regular?'

In addition, he is given the options of easy fit, relaxed fit, slim fit, baggy, or extra baggy.

Imagine if you were Schwartz. How would you know which jeans to buy? How are any of us supposed to wade through all these options?

The H&M store of my youth, bountiful as it was, seems downright frugal compared to the present-day stores. As young teenagers, my friends and I could always nip by the sales rack, find something we loved, pay for it, and be on our way.

Now, an innocent shopping trip, thanks to our wonderful options and multiple choices, seems almost Kafkaesque. I finally get why I love thrift stores so much; the sane part of my brain must be drawn to the limited options. It's just a lot easier to pick out a blouse when there are only five to choose from. At a mall, on the other hand, every single design comes in a wide variety of colours and shapes. And so the nightmare of having to choose begins.

Having too many options not only sucks, but it takes up a lot of time and energy. Think about Amy and her curtain dilemma, for instance. Had she only had three or four different kinds of curtains to choose from, there wouldn't be a problem. But what her curtain dilemma so clearly illustrates is that in this age of plenty, every single purchase, every single thing we buy, leaves us befuddled and bewildered.

Leonardo da Vinci said, 'The mind that engages in subjects of too great variety becomes confused and weakened.' He knew that our brains are not cut out for complex decision-making.

Another problem with choice, according to Schwartz, is the *outcome* we project about our decisions. When buying something new, we start to imagine how that purchase will make us feel in the future. Before we know it, we're not only comparing products, we're also comparing daydreams, and the more options we have, the more daydreams we have. Next thing you know, we're caught up in a spiral of insane expectations and predictions. Which leads to an increased sense of failure when we buy the wrong things.

I'm such a failure! Why did I buy skinny jeans? I clearly should have gotten the bell-bottom ones. Everything is wrong.

I now understand why not finding the perfect winter coat in a small gold-mining town in California was far less devastating than not finding one in London. The gold-mining town didn't have any clothing stores to speak of, so my expectations were low. So was my anxiety level. *Live and let live! Let's go to the movies instead! Who cares about a silly coat?*

Not finding the perfect winter coat in London felt like a personal failure, a reflection on my shortcomings as a human being.

Reading this book not only made me think about my shopping habits, but also about how much time I fret over lunch. When living at the Buddhist centre, we had a big communal kitchen that served breakfast, lunch, and dinner. Lunch meant going to the kitchen, standing in line, and eating whatever they served. One of the things I loved about moving away and getting my own apartment was that I finally could choose what to eat. Peach yogurt! Ritz crackers! Sugary treats! No more miso soup! As fun as this was, it never occurred to me how much time and energy this newfound freedom would require of me, or how neurotic I would become.

Now, almost every day I have obsessive lunch-related thoughts like, *Should I splurge on a Waitrose wrap, or should I be frugal and bring a packed lunch? How about fruit? Are bananas too boring? I need to become more inventive and eat things like dried mango and nuts. Aren't nuts fatty though? I do like carrots, but then there is all that peeling to deal with. Is there even a peeler at the Embassy? Maybe I can peel the carrots at home and bring them to work in a plastic bag. I guess I could buy a bag of baby carrots at the grocery store, but that seems so wasteful. Forget it. Yogurts are good, but should I buy Greek style, organic, or soy? Soy is supposed to have a lot of oestrogen in it. I can't remember if that's considered good or bad. If it's sunny, I definitely want to have my lunch in the park and read, but then I can't bring any food that requires utensils. Sandwiches are so boring, though. I should just buy an energy bar or something, but not the sugary kind. Do flapjacks have a lot of sugar in them?*

Those with real problems will undoubtedly laugh at this low-grade dilemma, but I can't help it. Every option is weighed, mitigated, and scrutinised. Choosing one over the other means forgoing all other options. What should be easy and straightforward, like buying a pair of jeans or eating a carrot, is all of a sudden an insurmountable task.

So to summarise: given that we shop more than before, and we only wear a fraction of what we buy, and we are less happy than we used to be, wouldn't you agree that if there was ever a time to scale back and embrace 'less is more' as a way of life, it would be now?

But then again, maybe we *are* scaling back? I'm about to find out.

Spring Trends

The new spring trends are here. Again(?). And once again the *Do's and Don'ts* lists make it into our newspapers and magazines, and they are long and surprisingly detailed.

I don't care about any of that. I'm just rummaging through the fashion pages to see if anything has changed. I want to know if Rana Plaza has changed anything.

Up until now, exploited textile workers and pollution, the two covert pillars that flank the fast-fashion industry, have methodically been pushed out of the way. Out of sight and out of mind. But now we're talking about it, right? Now everything is on the table and everybody is becoming more mindful and aware. Change is in the air. We're turning this ship around. No?

I'm afraid not. No one is even going *near* these topics. From where I'm standing, in the middle of Oxford Street to be exact, everything looks pretty much the same. To expect store signs with slogans like, 'If you already have enough clothes, keep on walking!' Or, 'Think Green! Buy less!' was maybe a bit unrealistic, but it seems to me that *something* should be different.

Have a look at these headlines lifted from the fashion pages this spring:

- This is what you should look like!

- It's time to invest in a new wardrobe!

- Add this to your wardrobe!

- Ready, set, buy!

Excuse me? After all that has happened, after Rana Plaza, the predominant message is still replace, replace, replace? Buy, buy, buy? I can't believe it. This is so messed up.

My own disappointment aside, I can't help but wonder how people will shop this spring. Are people still binge shopping? I fail to see why they would, but you never know. I also want to take a closer look at the clothes. Will they be gorgeous and timeless, or will weird and short-lived trends dominate the fashion scene? Just like I did in January, I'm going undercover. I'm ready to spy.

You don't need a blow-by-blow account of all the stores I went to, or a detailed account of all the manic shoppers I wanted to run away from. But I will tell you this: as I was lurking around in the background of the shops, I observed the same tendencies I'd noticed back in January.

People still binge shop.

People still hoard.

Not only that, from where I was standing, behind a rack of cotton tops to be exact, no one was enjoying themselves. People looked positively exhausted.

Show me a woman who doesn't revamp her wardrobe every spring, and I'll show you a happy soul.

Even as an observer, I found the whole experience loathsome. I can't believe people do this out of free will. But on the positive side, I did see some clothes I liked.

Liked. Just liked.

I wasn't tempted to buy them, I didn't drool over them, and I didn't feel deprived for not owning them. I simply admired them the same way I admire fine paintings in a museum.

Here are the styles that I liked:

- Oriental silhouettes and Japanese blossoms - *Love the oriental look.*

- Low-heeled shoes - *Thank you!*

- '60s silhouettes - *You had me at '60s.*

- Denim - *Denim can never be in, because denim was never out.*

Here are the styles I didn't like:

- Big and bold motifs - *Too mother-in-law-ish.*

- Striped skinny trousers - *Is it a spider? Is it a court jester?*

- Bermuda shorts - *I'm thinking toddlers and bald men.*

- Patchwork animal print - *What casino do you work for?*

As for the options, like how many different styles and variations were out there, inspired by Schwartz's book, with paper and pen in hand, I began to count.

At Gap I counted sixty-four different types of jeans; at H&M I counted over seventy dresses; Burberry had over fifty trench coats, and at Reiss I stopped counting the tops when I reached one hundred.

Schwartz is right, we're drowning in options. Albert Camus's question, 'Should I kill myself, or have a cup of coffee?' suddenly seems a lot easier to figure out than deciding on which coat to buy.

And I just can't get over the whole binge shopping thing. Am I overreacting, or is it a sign of illness? What's wrong with picking out one or two pieces, something special you know you will cherish for years on end? That's what Parisian women do, and I think we can all agree that they are some of the best-dressed women in the world, if not *the* best.

Speaking of Paris...

Paris

In the middle of May, Ben and I went on a pilgrimage to Paris. The trip was part Ben's birthday celebration, and part escaping from everyday life. We needed a break, and to quote Audrey Hepburn: 'Paris is always a good idea.'

Arriving in Paris, slightly tipsy from the bottle of champagne we shared on the Eurostar, we headed straight for our hotel, the luxurious Hotel Saint Germaine Des Pres. It was far more expensive than what I normally go for, but by staying there for only two nights instead of three, it all of a sudden became affordable.

See what I did there? Quality over quantity. I'm really getting good at this.

Over the next few days I came to realise three important things:
- Not living in Paris sucks.
- I have to move to Paris.
- I have to move to Paris and become a writer.

Before this trip I'd been anxious about breaking my non-shopping vows. I mean, who doesn't shop in Paris? But instead of being tempted by a new blouse or a new coat, I became tempted by the prospect of a new life.

That wasn't part of the plan, but it didn't exactly come as a surprise either. The Gunnerside events last month had been amazing and rewarding, but now I was back to feeling agitated and restless.

I tried to counteract those feeling by telling myself that, *At least I have a job!* And, *At least I don't work in a factory in Bangladesh!* But somehow that only made it worse.

Chaos! Chaos! Chaos!

Feeling stuck at work was one thing, but part of the mental chaos had to do with my restless nature. Growing up I had wanted to become everything from Indiana Jones to a hermit, and if it were up to me, I'd just clone myself and live out all my different lives all at once.

Having an abundance interests and hobbies makes for an interesting life, but career-wise it's suicide.

When it comes to big questions like these, Amy and I are fundamentally different. She lived in the same house her entire childhood, while I moved about sixty million times. Her parents are still together, mine are divorced, plus my father is dead. Amy's been with the same guy since college, and they're married and have two kids. I didn't even *finish* college, and I'm on my second husband. When I left the Buddhist centre I was battling my own *Eat, Pray, Love* crisis, only I wanted to escape *from* the ashram, not to it. Amy hasn't even read *Eat, Pray, Love*. I'm great at cutting through all the bullshit when it comes to curtains and closet clear-outs, but Amy is far superior at knowing what she wants in the big scheme of things. She's not afraid of settling down and growing roots. I'm afraid of settling. While she freaks out over everyday stuff like lunch boxes and play dates, I'm sick with worry that no one will come to my funeral and that my eulogy will totally suck.

I had hoped that by going to Paris all these unhappy feelings would just go away, vanish for good, but being away from home only seemed to intensify them. While busy at work, 'Be happy with what you have,' had sounded like decent enough advice, but under the Parisian sky it sounded like a coward's mantra.

Walking the streets of Paris, all my dreams and aspirations came rubbing up against me, reminding me, telling me, that my life could be free of Outlook calendars, meetings, and office space. I could be released from email, cell phone, and admin duties. I could just be me. I could write. What would that be like?

I could write? That old dream again. *OK. I'm listening.*

I don't talk about my writing much; I've been strangely quiet about it. Normally I can't wait to talk about my latest passions. 'Wouldn't it be great to be a chocolate taster?' Or, 'Wouldn't it be great to be a lawyer, like Alicia Florrick?' Or, 'Wouldn't it be great to sell everything and buy a yurt in Nepal?'

Those things sound exciting. Fun! Adventure! I'm living the dream! Nice! But wanting to become a writer? That's only the world's biggest cliché, and talking about it makes me feel foolish, so I keep quiet. Even when I *almost* got a book deal, a few years ago now, I only told a handful of people about it.

I'd never *almost* had a book deal before. I could practically smell the contract, everything was lining up perfectly, but then a tall, thin, young, celebrity woman — basically, your worst nightmare — arrived on the scene with a similar book idea. And surprise, surprise, I was cast aside and the publisher went with her instead.

I should have felt crushed, but I didn't. I felt hopeful. If I had come that close on my first try, what would I accomplish if I kept going?

But then life got busy, the years went by, and the dream of getting published slipped further and further away.

Now, however, the writing dream was resurfacing and coming back to life. Paris can have that effect on you. I was waking up from a coma. I saw everything in a new light. What had I been waiting for? Why had I stopped writing? What kept me from starting again?

Filled with new energy and hope I thought: I should do this! I should just rent a loft! I should get back into writing! All I had to do was quit my job! Just go for it! Do it!

I could eat croissants for breakfast every day. I could befriend fellow artists and become the new Gertrude Stein. At the very least I'd be working on my book.

How amazing would that be?

Inspired by this idea, in the early mornings, while Ben slumbered past six, seven, and eight o'clock, I tiptoed out of the hotel room and walked down to the corner café. There I found a table in the sun, ordered a latte, and began to write. Fresh coffee. A notebook. A pen. Happiness. I couldn't help but think, *Scribbling away at a street café in Paris is only the most natural thing in the world. I'm clearly in my right element, my seat of residence. I can't believe I was worried about being tempted by shopping. Ha! How pointless. How juvenile. Who needs shopping, or a job for that matter, when you have writing?*

But then some other thoughts weighed in. *What about money? Everything in Paris is so expensive. Could I really afford to live here?* And then there was the whole language barrier thing. Also, I reminded myself that I wasn't twenty years old anymore. I wasn't exactly old, but I wasn't young either. It's just not the same to pack up your bags and leave everything behind when you are twenty-something as when you are thirty-something. For a twenty-year-old it's considered brave and adventurous. *You go, girl! Good for you!* At thirty-something, you're a loser who hasn't figured anything out yet. *She's doing what?* No one wants to be that person, not even me.

On our last evening in Paris, we celebrated Ben's birthday at a quaint little jazz café. It was the ultimate Parisian hang-out spot: velvet curtains, carafes with red wine, and a live band. The only thing missing was the cabaret stage and Marlene Dietrich.

I loved being there, and I hated that by tomorrow evening all of this would be gone. I would be back in London. I didn't want to be back in London. Why couldn't I stay? *Why can't I have the life I want now? Do I really have to wait until retirement?*

When the band began to play *Fly Me to the Moon,* I was on the verge of tears. I turned my focus to Ben. What was his secret? Why was he always so happy? Did nothing ever faze him?

We ordered dessert and tea and coffee. I sipped my coffee slowly, almost like in a dream. I was stalling for time. I didn't want the evening to end.

To my great relief, as soon as we left the restaurant, my heavy heart felt lighter. It must have been the healing presence of the clear night sky, or the fresh air, or the soft piano music coming from the house across the street. Whatever it was, it worked.

Ben put his arm around me and we walked back to the hotel.

Shopping as an Antidepressant

Do you think it took me long to get over Paris? I'm still not over it. But I have a plan. My plan is to never think about it again, and my goal is to figure out a way to move there.

In the meantime, I take back what I said about shopping being pointless and juvenile. Never mind what I said about climate change and scaling back. I've come to the conclusion that we need shopping, for medicinal reasons. Shopping is clearly an antidepressant. You know I'm right about this. We shop in order to keep the dullness of ordinary life at bay. What other reason could there be? This also explains why shoppers look so sad. That's because they are.

When you have a rich and rewarding life, shopping is the last thing on your mind. The only thing I bought in Paris was a red spatula. Case closed.

While in Paris I read, I wrote, and Ben and I went to Ladurée and ate macaroons and chocolate cakes. We drank wine. We went on walks. We sat in the parks. We held hands. It was like being in an old black and white movie. Even my existential angst seemed to go with the theme.

But now, being away from Paris feels so horribly wrong that I need to distract myself by going shopping. I don't know what else to do. My only problem is - as you well know - I can't shop. I'm denied the only medicine that will cure me.

At least work is busy, which is good. It keeps my mind off things.

Part of my job is to plan and execute all the events at my Ambassador's residence. I'm in charge of sending out the invitations, keeping track of the guest list, and coordinating the logistics (food allergies, number of waiters, wine list, piano tuning...) with the chef and the housekeeper.

Since the administration frowns on overtime, I don't attend many of these events, which is fine. But sometimes I just have to be there, like this Thursday, and that's also fine.

If the weather is nice, I prefer to walk to the residence. I cut across Belgravia and walk over to Hyde Park, thus avoiding busy streets and traffic altogether. And if I have extra time on my hands, I like to sit in the park and read before the event starts.

Not this Thursday, though. I'm too restless. I feel like a zombie. I clearly woke up on the wrong side of the bed. All I want to do is crawl underneath the surface of the earth and disappear. I just can't shake the feeling that life is passing me by. Why haven't I found my true calling yet? Where is my destiny? *What* is my destiny? And why don't I live in Paris already?

If you think this book has taken a weird turn, you're not wrong. When I planned to write about my year of not shopping, I didn't factor in career unrest. My first instinct was to leave my work struggles out of the story completely, but that felt dishonest. Plus, it seems to tie in with everything else that's going on, so even if I had wanted to leave it out, I wouldn't know how. I'm just so grateful that this isn't the year I caught Ben cheating, or the year Amy died of cancer, or the year I fell off a cliff and became paralysed from the neck down. Then this book would had taken a really weird turn, for sure.

At any rate, walking around in Kensington, killing time before the event begins, I look up at the sky, hoping to see a chopper. I want to be lifted out of this mundane existence and dropped into a new and fabulous life. I want this transition to be effortless and easy.

I hate feeling this hopeless. Why can't I be happy with what I have? I honestly don't know what to do.

Maybe I should go to Hampstead and visit my favourite bookstore. Maybe that will resuscitate my brain cells. They need reprogramming. There's been too much moping and drama lately. I just need to get over it and move on with my life. What time is it?

That reminds me: I need a new wristwatch.

I cross the street and see that American Apparel has a sale on watches. Lucky me. I buy the one with the red leather strap. It looks like something I would wear in Paris. I'm happy with that.

Then I walk over to a thrift shop that is just around the corner. There is always so much fun to look at, and looking is free. I arrive at the thrift shop only to find that the window display features a marvellous Mary Poppins bag.

I'm not interested in handbags. You know this about me. But this is different. This bag is vintage, and clearly something Mary Poppins would carry. And since it's not clothes, I buy it. It feels healing. Even though I'm clueless about what to do with my life, this bag will be a symbol, a reminder of sorts, of whom I will become.

On the way out of the shop I notice a pair of shoes by the door. It's a pair of dark brown, high-heeled shoes with an inserted suede panel and a little velvet bow. Very nice. Very unusual. The most unusual thing about these shoes, however, the only reason why I'm even looking at them, is that they appear to be in my size. *Really?*

I try them on, and sure enough, they fit. Wearing these shoes, my feet look like they belong to a lady who lunches at Ladurée. That means I must have them. I walk over to the cash register and pay for them.

Back out on the street I'm a brand new person. I both look and feel amazing. And, just to be clear, I didn't break any rules here. None of these items were clothes, therefore they don't count as shopping. Also, for your information, I acted purely out of self-defence. Now that I'm back from my fantasy life in Paris, I need cheering up.

The Primark Incident

Next morning, sitting on the bus on my way to work, the streets are almost deserted. By the time I get to Oxford Street I'm a full hour ahead of schedule. There is no way I want to arrive at work *that* early, so I get off the bus at Selfridges and wander over to Primark. I don't *want* to go to Primark, I'm just being practical. It's the only shop that's open this early, so I walk inside.

When I was here before, when I was doing research and spying on the shoppers, I couldn't see much for all the people. Now I'm delighted to discover I have the entire store to myself. *Will you look at all these clothes?* I don't remember seeing all those linen outfits before. They're nice. That reminds me: my own linen trousers are hideous. They make my ass look like the size of Brazil. I need to replace them.

Stop.

I move away from the linen selection and take the escalator up to the second floor where all the bags, shoes, and accessories are on display. Suddenly I want to buy something. Anything. I feel confused.

Big time. Scary.

Stop.

It's as if I'm treading on thin ice, but I quickly dismiss that notion. I'm not doing anything *illegal*, we're not talking major crime, I'm just looking at sunglasses. I'm casually looking at a pair of sunglasses and trying them on. But before I can stop myself I've moved over to the hair section where I try on a jet-black fascinator with a huge bow and giant black feathers. It's like an elegant little hat. *Haven't I always wanted to wear more hats? It's so Jackie O!* I like the way it feels on my head. Looking at myself in the mirror I think, *Wow! Look at me!*

Stop!

Hm. But when would I wear it? Who cares! I should just get it, you know, in case someone dies and I have to attend a funeral or something. Everybody knows you have to wear a hat at funerals.

STOP!

Wait.

Wait!

Why am I standing in front of a mirror? Why is there a black fascinator on my head? What is happening to me?

I'm actually asking you.

And what's this talk about a funeral? When did I buy funeral-wear on a whim? When did I *ever* buy funeral-wear at all?

Oh, last month actually. I had forgotten about that.

Last month, when Margaret Thatcher died, I was sent to Moss Bros to buy a black waistcoat for my Ambassador. The funeral service was at St Paul's Cathedral, and the dress code was morning dress (black waistcoat and black tie). The salesperson nodded solemnly at my request. 'You know, Baroness Thatcher's grandson was in here only yesterday, buying that very same waistcoat.'

But for myself? I've never even *thought* about what to wear to funerals before. *So why did I think I wanted this fascinator thingy?*

The only logical explanation is that Primark has developed a special pheromone that causes customers to crave shopping. Either that, or there's something spooky about the lighting. That must be it.

The fluorescent lighting must trigger some primordial shopping gene. Good! An explanation! Or...

There is, of course, another possibility. Which is: I may, or may not, have cracked.

I always thought that if I cracked, if I broke my non-shopping pact, it would be somewhere like Paris, or at Fortnum and Mason, somewhere where my lack of willpower would be excusable, or at least explainable.

But Primark? I was almost brought down by Primark?! How humiliating! I feel there is salt, lemon, and vinegar in my non-shopping wound. Where is Amy? She needs to be here and support me. I'm so tired of her living in Glasgow.

I scurry downstairs, hurry outside through the giant doors, pass the bewildered security guard, and quickly make my way over to Park Lane. There I stop and catch my breath and conjure up sobering thoughts. *Think Bangladesh. Think dead people. Think carbon footprint.*

This actually helps, and I start to calm down.

I knew it was a mistake to let myself buy the watch. And the bag. And the shoes. All these purchases must have brought my consumer personality back to life. Maybe not shopping is like being in AA. You either stay away from alcohol, or you go under. I don't want to go under.

What am I feeling right now?

I'm disappointed, obviously, but I'm also sick of having to have self-control. I'm sick of having to be smart and think up clever anti-shopping solutions all the time. I'm sorry, SUSTAINABLE solutions. *'Ooooh, non-shopping strategies..! La-di-da!'*

Who do you think I am? Nietzsche's Ubermensch? This is bullshit. It's too much pressure. I just want to forget all about this shop-stop nonsense, go home, and bake a giant tray of brownies. I make good brownies. No, I take that back. I make *fantastic* brownies! Why can't I do more of the things I'm good at? London is one giant shopping trap. I can't take three steps in any direction without running into a shop. How can I expect consumer me to change when my entire environment is geared toward consumerism?

Pema Chödrön once said, 'Nothing ever goes away until it teaches us what we need to know.'

Snore. I'm sick of learning. I *hate* learning. Stop teaching me things. I need caffeine.

I cross the street and speed-walk through Hyde Park. I almost knock a guy off his bike. At Prêt A Manger I buy a large latte. 'Double shots of espresso, please.' *Ah, the taste of Paris! Maybe my life isn't so bad after all.*

Unlock the Prison Door

Later that evening I began to question my attachment to the shop-stop challenge being nothing but fun and easy. *We're going to have FUN here, damn it!* I had barked that order like a prison guard. All other possibilities had been issued a gag order. Even when I said, 'I'm in the messy middle!' I'd secretly thought that the next few months would be like sliding down a sparkling rainbow. *Woohoo! Look at me! I'm not shopping!!!*

Ironically, being hell-bent on this outcome had produced the exact opposite result. I'd grown tense and tired.

Since I know a little bit about how this world works — that life is like a mirror, not a window — I was reluctantly beginning to see that the problem wasn't the shop-stop, the problem was my attitude. By attaching all kinds of unrealistic expectations to the shop-stop journey, I'd made everything difficult and draining.

As soon as I formulated this thought, my resistance flared up. I felt provoked, which always happens when I'm hit with a solid dose of truth. When my lama told me that everything in this world is impermanent, I wanted to punch him in the face. I knew he was right, and so I resented him for it.

Contemplating this, I knew what I had to do next: I had to unlock the prison door and release my expectations. And I had to relax. I had to roll with the punches. I had to accept the fact that I love clothes. I had to accept my limitations. I still had to be accountable, I still couldn't shop, but I had to make peace with the fact that I was still learning. I still had a long way to go.

Chapter Eight

6 *To be beautiful means to be yourself.* **9**
- Thich Nhat Hanh

In the month of June I embarked on a mission of figuring out how many different ways I could get my hands on new clothes, but without going shopping. This was part of my 'I have to accept that I love clothes' strategy, and it was a lot more fun than sulking over how difficult this challenge was. Pema Chödrön is famous for having said, 'Start where you are,' and this was my new starting point.

How to Get New Clothes for Free

And just so you know, this is not about finding loopholes or trying to make the best out of a crappy situation. None of the following methods involve stealing, tricking people into buying you things, or telling shop clerks that you have cancer. This is some serious, genuine, guilt-free clothing fun.

The Freebox

At the Buddhist centre, sitting in the corner of the communal laundry room, was a huge box full of free clothes. We called it the Freebox. The deal was that everyone could either drop off or take home as many clothes as they liked. What got recycled through that box was a fashion miracle.

But where did all these clothes come from? Neighbours dropped things off. So did people who came for events. Other donations arrived in the mail, in the form of giant cardboard boxes filled with clothes. When that happened, it felt like Christmas.

As much fun it was to find a great new outfit, I was equally touched by people's generosity. Thanks to all these donations, I could live in the middle of nowhere and still have access to great clothes.

I never thought of the Freebox as being green, or part of an ethical fashion trend, but the spirit of the Freebox is undoubtedly the very essence of sustainable living.

Swishing

London could use a Freebox, I thought to myself. Researching to see if there was one, I stumbled upon something called swishing. I immediately wished I'd invented it, because it ticks all the right boxes:

- It's eco-fabulous.

- It's social.

- It's free.

- It's fun.

And it's easy. Gather up your unwanted clothes and bring them to a swishing venue (you can find them online). Hand your clothes over to the swishing ladies, who in return will give you a set of coupons. Now you can pick out any clothes, shoes, or accessories in equal value to your coupons.

I found a swishing event near Highgate, and this being my first time and everything, I wanted to make a good impression. Handing over my Prada skirt, my polka dot spring coat from Camden, my Gap trousers, and the Karen Millen blouse, one of the organisers threw her hands up in the air and said, 'What great clothes!'

Unfortunately, the selection from which I could choose was less impressive, but that didn't dampen my spirit. I weaved through all of the clothes and landed on a grey bohemian Topshop sweater. It was the perfect blend of cool and formal, one of those super practical 'goes-with-everything' tops.

I was allowed to keep the unused coupons for the next swishing event.

Swapping Party

If you can't find a Freebox, and you don't live near a swishing venue, organise a swapping party. Swapping parties are earth-friendly, ethical, and a great way to get a ton of new clothes without spending a dime.

Begin by inviting a group of friends over and tell them to bring all their unwanted clothes, shoes, and accessories. Put all the donations in a designated area (you can either get all neat-freak about it and sort everything into categories and sizes, or you can just throw everything in a pile on the floor), serve wine and nibbles, and let the trading begin.

This might not sound so glamorous and fun in writing, but believe me: it is. When I hosted one of these babies in Norway, I got so many 'new' and amazing outfits that I could hardly believe it. And for some weird reason, it was a lot more fun to wear clothes that were basically given to me than clothes I'd spent money on.

In a world where most people are burdened with too many clothes and nothing to wear, swapping might just be the perfect solution.

Re-sewing

What could be greener and more creative than breathing new life into the clothes you already have? If you don't know how to sew, take your clothes to a professional seamstress. Fixing and upcycling ticks the sustainable box, and it's totally in line with the Mend and Make Do mentality currently sweeping the nation.

Knitting

Knitting, like sewing, is creative, fun, and sustainable. What's more, you get to play fashion designer, which is a lot more rewarding than being a helpless shopping victim.

Last year I knitted the star-patterned jumper made famous from the Danish TV series *The Killing*. 'Is that a Sarah Lund sweater?' my Ambassador asked. He was impressed I had knitted it myself. I was impressed he recognised the sweater.

I've been knitting since before I can remember, but strangely enough, so far in this shop-stop year I hadn't knitted single thing. Between the shop-stop challenge and figuring out my destiny, it must have slipped through the cracks somehow.

Grandma had sent me a shipment of silk yarn that I'd been saving for a blanket, but now I thought, 'Why knit a blanket when you can knit clothes?' I called Amy and said, 'Guess what? I'm knitting a sweater!'

She immediately began to knit one herself.

If you don't know how to knit, you can learn. My friend Nicole learnt how to knit by watching YouTube videos. Where there is a will, there is a way.

Borrowing

Who borrows clothes anymore? Not nearly enough people, if you ask me. When Amy was my maid of honour, she showed up at the wedding wearing a borrowed bridesmaid gown. Tina, the girl I went wedding dress shopping with back in February, borrowed my veil for *her* wedding. My sisters and I used to borrow clothes from each other all the time, and in the past I didn't think twice about borrowing clothes from my uncles. One of them had a t-shirt that said in a blood-red script, *I Killed Laura Palmer.* Of course I had to borrow it!

Borrowed clothes are just like new clothes, only they're not ours to keep. Given how quickly we grow tired of our clothes, does it really matter that we have to return them?

Closet Clear-Out

Offer to help your friends with a closet clear-out. You help them create a clutter-free and beautiful wardrobe, and in return you can help yourself to their rejected clothes.

A word of caution: never encourage them to get rid of clothes you yourself want. Every time I've helped Amy with a closet clear-out, I gently suggest she should get rid of her butterfly blouse. Does she still have it? Yes. I think it's because she knows how much I want it.

I've helped many a friend with their closet clear-outs, but Gigi is my favourite decluttering pal. She is such a fun person to be around, and she says things like, 'I used to be young and gorgeous, now I'm just gorgeous.'

Gigi shops. Gigi shops a lot. When she runs out of closet space, she calls on me for help. 'I just don't know where to start,' she says. Her clothes are expensive and of superb quality, and parting with them is hard for her. But I firmly point out that she doesn't need eight pairs of jeans. I also point out that no one needs *four* pairs of Wellies. Then I pull out three identical suits and tell her she can keep *one*. Even though this makes her want to shoot me, she sees my point.

We can spend a whole day doing this, going back and forth, negotiating, gossiping, laughing, and disagreeing. When we're done, I'm free to help myself to any of her rejects. This is why I'm the proud owner of a pair of swanky Burberry shoes, a pink Ralph Lauren nightgown, and a pair of chic Wellies with tweed. It's also thanks to Gigi I have so many cashmere sweaters.

Who can *you* help with a closet clear-out? Maybe you can help each other?

Green Fashion?

As I was coming up with all these creative new ways of getting new clothes, I couldn't help but wonder how the Bangladesh disaster would have affected me if I wasn't on a shop-stop.

Maybe I would have shopped less, or at least paid more attention to where the clothes are made. But would I have found swishing? Would I have bothered with sewing? Would I have noticed that several of the big names in the fast-fashion industry were publishing sustainability reports and pulling out of the worst factories? Would I have cared about any of that?

And what about the rest of the world? What had changed?

I noticed *one* curious thing.

In a post-Rana Plaza world, celebrities were being praised for wearing the same outfits twice. This was described as 'fronting green fashion'. Kate Middleton was called thrifty due to her 'willingness' (strange choice of word) to wear an outfit more than once.

Can I just point out that Diana often wore the same clothes many times over, but no one ever called her *thrifty*, or eco-friendly for that matter? And when Jackie Kennedy married Aristotle Onassis, she wore a beige Valentino creation she had worn at a party a few months earlier. Did the journalists covering the wedding call her *ethical*? No, of course they didn't.

I'm sorry...*thrifty?!* I need hardly point out that when normal behaviour gets labelled as *green* or *ethical*, it's a sure sign that something is totally out of whack.

Event Planning

'Hey, Inger! Do you want to go to Turkey?'

Do I want to do what?

The voice came from the Press and Culture office. That office is right next to mine, and it's something out of a '30s movie. It's dark and messy, there are books and papers everywhere, and it's occupied with brilliant people who are passionate about their work. You can almost imagine them chain-smoking while discussing literature and emerging jazz trends.

Curious about this question, I stepped away from my desk and peeked through the door. Alice waved me over.

Alice is as sharp as a tack and has an understated sense of humour. She knows everyone, or knows someone who knows everyone.

'It's the Ankara Embassy on the phone,' she said. 'They're looking for someone to give a course in event planning.'

'And?' I looked at her plainly.

'*And*, I immediately thought of you!'

Over the years I'd developed something of a reputation for being an expert on event planning. I know this is not the same as being an expert on the Syria crisis, or the human genome, but it's great to be best at *something*.

People think event planning is a walk in the park. 'Event planning is easy,' is how they put it. Which just goes to show that they don't know the first thing about events, or how to plan them for that matter. You'd be surprised how many diplomats think they can get away with planning for big events by using amateur tools like Word documents and Excel sheets. On top of that, they frequently leave out important details.

One time, when fact-checking a program for the Norwegian Prime Minister's visit, I asked the diplomat in charge, 'When will he eat?'

'What do you mean?' she said.

'According to this program, the PM goes seven hours without eating. Unless he's on a new diet, I don't see how that's possible.'

Another time I pointed out that they had forgotten to book a restaurant table for the royal security guards.

'They don't need to eat at fancy restaurants,' they said.

'I know,' I responded. 'But how are they supposed to protect the King if they can't see him?'

Alice handed me the phone.

I cleared my throat and said, 'Hi, I'm Inger, and I'll be thrilled to teach an event course for your staff! When do you need me?'

Two weeks later I'm on a plane to Istanbul.

Istanbul

When preparing for the trip, the staff in Ankara told me, 'There is nothing to see in Ankara. It would be a shame to come all this way without visiting Istanbul first. It is such a magnificent city. We'll cover the extra ticket if you want to stop there on the way.'

Arriving at my hotel, I quickly unpacked and changed into my Istanbul dress. This dress had been a gift from a flower-power girl from Oregon, and wearing it makes me feel like I should be able to heal people, or write the next great novel. It's what I wear when I feel adventurous, and what could be more adventurous than spending the next forty-eight hours alone in Istanbul?

This dress is also the perfect 'East meets West' dress, which is precisely what Istanbul is so famous for. This city stretches over two continents, linking Asia to Europe, with the Bosporus Strait in the middle. I don't think anyone should get away with wearing an ordinary dress in a city like that.

I should move here!

That's what I told myself while sitting down for lunch. *Why not?*

Unlike Paris, everybody spoke English, things were dirt-cheap, and there was no real reason why it wouldn't work. *I even have the perfect dress to go with my new life here,* I thought enthusiastically.

But what would I do exactly? *I could write...?* I could write! Both Hemingway and Agatha Christie wrote here, that had to mean something. But what else could I do? And what about the whole visa thing?

Maybe I didn't have to do something as drastic as *move* here. Maybe it was enough that I got to spend the next two days in a foreign, exotic city. Anything could happen. It would be an adventure! And I could write! Yes! This could be like a mini-writing retreat! How great would that be? In the evenings I could sit by the window with my laptop, looking up at the sky for inspiration, just like Carrie Bradshaw in *Sex and the City*.

Ironically, if Carrie had been here, I'm sure she would have slammed shut her laptop and gone straight to the Grand Bazaar. The Grand Bazaar is only one of the oldest and largest markets in the world. We're talking over three thousand shops under one big roof. How could Carrie resist something like that?

I could, but that's because I had my eyes on the Egyptian Bazaar instead.

The Egyptian Bazaar

Reading in my travel book, I learnt that the Egyptian Bazaar dates back to 1660, and it's a mecca for spices, tea, dried fruit, perfume, cheese, and Turkish Delight. In other words: a clothes-free zone. In other words: perfect for me.

After a leisurely walk through the city, I arrived at the entrance to the bazaar. I felt my pulse quickening. I couldn't believe I was about to buy tea from a stall that had been around for over three hundred and fifty years! I used to study archaeology; old things are like catnip to me.

I stood still and closed my eyes. I took in the smells of cinnamon, strong tea, honey, mango, perfume, cumin, rose petals, coffee, spices, and incense.

I'm just kidding.

I didn't smell any of that, but I *felt* like I should be able to smell all of those things, and in any case, it *did* smell delicious.

When I opened my eyes, the camera in my head panned to heaps of earth-coloured spices, big cheese wheels, baskets filled with tea, and tea sets that looked like relics from *Lawrence of Arabia*. I had always wanted one of those! There were also mounds of dried strawberries, mango, papaya, pineapple, and dates. Everything was inviting and mouth-watering.

The bazaar was buzzing like a beehive, but in a thoroughly enjoyable way, and I began to make my way down the labyrinth of stalls. I smelled, I tasted, I looked, and I bought. The vendors were quick to offer me free samples of Turkish Delight, dried fruit, and nuts. One of them leaned out of his stall and shouted, 'Nice dress, lady!' and I turned my head and smiled.

Absorbing everything around me, it was becoming painfully clear to me that my life, culinary-speaking, up to this point had been a colossal mistake. Turkish food was more than just food. Why do you think they call it Turkish *Delight?* Every meal was like a feast, every sesame seed a taste sensation. I had only been in Istanbul for less than twenty-four hours, but I knew I could never go back to eating regular food again. Absolutely not.

And sailing through the ancient bazaar, I knew I could never go back to shopping at a normal grocery store again either. Even a politically correct farmers' market paled in comparison to this. This was not shopping; this was an enlightening activity. I was taking part in an ancient ritual of trade and commerce. By stocking up on tea and dried papaya, I was honouring ancient traditions and cultures. To call this shopping would be insulting.

Ahead of me I saw a perfume stall. It was something out of *One Thousand and One Nights.* The owner, a small man with big round eyes and a swirly moustache, reminded me of Hercule Poirot.

'Can I help you, Madame?'

Of course he could help me!

'But first, can I offer you a cup of pomegranate tea?'

Of course he could offer me a cup of pomegranate tea!

I discovered that I love pomegranate tea. *Why am I only discovering this now?*

At Selfridges I had been reduced to smelling the perfumes on strips of paper, which made me feel both silly and irritated. Here I got to sniff directly from the beautiful bottles, and Poirot acted like it was his sole mission in life to find me the perfect scent.

Just like the real Poirot, this man was quick and intuitive. With a gleam of playfulness in his eyes he suggested, 'No rose for you, Madam. How about Egyptian orchid?'

I sniffed my way through countless orchid samples, and in between each sample I was handed a small cup filled with coffee beans.

'It clears the nose, Madam.'

Coffee beans! How adorable! I didn't remember the little man at Selfridges having coffee beans behind *his* perfume counter.

I found the orchid scent that was *me*, and Poirot sniffed and agreed.

Can I just tell you what a difference all this attention to detail made? Western retailers have a lot to learn. Something has clearly been lost in between 'More tea, Madam?' and 'Hello, my name is Steve and I'll be your server today.'

The Escape Manifesto

The next morning I woke up to the wonderful melody of the Call to Morning Prayer. I pulled my covers up and smiled. This was already shaping up to be a great day.

After lunch (grilled vegetable platter, halloumi cheese, fresh bread, and a mango smoothie) I went on a mini-cruise on the Bosphorus strait. Seated near a window I opened up my new book, *The Escape Manifesto*.

I'd bought the book at the airport, intrigued by the blurb. It read in big bold letters, 'LIFE IS SHORT. QUIT YOUR CORPORATE JOB. DO SOMETHING DIFFERENT.'

Reading this book was like medicine to me. All my bewildering thoughts about my own job, about what to do with my life, my worries, my hopes, all of it had finally been given a vocabulary and a clear voice. It was like the author was speaking directly to *me*. The book was like a ten-step program, a roadmap to sorting out my priorities. It offered an exit strategy. Above all, this book made it seem possible to leave my job and follow my dreams. Not easy, but possible.

This all might sound cheesy to you, like just another pathetic self-help manual, but you have no idea how refreshing it was to see my own thoughts in print like that. What's more, it was a huge relief to discover that I wasn't the only person struggling with career unrest and feeling confused about my direction in life. I was not having a midlife crisis. I was not going mad. I just wanted to quit my job!

I closed the book and looked out the window at the sea. I tried to digest everything I'd just read. There was so much to consider. On sudden inspiration I walked outside.

Had the boat been bigger, I could have stood on the bow and stared dreamily into the horizon, like Kate Winslet in *Titanic*. But leaning over the rickety rail and watch the waves roll by felt equally dramatic. And if this had been a movie, the film score would reach a crescendo, and over the music you would have heard me say: *You can do this! You can quit your job! Just take a leap of faith! What are you waiting for?*

What *had* I been waiting for? To be saved. To be rescued. By someone. By anyone.

But *I* was the one in charge, as this book had just reminded me. *I* was in control. I don't know why I had to be reminded of that, but that just goes to show how far off course I'd become. I'd been drifting.

Rediscovering that I was in control made me feel like a genius. Not to mention relieved. *I won't become one of those regretful and bitter people after all! I can turn this around! I will turn this around!*

I looked out over the ocean. A plan was brewing. A plan! Finally! I just stood there, watching my thoughts as the plan took shape. It was so simple. So straightforward. So perfect!

I *was* a genius!

The Plan

The plan, in case you were wondering, was to stay put. That wasn't the genius part. The genius part of the plan was that in a year from now I would hand in my notice. Yes. I would allow myself twelve months to save up more money, twelve months to find a cheaper place to live, and twelve months to get serious about writing again. Everything I did over the next year would serve my exit strategy.

That was my plan. It seemed achievable, almost religious –

original even!

Back on land I felt less brave. Hold on! *Oh God. Nobody leaves a secure job in the middle of a double-dip recession. Or do they? (Some do.) Who says I can't? And what if I did? (Who are you taking to?) Do I have to get cancer before I manage to sort out my priorities? (Stop being so melodramatic.) Too many thoughts all at once. (What else is new?) I need to sort them out. (How?) Shit. At least I don't have to decide right away. I have a full year to figure this out. And I have to talk to Ben. He'll know what to do. I miss Ben.*

Great, just great. Here I was, in the beautiful city of Istanbul, turning into some soul-searching, hysterical female. That's not at all what I had in mind when I said I wanted adventure. I just wanted to have a good time. But now I had to work through all my *issues*? It was most uncharacteristic. It was unbecoming. I needed a drink.

Actually, what I needed was a quiet place to sit and reflect.

I'm a shrine junkie, and holy places are incredible. And as fate would have it, Hagia Sophia was right behind my hotel. Operation Soul Searching could begin.

Operation Soul Searching

Part of me wished I'd gone to a bar instead. Then I would have something normal to write about. I would be able to tell you about the cheesy songs playing on the jukebox, and how I almost slid off my barstool, and how the bartender pretended to listen to all my troubles while I threw back vodka shots. Now I'm afraid you will think I'm the kind of person who believes in fortune cookies and will bombard you with carpe diem gibberish.

But the second I stepped over the ancient threshold to Hagia Sophia, I knew I had come to the right place. Hagia Sophia, which means Holy Wisdom, has been a place of worship for over fourteen hundred years. It's now a museum, but it used to be a mosque, a basilica, and a church.

Inside this building, which is so big that you can see it from over a mile away, I felt soothed almost at once. It had something to do with the light, I think. It was hushed and dim, like dusk or dawn, only more vibrant. In addition, it was remarkably quiet.

After wandering around for a while, I found a tucked-away corner where I sat down and allowed my thoughts to run free. I didn't attempt to control them, understand them, or even judge them. They had to sort themselves out without me getting in the way.

I was convinced that my emotions would prove too strong for me, and this mental exercise would end with me sobbing uncontrollably and being escorted out by the guards. But so what? I was too confused to feel self-conscious. Besides, no one here knew me.

Sitting in that golden light, hidden from the outside world, I felt at peace. I felt translucent, much like the golden light shining down on me. It occurred to me that if I hadn't been on a shop-stop, I would never have bought that book at the airport before coming here. I would have looked for sunglasses, or trying on lipsticks, wondering if I could get away with *nude shine* or stick with *cinnamon red* like I always do. It also occurred to me that if I hadn't been on a shop-stop, I would never have spent so much time in this city reading and writing. I would have busied myself with browsing, sightseeing, and shopping. I didn't know what all of that meant, but it felt significant.

Walking back to the hotel I felt elated. Thanks to my new plan, everything would fall into place. Everything would be OK. More than OK. I had finally, after weeks and months of moping, set in motion the energising process of taking matters into my own hands.

Ankara

That night I fell asleep the second my head hit the pillow, and by the next evening I found myself in Ankara, the capital of Turkey.

The event course went swimmingly. I talked about things like importing and exporting guest lists (makes life easier), mail merge (saves time), and event briefs (crucial).

Everyone was welcoming and kind. They actually seemed glad

to have me there. I'm not sure what I had expected, but certainly not all this eagerness to learn.

In the evenings I went out for dinner with the Embassy staff, including the Ambassador. The food was scrumptious (as always), and the conversations were pleasant and flowed freely. They asked me how long I'd been with the Embassy in London, and if I planned to stay there for a while. I kept a solid poker face and said, 'yes' and 'sure', patting myself on the back for having a secret plan. I wasn't ready to say, 'Actually, I want to be a writer, so as soon as I've saved up some more money I'll be leaving.' I had a full year to work up to *that* conversation.

Then it occurred to me, if I had a secret plan, who's to say these people didn't have one also? I studied their faces for clues.

The days went by very quickly, and before I knew it I was back in London again.

A New Plan

I wouldn't go so far as to say that I was *thrilled* to be back at work again, but to tell you the truth, I wasn't hating it either. That's because I no longer felt trapped.

On Friday night the Ambassador and his wife hosted their annual BBQ party. The Ambassador actually wears an apron, and all the men gather around the grill like a flock of cavemen. From the way they act, you'd think they'd shot the meat themselves. They sip beer and say things like, 'Better flip that one.' And, 'What a beauty, nice and juicy.'

It's always fun to socialise outside the office and relax together; we're good at that.

Ben had been away at an NHS (National Health Service) course, but he returned just in time for the BBQ.

I couldn't wait to talk to him about The Plan, but this was neither the time nor the place for serious, life-altering, conversations. Keeping it light, I kissed Ben hello and mingled with the other staff.

Sitting down with a glass of champagne, on the manicured lawn, in the very same spot that used to be Henry VIII's herb garden, a harsh reality came crashing down on me: *Alone I'm nobody. Nobody! As the Ambassador's secretary, I might be lost, but at least I'm SOMEONE. The job ensures that I'm included in a very exclusive way of life, and I can't deny that it's comforting to bask in the shadow of other people's glory.*

These were disturbing thoughts, but at the same time I knew I had higher aspirations than getting my feet underneath somebody else's table.

I hoped nobody could sense the panic and confusion in my eyes. *Keep it together,* I told myself. *And remember, you have a full year to figure this out. Relax.*

I got up and helped myself to some more champagne.

The next morning, over tea, Ben and I talked about our future.

Here is what you need to know about me and Ben: we have never been big planners. In fact, we pride ourselves on being spontaneous and carefree. When we first met, years ago in California, I was still happily married to husband number one, and Ben was busy visiting with his aunt and cousin. It wasn't until we met up again in London, almost a decade later, that I noticed him. This time I *really* noticed him. We fell madly in love, and the fact that I lived in Norway and he lived in London didn't hold us back at all. Not for a second. We visited each other as often as we could, and after spending only twenty-one days together we got engaged. Then I quit my job and moved to London. We found a place to stay, bought some teacups, and began our lives together. A year later we were married.

Now, this Saturday morning, as I was about to tell him I wanted to quit my job and do something else, I was nervous he would think I was being foolhardy and silly. But as it turned out, his NHS course had been a disaster. It confirmed everything he disliked about his job, and now he was ready to quit as well. He no longer wanted to be a radiographer. 'What will you do instead?' I asked, half surprised, half relieved.

'I could be a drone pilot, an aerial photographer,' he said.

He was right. He *could* be a drone pilot. For the past few years he'd been out flying every free evening and weekend. Why *not* turn his hobby into his job? People do this all the time.

'I'm so glad you agree with me!' I said. 'Let's do this! Let's resign! We'll do it next year, next year on my birthday. How great will that be?'

'Why wait?' he said.

'What do you mean?' I said.

'Just think about it,' he continued, pacing around in the room, perfectly imitating a tiger in a cage. 'What will really be different in a year's time? We will have saved up a bit more money, but that will be it. In the meantime, we will have wasted a whole year not living our dreams. I'm telling you, we should do this now.'

Feeling dizzy, I went to fetch my diary. I thought about it, paused for a second, then I said, 'How does Monday sound to you?'

'I need to lie down,' he said.

Handing in My Notice

On Monday morning I put on a pair of jeans and my new grey Topshop top from the swishing event. If felt like something an author would wear. It was important to me that the Ambassador and my colleagues would see me and think, 'Of course she's resigning! Look at her! She looks like Zoë Heller. She's wasted on us!'

I knocked on my Ambassador's door, sat down in the chair in front of his desk and said, 'Ben and I have decided to quit our jobs and pursue our passions.' The words rushed out of my mouth like bejewelled unicorns. It was one of the most liberating experiences of my life.

Fast forward to eight hours later and you'll find me crawled into bed with a mountain of chocolate.

I love a good bed. I love how the duvet feels on my body. I love propping up the pillows and nestling in, and I'm one of those people who can't wait to make the bed in the morning. When Grandma showed me how to make hospital corners, I felt I'd been handed the secret of life.

Now, under the covers, I felt unrest stirring. *Was this really what I wanted?*

Yes, but...

But what?

What was my next move? Should I be brainstorming? Should I make a graph or something? Should I make a Vision Board? Did people still do that?

Er...maybe not, there was no reason to get all weird about it. A plain to-do list seemed appropriate. I grabbed a pen and paper, started in on the Toblerone, and began to jot things down.

- We have to find a new place to live.
- We have to pack.
- I have to tell my family and friends.
- I need new clothes.

I need new clothes? I need new clothes! Absolutely! Now that I was finally getting the right kind of life, all my clothes were plain wrong. Office wear? Evening gown? What a joke. When would I ever need clothes like that again? Only *never*.

There was no way around it, I needed a brand new wardrobe.

Since I get a lot of my education from TV shows and movies, I've learnt that getting new clothes in preparation for life-altering events is an important part of the process. What did Lorelai Gilmore do when she got back together with Luke Danes? She bought a brand new get-back-together-dress. Of course she did. Wearing brand new clothes is cathartic and signals renewal and restoration. History will also back me up on this. When Elizabeth II was crowned the Queen of England, her brand new coronation gown took eight months to make, and her robe was hand-woven. Of course it was. Young Elizabeth wasn't about to show up for her coronation in an *old* dress. How inappropriate.

So what about me? Where were my larva-transforming-into-a-beautiful-butterfly dress? Why did I have to resign in a shop-stop year? I should have waited. I knew I should have waited!

I dropped the clothes issue and returned to a more pressing matter: where to move to. Paris or Istanbul? Staying put in London was out of the question. It was way too expensive, but more importantly, we wanted a change of scenery.

When Ben returned from work that evening, he couldn't stop smiling. 'We did it! We resigned!' He was spooked too, you can bet your sweet face he was. He would be leaving a secure NHS job, and I was dropping out of the gilded life of diplomats.

'Ben,' I said, 'where should we move to?'

'What about the Cotswolds?' he said.

Was he pulling my leg? The Cotswolds? *Move* to the Cotswolds? The Cotswolds? But we love the Cotswolds. It's where we escape to, it's our hide-away happy place. Was he being serious? Who moves to their...Oh...I see.

I'd been so busy thinking about exotic cities and foreign countries that I didn't even stop to consider something closer to home. Which just goes to show how weird my mind is, because ever since I was a little girl I've been dreaming about moving to the English countryside. My diary from 1992 reads, 'When I grow up I'll move to the English Countryside.' However, I only pictured this happening in a faraway future, in another life somehow. If I became a totally different person, or if I switched places with someone. Like Cameron Diaz and Kate Winslet in *The Holiday*. It was never a place I could just *move* to. But apparently it was, because that's where we were headed!

The H&M Incident

Later in the week I went to H&M to buy a six-pack of black socks. I had resigned to the fact that I wasn't allowed to shop for a my-life-is-about-to-change wardrobe, but I simply refused to move to the countryside with worn-out socks.

Inside the store, on a table near the escalator, I noticed an attractive stack of corduroy trousers. I'd forgotten all about corduroy trousers. Haven't I always liked them? Didn't I used to have a pair? A brown one?

I made my way over to the table, as if summoned by decree. These trousers came in every colour of the rainbow. I picked one of them up, just to have a look.

That's really soft. These are incredible.

With razor-sharp clarity I knew I needed a pair. Not wanted, but *needed*. These were exactly the kind of trousers I had to wear in order to fit into whatever village we'd be moving to. We've all read Agatha Christie novels. We all know how villagers are suspicious of newcomers. If I arrived looking like a city slicker, everyone would hate me.

I immediately pictured all the things these corduroy trousers would go with. My cashmere sweaters, my tweed Wellies, my winter coat, and my cute black top.

I was not in control over my thoughts, but I didn't know that. I just knew I needed those trousers.

I grabbed a green pair and marched toward the changing room. *These will look so good on me!* I sang to myself. *I'll blend right in. I'll wear them to the country fair where my brownies will win the first prize in the baking competition. 'She can write AND bake,' the vicar would say approvingly.*

So what if it wasn't strictly November yet? So what if the shop-stop wasn't really over? Real life didn't work like that. And besides, I didn't have time for all this negativity. Who cares about a silly shop-stop? I had a new life to start.

Once inside the changing room I saw something that made me jump out of my skin. *Good God!* I dropped the trousers and backed into the corner, staring at the trousers like they were a poisonous snake.

Made in Bangladesh. The label inside the trousers read, 'Made in Bangladesh'. For all I knew they could have been made in Rana Plaza. The person who made them could have died in the ruins.

I felt hot with shame. I felt sick. Made in Bangladesh or not, the trousers were off limits. All clothes were off limits! I knew that.

But even though I knew that, and even though I should have known better, I almost fell for one of the oldest fashion lies in the world, which is: this outfit will change my life.

Or to get more specific: this outfit will set me up for life.

Meaning, I will justify my craving by promising myself that it will be the last thing I buy EVER, plus I will wear it *all the time*.

I recognised that lie, because that's what I told myself when I bought the Anthropologie coat, and the pencil skirt, and the white silk shirt, and the brown faux-fur coat.

'I'll become the girl in the pencil skirt,' I told myself.

'I'll wear nothing but faux-fur from now on.' Yeah right.

'I'll only wear white silk shirts. How elegant!' I wore that blouse once. Once!

Days later I was still thinking about the H&M incident. I couldn't believe I'd been *this* close to buying a pair of trousers made in Bangladesh. In a shop-stop year! *And why did it have to happen on an afternoon that was originally designed for some innocent sock-shopping fun?*

And how did it fit into my non-stop journey? I prefer things to be linear and progressive. There should always be a clear and straightforward way of measuring success. This was nothing like that. My only conclusion was that I'd graduated from the *Messy Middle* to the *I'm Getting Nowhere With This* part.

Hmmmm.

Could I accept that?

Oh, yes.

Really?

Many years ago, when I was going through a really hard time, a close friend of mine asked me, 'Is there a part of you that can accept the situation you're in?'

'No!' I fired back at her, thinking she was mad. 'Of course I can't accept this situation. Don't be STUPID.'

To me, this was just another perfect example of how all Californians live in la-la land. *Accepting a difficult situation? What a preposterous notion!* It defied all logical thinking.

But, and this shouldn't surprise anyone, the moment I accepted that I was in a world of hurt, the healing process could begin.

The same pattern had emerged with my shop-stop journey. It's no coincidence that the very moment I let go of my 'this should only be fun and easy' expectations, was the exact moment it stopped being difficult and draining.

Not shopping in Istanbul had been child's play. The swishing event was super fun. I was knitting a gorgeous sweater. I'd resigned! I was getting ready for a brand new life.

With all of that going on, can you blame me for thinking that I'd arrived at the 'veni vidi vici' part of the shop-stop journey? Around clothes, my mind should now be as reliable as a Swiss watch. Except it wasn't. I'd just been sandbagged by a pair of corduroy trousers.

Meanwhile, I was beginning to notice that when I had thoughts like, 'It's only clothes! What's wrong with you? Get a grip!' everything got harder. It made me want to give up, and everyone was stupid. But interestingly enough, when I told myself, 'Shit, this sucks. Now what? What's my strategy? How does it all fit together?' it had the opposite effect. These questions made me feel calm and contemplative.

Noticing this felt like progress.

And the fact that I could say, 'YES. This is tricky! And I accept that,' felt like a progress as well.

If you think this was a jubilant YES, you're wrong. No balloons floated down from the ceiling, and nobody handed me a glass of champagne. But it wasn't a pissed-off YES either. I can't tell you how liberating that was. I wasn't upset, I was mostly...*puzzled*. And that, strangely enough, felt like progress as well. Not a breakthrough, but a step in the right direction. What's more, even though it was still hard for me to wrap my mind around how quickly my mind jumps into craving mode, at least I was beginning to recognise my own patterns.

Goethe said, 'Everything is difficult before it's easy,' and that goes for not shopping as well.

After the H&M incident I realised that becoming a mindful

consumer was never about being *cured*. Mindfulness doesn't just *happen*. It's a skill that requires regular practice over long stretches of time. Saying NO to shopping was something I had to practice over and over again. In theory, thinking about climate change and being happy with less should have made me allergic to stores and shopping, but until this new learning seeped into the very marrow of my being, I had to draw from the wholeness of my experiences. Motivation alone wasn't going to cut it. This journey required a combination of paying attention, being committed, and finding strategies for getting back on my feet again. Like a tightrope walker I had to move with courage, grace, and discipline.

As I was making my way from a mindless to mindful consumer, every step of the way had produced small but significant insights that caused drip-drip shifts in my mind. With only four months to go, I had to pay close attention to those shift. They would keep me on the straight and narrow.

But even if I kept a close watch on all my thoughts and actions, there was one more thing I had to deal with before moving on: my consumer identity.

Chapter Nine

July

> **6** *Do not trouble yourself much to get new things, whether clothes or friends.*
>
> *Things do not change, we change.*
>
> *Sell your clothes and keep your thoughts.* **9**
> - *Henry David Thoreau*

Looking at it from the outside, this shop-stop pact was nothing more than learning what to say **yes** to (not shopping), and what to say **no** to (shopping). But eight months in, I was finally starting to appreciate the fact that becoming a mindful consumer cuts right to the core of my identity.

Letting Go

My identity has always been invested in being carefree, spontaneous, and impulsive. I despise rules and restrictions, and I love to feel free and frivolous. I worship rituals, but I'm allergic to routines. I want to be in control, and I don't always like change.

In my fourth quarter of the shop-stop challenge, I couldn't wait to become a virtuous and mindful consumer, but I also wanted to run the other way. Why? Being a mindful consumer was vastly superior to being a mindless shopper. It meant being green! It meant being part of the solution! It meant being one of the good guys. So why was I dragging my feet and depriving myself of this glorious transmutation?

In retrospect, I think I was holding on to an idealised Free Spirit persona. *No responsibilities, that's me! Let's wear diamonds and pearls and sleep in!! Let's eat breakfast at Tiffany's! Don't talk to me about rules!* Serious stuff like paying attention, making sensible choices, and being *responsible* (gag alert) felt like too much work. Worse, it felt boring. Who would I become if I changed?

- Would I only eat kale?

- Would I sleep on a futon mattress on the floor?

- Would I stop listening to Taylor Swift?

- Would I stop (gasp!) wearing lipstick?

- Would I become a stick in the mud?

- Would I die alone?

I could go on and on. Deep down I knew that all my old shopping habits, my mindless shopping sprees, had been as carefree and fun as a chain collision, but I also knew that the only way to walk away from the wreckage was by dealing with a peculiar sense of identity loss. As silly as this felt, I had to give myself time and space to grieve.

But what was I grieving? Well, I knew I could never bring myself to buy a pair of trousers that were made in Bangladesh. That part of my life was over, gone, nevermore, and that made me feel sad. Ignorance is bliss. I also knew that I could never go shopping out of boredom, or to kill time. This made me feel like I was being grounded, by my own virtuous aspirations.

What else?

The new me would forever pay attention to quality and

craftsmanship, which in some strange way felt like a loss, not a strength. *Why can't I just keep on buying cheap plastic crap like the rest of the nation? What's so special about me?* my mind protested.

As weird as these feelings were, they deserved to be heard and honoured. Only then would I be able to let go and move on. Out with the old, in with the new. Right?

The old me was in a state of grieving, but through this process the new me was growing stronger.

If this sounds dramatic, that's because it was. It felt like recovery, and it reminded me of what a friend once told me about getting sober.

'In a way, not drinking was the easy part, but the urge to go to the bar and hang out with the cool kids was overwhelming,' she said. 'I didn't like being the sensible one. I hated feeling so mature.'

My situation was totally different, but the same principles applied.

But now that I was getting a sense of what I was holding on to, it became easier to let go.

The Ten Stages of Not Shopping

Inspired by everything I was learning, about myself and about this journey in general, I began to take more notes. I scribbled away in my journal and made all kinds of far-reaching observations. Some of them are too private, and too off-topic, to be included in this book, but I want to share with you my *Ten Stages Of Not Shopping*. I told you I like lists, and working on this one felt like I was being wrapped in a big cosy blanket. It allowed me to relax, sort out my impressions, and to organise my thoughts. This is what I came up with:

1. **Panic** - *I have nothing to wear!* Relax. This is a common reaction. Just take solace in the fact that everybody think they have this problem, even people who shop every single day. The wardrobe is a state of mind, not a solid thing. And remember, getting new clothes is not tethered to shopping. Swap, borrow, sew, and go swishing. Use

your imagination.

2. **Denial** - *What is this non-shopping thing you speak of? But that's my dream coat! On sale! This can't be happening!* It is happening, so just remember to breathe. You can't shop. The quicker you take this to heart, the easier it gets. Besides, you won't remember half of the clothes you told yourself you couldn't live without anyway.

3. **Isolation** - When you start to avoid situations and people you fear will trigger your shopping button, you've reached stage three, the isolation phase. But please don't be a scared and timid non-shopper. Go out into the world and be brave. Be open. Be the best non-shopper you could possibly be. Rejoice in other people's purchases and quietly congratulate yourself on being a better person.

4. **Envy** - Do people have more clothes than you? Is that a new sweater? Do you resent all your clothes? If these thoughts come sneaking in, recognise them for what they are (just thoughts) and move on. And remember, shoppers have problems too, and don't forget that you're doing this for a good cause. You might not have a new blouse, but you're standing up for important issues. If anything, people should be envious of *you*.

5. **Anger** - At times, you will feel that you aren't ready to give up shopping yet, and everybody should just be cool and mind their own business. You feel angry and frustrated. When that happens, call on your inner saint. Be patient. Don't turn into the Hulk. Not over clothes.

6. **Bargaining** - There will be times when you want to make deals with higher powers. *Pretty please, pleasepleaseplease,* you beg. *If you let me have these jeans, I promise not to gossip.* Do not go down this road. Do not look for loopholes. Do not try to outsmart yourself. It's not worth it. You'll only

end up disappointed and angry, which leads you right back to stage five.

7. **Contentment/Pride** - By now you actually enjoy not shopping, and you congratulate yourself on being a perfect person. You have reduced your carbon footprint! You upcycle! You are sticking it to the man! Just be careful that these feelings don't turn into notions of superiority and smugness. So what if you don't buy clothes? Big deal. Stay grounded.

8. **Grief** - Laid back browsers and shopaholics alike will go through a period of mourning. Feeling sad about not being able to buy new clothes is a natural part of the process. You feel alone. You feel left out. You're losing a sense of who you are. The old ways no longer apply, and that feels scary. These feelings will pass; just stay present and honour the process.

9. **Hope** - Not shopping is starting to feels as natural as breathing. Less is more, and you no longer remember what it's like to be a mindless consumer. As you go mountain climbing with your best friends, or plan a surprise party for your sister, you feel hopeful about the future. Stay here for as long as you can. It's a great frame of mind to be in.

10. **Accepting** - You finally accept yourself as a non-shopper. This is who you are now, your new identity. Even when you are allowed to go shopping again, your approach will be different. Bargains mean nothing to you. You look for quality. You invite friends over for a swapping party. In your own quiet way you're becoming a role model for the Shop Less Live More movement. Congratulations!

If you ever embark on an non-shop journey, and I truly hope that you will, now you know what to expect.

You can also expect bursts of energy. You will discover new likes and dislikes. You might want to learn a new language. You might want to quit your job. Half your wardrobe might seem wrong. You start to question everything. It's like being under water. You feel disconnected from your old ways of being, but that doesn't stop you from yearning for how it used to be. You want a breakthrough. Short of that, a break. This is normal. Just lean into the changes and allow new habits to form. Our willingness to shed the old ways is the key that opens the door to new possibilities. These are exciting times.

My own journey, as you all know, was like running around in circles. Stage six, bargaining, was the hardest one to overcome, but now I was finally settling into a calmer place with it all. (Here calmer means realistic.)

Low Point

Before we move on, I need to tell you about the sweater incident.

A while back Amy got a weird rash on her arms. This allowed her to buy hypoallergenic cotton tops, doctor's orders, and so I found myself thinking that maybe I had a rash as well. Like a meticulous archaeologist, I studied every inch of my arms, hoping to find the smallest sign of redness, itchiness, or swelling. If a rash was the ticket to getting a new top, I was going to find that rash.

That's not the sweater incident, I'm just building up to it.

A few months ago I bought a new sweater. (*That's* the sweater incident.) I went shopping. Don't ask me what I was doing in a store shopping for sweaters; I couldn't tell you. I have no idea what came over me. It was like I'd been drugged or something. But the way I saw it, the way I justified it to myself, was that nobody needed to know; therefore, it didn't count. Furthermore, this guy had been a real arse, so I needed to distract myself by going shopping.

What can I say? I temporarily lost my mind.

In all fairness, it was a very alluring sweater. It was unique, it was timeless, and most importantly, it was *me*. *Of course I can buy it.*

Who's going to stop me? Gestapo? Please!

I would just bring the sweater home, start wearing it, and pretend I'd had it all along.

I *did* bring it home, and I *did* put it on, but ten seconds later my conscience caught up with me, and so I ripped it off and threw it across the room.

The very next day I gave it to my sister Elise. She loved it. 'This sweater is so *you!*' she said.

'I know,' I said.

Buying that sweater was definitely a low point, I won't deny that. I wanted to erase it form my mind and move on. But after writing about *The Ten Stages of Not Shopping* I couldn't keep it a secret any longer. I had to come clean.

I'll tell you one thing, I'm normally a very private person, and if I have to tell stories about myself, I would prefer them to be about rescuing children from burning buildings, or heroic tales about the time I defused a bomb and saved an entire village. Instead you're stuck reading about me freaking out over a dress, lusting after corduroy trousers, and confessing my past shopping mistakes. My only hope is that you will read all of it with a flicker of recognition and think, 'Me too, sister! Me too! We've all been there.'

I'll tell you another thing, had I written this book in my twenties, I would never have told you about the sweater incident. Or the H&M episode. Or the Primark meltdown. I basically wouldn't have written this book at all. I would have been like, *I'll take all my mistakes and struggles with me to the grave. No one must ever know!*

But then again, who wants to read about someone getting it right all the time?

Lotus Feet

This feels like a good time to tell you something about myself, something I don't normally talk about. It's not by any stretch of the imagination shopping-related, but it fits nicely into this whole 'full disclosure' theme we have going on here.

I'll just jump right in and say it: I'm a club foot baby. (Just writing *club foot* makes me wince.) That's a truly unflattering medical term that means I was born with my feet twisted inwards and with no real heels to speak of. My feet were basically in the shape of two clenched fists.

This had to be corrected. I had my first surgery when I was two days old, and the last one when I was nine. The doctors loved me. I was exactly the sort of patient doctors love. I got better. I didn't complain. I was brave. But it was more than that. I was a miracle baby! I didn't end up in a wheelchair, like they predicted. I didn't have incurable back pain, like they predicted. I learned to walk, which was *way* outside the realm of possibilities. 'She can walk!' my surgeon said, while parading me in front of a room full of curious doctors. Had I been a character in one of the Harry Potter novels, they would have called me 'The Girl Who Walked'.

In person I'm very nonchalant about the whole thing (*in and out of the hospitals, so what?*), but that's not to say I wasn't in pain. Hospital stays were lonely affairs, and no amount of gifts or attention had the power to make me less scared of needles, operating theatres, and the mind-numbing anaesthesia machine. That machine was the worst. Every time the nurse placed the jet-black inhaler nozzle over my nose and mouth and said in a hushed voice, 'Breathe in deeply and start counting backwards from ten,' I was gripped with an all-consuming fear that I would never wake up again. And then I passed out.

But I did wake up, and I did get better, and one day it all went away. No more check-ups, no more blood tests or x-rays. I was free to go. After fourteen surgeries my feet were almost like normal feet. Only really tiny. And slightly wider than normal feet.

So now, put yourself in my shoes, with feet like that, what would you do? Be discreet about it and pretend it never happened? Try to hide the scars? Never talk about it?

The reason I'm asking you this is because I want you to know that there is a tipping point from where having surgical scars goes from being *meh*, to becoming something sick and disturbing. Also, scars from a motorcycle accident, or from wrestling with an alligator, are cool and intriguing. Scars from a birth defect, on the other hand, mean you're only few steps away from being the Elephant Man.

When I was in China, an old lady with small bound feet looked at me with wide eyes and cried out, 'A western girl with Lotus Feet! A western girl with Lotus Feet!'

She acted like she'd just seen a ghost, but who could blame her? My feet are, after all, only a tiny bit longer than the Chinese Lotus Feet standard, which measures about four inches.

I wanted to hug this old lady. She deserved a medal. I *loved* being mistaken for a ghost with Lotus Feet. It was so much nicer than being mistaken for some sort of handicapped person. Which I'm not. Not really.

To hide my 'condition' I mostly wear long trousers, not short skirts. I pull my socks up. I try not to limp in an obvious manner. You shouldn't know something is up with my feet. I try to ignore them, and so should you. And whatever you do, don't feel sorry for me, that's the worst.

But now I'm like: why so secretive? Why pretend? *Just tell them about your funny feet so they understand why you hate buying shoes.* Which, all things considered, isn't so bad. We all have to work with what's on the table, and in my case that's small feet.

Possessions Versus Experiences

Even though I was terribly pleased with my *Ten Stages of Not Shopping* list, it didn't explain why so much about shopping is counterintuitive. It still puzzled me that when out shopping, caught up in the moment, we're wholly convinced that our new clothes will give us boundless joy. And yet, at the same time, we must know this to be untrue. You only have to look inside your own closet to get a sense of your own shopping mistakes. Can I just remind you that we only wear thirty percent of all the clothes we buy? That is a shockingly low figure. And yet, we keep buying more.

So what was going on here? I was no longer satisfied with the mere-exposure explanation, or the hunter-gatherer explanation. I had to dig deeper. What I wanted to know was this: why is our mind on shopping so unreliable? It's like normal rules don't apply.

In search of answers, I turned to science. That is to say, I listened to a bunch of TED Talks.

I listened to Graham Hill's talk on 'Less Stuff, More Happiness.' I listened to Barry Schwartz's talk on 'The Paradox of Choice.' I listened to Jessie Arrington's riveting talk on 'Wearing Nothing New,' and I listened to Joseph Pine's talk on 'What Consumers Want.'

I was on a roll. I also listened to Benjamin Wallace's talk on 'The Price of Happiness,' and in addition I surfed the net for articles on happiness, experiences, possession, and memories.

What I extracted from my unscientific research can be distilled into two main points.

Point number one: our satisfaction based on what we buy quickly fades. Like *really* quickly. Surprisingly so. This doesn't explain why we go shopping in the first place, but it helps explain why we go out shopping for more. Because once the initial high we get from buying something new has been reduced to a faint *whatever*, we can't wait to go out shopping again. By buying more stuff, we're subconsciously hoping to reclaim that happy feeling we experienced the *last* time we went shopping. So in a way, we don't really want more stuff, we just crave the euphoric feeling that comes with strolling out of the store with shiny new shopping bags.

This is a bad strategy. Here's why: **no amount of shopping can ever bring us to a place of contentment and lasting satisfaction.** It just doesn't work like that. We're barking up the wrong tree. But since we don't know that, in good faith we go out shopping again, and again, and again.

Point number two: our satisfaction based on our *experiences*, on the other hand, grows over time. Over time we become more and more pleased with experiences like our chocolate baking course, or our vacation to Egypt, or our evenings out with good friends. The sheer memories of these events make us happier and better people. Wonderful experiences will never fade into a big meaningless nothing, they sustain and inspire us. Of course, no one tells us this. We don't live in a culture that values experiences over stuff. We live in a culture that glorifies better, newer, and more.

These two points brought everything into focus for me. Everything clicked into place. This was the last piece of the puzzle I'd been waiting for.

At different times in my life I've sort of known this to be true, *of course* experiences like hanging out with friends, traveling, or seeing a play, beats buying a silly new sweater, but without having the vocabulary to put my feelings into words, it was hard to know what was really going on. Now, at last, my intuition was firmly backed up by research and science. *Finally a clear explanation!*

To me this also explains why people on their deathbeds don't have crippling regrets about not hitting the mall more often. No dying person has ever said, 'Life is short, you have to shop while you can.'

Based on this, the Emergency Shopping Guideline for July has to be:

Invest in experiences, not possessions.

Inspired by this, I wanted to collect as many new experiences as I could. I wanted to rappel down a building or enrol in a truffle-making class. Where to begin? What to do first?

Occasion Right Clothes

Unfortunately, there wasn't much I *could* do. I was itching to gather new experiences, but I was stuck at work. Even though I had handed in my resignation, I still had two months left. This put me in a foul mood.

First I tried to put a positive spin on things. I believed that having the end in sight would make me insanely energetic and motivated. During these last months, I imagined, I would be at the top of my game, and as my last day approached, all my colleagues would freak out and say, 'How will we ever manage without her?' sending the new PA pitiful looks.

Instead I felt increasingly sluggish and bored, and it certainly didn't help that my clothes were all wrong. Yes, that still bothered me. I was still yearning for a 'transition' wardrobe.

All the same, I had to admit, expecting my clothes to effortlessly represent every emotion, feeling, and mental state known to man, was maybe too much to ask.

Just think about it: having the correct outfit for every single situation is kind of ludicrous. There is nothing wrong with having a cool blouse that catches my carefree spirit of the day, but what I needed more than anything else was emotionally neutral clothes. That's what mature people have. My wardrobe needed to be more like Switzerland, and less like a Pride Parade.

So what if my sweater wasn't Morse code for my complex inner life? What did I care if people didn't 'get' me based on what I was wearing? OK. But if I didn't care, why did it still feel like it mattered somehow? *Who cares, it's just clothes?* And yet I cared deeply.

Caitlin Moran once said: 'For a woman, every outfit is a hopeful spell, cast to influence the outcome of the day. An act of trying to predict your fate, like looking at your horoscope.'

But who has time to get dressed in the morning *and* predict the outcome of the day? It's too much work!

In my case, I think this 'let's predict the outcome of the day' madness stretches back to my childhood where I grew up with, 'Remember to always wear nice underwear; you never know when you might get hit by a car.'

This taught me that there is a right way and a wrong way to dress, and that people will judge you for it.

There's a small chance I took this advice more seriously than it was intended, but I just couldn't shake the image of myself lying on a gurney, bleeding to death, while wearing the wrong kind of panties. The shame of it all! What would the doctors think?

Had I grown up with, 'Invest in gold' instead, I would have been far better off. I'm sure of it. Which leads me to this month's second Emergency Shopping Guideline:

Don't worry so much about clothes.

Invest in gold instead.

Visit Number One: My Sister and Her Family

The beginning of July had been slow and painful, but by mid-month things began to pick up. The first thing that happened was that my older sister Maya and her family came to visit. The second thing that happened was that my grandmother, mother, and my younger siblings came to visit. The third thing that happened was that Amy came to visit.

It occurred to me that I still hadn't told my family about resigning. I wasn't being secretive, I just didn't know how to start the conversation.

Hi! How are you? I have resigned. No, I don't have a new job. No, no book contract either. Not yet. Where are we moving to? Out of London. Probably the Cotswolds. We're still looking. I'll keep you posted.

See? Not great.

I had to find a way of telling them that didn't make me sound like a total flake. But how?

On Saturday morning I took my sister and her family to a quaint little bakery in Hampstead.

Hampstead is like a village, a city within the city. It's renowned for its liberal, intellectual, and artistic flair. The bakery I had chosen for this family breakfast used to be a bookstore. George Orwell used to write in that bookstore. Hampstead is that kind of place.

I took a bite of my hazelnut-filled croissant and said in what I hoped was a casual voice, 'Oh, by the way, I've handed in my notice. Ben and I are moving to the country.'

Maya turned her head and looked at me, cigarette in one hand and a strong cup of coffee in the other. Her face lit up and she said, 'About time!'

Wait, *what*?!

Where was this coming from? I'd prepared some lame speech about how we only live once, and that life is a daring adventure or nothing at all, and how I don't care if I don't know what's going to happen next.

I was sure I had to defend myself. Instead she was being *supportive?*

I looked over at my cute niece and nephew. Both of them were enjoying a giant pastry and comparing fruit-smoothies. They were totally unaffected by my 'big' announcement.

Hello! I'd just walked away from a super secure job. I would no longer be working in Belgravia! Belgravia, people! Only the most exclusive area in all of London! This didn't bother anyone? No one was freaking out over this? Fine. Not another word from me then.

The next few days disappeared in a flurry of events. Best of all was the visit to the Harry Potter theme park. We flew over Hogwarts on a broomstick. We drank butter-beer. We wandered down Diagon Alley like any old group of Gryffindor students. It was fantastic. Talk about having experiences! Talk about having memories for life!

At Harrods I impressed everyone by knowing where everything was. At Southbank I showed my nephew where the skaters hang out. His wish was my demand. Best hamburger in town? Follow me!

My niece didn't care about burgers or skating; she was dying to go shopping.

Shopping? What? No!

I felt like telling her to buy silver instead, but I keep quiet. I didn't even tell her I was on a shop-stop, or that I now viewed shopping as an abomination.

Part of me was afraid I'd come across as a killjoy, and another part of me didn't want to destroy shopping for her. She was only thirteen years old. She should keep her innocence a little bit longer. So I kept my thoughts to myself and assumed the role of a kindly chaperon.

We covered a lot of ground. Leaving my brother-in-law and nephew behind, I took my sister and niece to Reiss, Hobbs, and Monsoon. We went to Topshop, American Apparel, and Laura Ashley. Places like that.

Shopping with my niece and sister was a lot less stressful than I thought it would be. Maybe because I wasn't there for *me*, and maybe because my niece turned out to have an excellent eye for quality. She didn't need me to tell her Quality over Quantity. She was already living it. That's my girl!

But what about me? Did I get tempted? Did I see some clothes that I liked?

Daydreams and Storytelling

Only a ton of stuff. There was that Laura Ashley skirt suit (perfect for a walk in the Cotswolds), the blue and white blouse at Reiss (perfect for a walk in the Cotswolds), and the green felt hat I tried on at Accessorize (perfect for a walk in the Cotswolds).

Holding up the green felt hat, suddenly aware that I was having my third vision of walks in the Cotswolds in a two-hour period, I realised that one of the main things I love about clothes, one of the main things I love about shopping, is the storytelling.

Within seconds of seeing an outfit I like, I get lost in an elaborate daydream about where and when I will wear it, and how my personality and life in general will greatly improve when wearing it. This is not a super-conscious effort on my part, but I do love a good daydream. The funny thing is, while I'm preoccupied with the storytelling and the daydreaming, logical thoughts like, 'Will this look good on me?' or 'Do I need this? Will I ever wear this?' get pushed aside. I jump straight to, 'This hat would look perfect on me for a walk in the country That means I must have it!'

Upon discovering this daydream tendency of mine, my next thought was: could it be that I liked the daydreams more than the clothes themselves?

I'd never asked myself that question before. Why would I? *How* could I? Swept up in the daydream, there was virtually no gap between the storytelling and the impulse to buy, which made it impossible to sort out my thoughts and impressions. Everything got meshed together. But now I thought, *Maybe I do like the daydream more than I like the clothes.* Maybe the storytelling part *was* more fun than the shopping part. In light of everything I'd just learned about possessions versus experiences, that sounded right.

Putting the felt hat back on the shelf, I asked myself, 'So you're telling me that daydreaming about an outfit is not an incentive for buying it?'

'That's right!' the other voice in my head chimed in.

'So what you're saying, just to be clear, making up a story about an outfit is not code for owning it?'

'You've got it!'

Well, I'll never!

Was I finally beginning to understand how my mind works around clothes? Was I having a breakthrough? Had I cracked my own shopping code? It certainly felt that way. And even if I didn't understand *all* of it, I knew that for the first time in my life there was a space between the voice in my head that mused, 'That jacket is perfect for a walk in the country,' and the voice that demanded, 'Get it!'

If that's not a personal breakthrough, I don't know what is.

I think all the TED talks I listened to deserve some of the credit for this. Thanks to these people, I now knew — as a fact, not as a feeling — that less is more, that our mind is counterintuitive, that our thoughts betray us, that our culture keeps feeding us the wrong message, and that it's only by scaling back and saying, *No thank you, I already have enough,* that we can find true and lasting happiness.

I wish I could round up all these people and thank them face to face. Their research is groundbreaking, and the world needs more people like them.

Visit Number Two: A Clan Gathering

On the cusp of my sister's family leaving, my mother, grandmother, and my two of younger siblings arrived in London. It was like a clan gathering, like Vikings arriving in longboats.

I have three younger siblings. Elise, Peter, and Selma. At the time Elise was living in London and studying at King's College, but the rest of the family was living in Norway.

Grandma was getting a bit forgetful, I noticed. It was almost like she was getting old. I mean, she's well over eighty, my entire life she's been old, but now she seemed fragile. I worried about her falling over, or leaving her purse on the bus. She kept asking me, 'Are you sure this is the right way?'

Maybe it was the heat, and besides, who doesn't get disoriented when abroad in a big noisy city?

To get away from the busy streets of London, I suggested a day trip to Hever Castle, Anne Boleyn's childhood home.

Hever Castle is a genuine medieval castle. It's actually quite breathtaking. It has a proper moat, a drawbridge, and looks like something out of a fairy tale. I can't believe people used to live like that. Well, maybe not *all* people, but some people did.

In any event, it's the perfect destination for a day of multi-generational family fun. And also, inspired by my recent TED Talk binge watching, I knew that visiting Hever Castle would crystallise into a beloved memory that I would cherish for the rest of my life.

Walking down the big entranceway to the castle, which seemed to stretch on forever, I studied the visitor's guide.

Should we walk through the Tudor Garden, or the Italian Garden first? Were there really four thousand rose bushes here? Could that be right? Maybe we should venture into the woodland area and take the famous Anne Boleyn's Walk? I also wanted to visit the dog cemetery, and maybe try out the Water Maze. And what about the jousting event?

In the end hunger took over, so we spread out on the lawn and had a picnic by the lake.

Later on, while walking around that same lake, I kept noticing new and interesting features. Italian statues. Water fountains. Cute little boats. Acres and acres of land. A forest.

This was a different world for sure. I couldn't help but feel a tiny bit jealous. I wanted to own a family castle. Where was *my* family rose garden? Where was *our* family land? All of a sudden I had this irrational urge to buy land. Lots of it. Maybe Ben and I could become landowners in the Cotswolds? Cheered up by this thought, I treated everyone to ice cream.

Sari. Silk. Sewing.

The next day, Grandma came over to our place. It was just me and her. Big Inger and Little Inger. That's what people call us.

I had prepared a big pitcher of pomegranate iced tea from Istanbul, and I put out some biscuits and fruit.

'What have you been working on lately?' she asked.

By 'working' she meant sewing. We *always* talk about sewing. Or knitting, or crocheting, or different types of fabric. These are inexhaustible topics.

My latest sewing project was a maxi dress for Selma. Selma had been looking for a maxi dress for ages, but all the ones in the stores were made from polyester and other synthetic crap. That wouldn't do, so I thought to myself, *Where can we get a maxi dress that isn't made from plastic?* And that's when I remembered my blue silk sari.

Sari. Silk. Sewing. Perfect!

I explained to Grandma that in making this dress, I finally got to use shirring.

'Ah, shirring,' she nodded in recognition. 'That's a great sewing technique.'

It really is. And it's dead easy.

You wind the bobbin with elastic thread. Start sewing. The back of the seam will be elastic, which creates this beautiful effect of pulling the fabric together, yet at the same time making it...elastic. If you're using shirring on a bodice, like with this maxi dress, sew parallel seams the width of the bodice until you've covered the entire area. That's all. You're done. (I told you it was easy.)

The next day I brought Selma to work with me. She floated down the quiet streets of Belgravia looking like an Indian Maharani. The skirt part of the dress fluttered around like butterfly wings, while the bodice part was nice and fitted.

'What a great dress!' my colleagues said to her.

'Inger made it,' she replied, which didn't surprise anyone.

I might not have told you this already, but in addition to being the Ambassador's private secretary, I was the self-appointed Embassy in-house seamstress. With that many people milling about, there was always something that needed mending and fixing. Ready to tackle any sewing emergency at a moment's notice, my office drawer was fully equipped with needle, thread, and scissors.

With Selma by my side, being stuck at work (in a job I had resigned from) became a lot more enjoyable. For someone who is twenty-five years younger than me, she is remarkably great company. In the words of Toni Morrison, 'A sister can be seen as someone who is both ourselves and very much not ourselves - a special kind of double.'

This is true for all of my siblings. I see parts of me in all of them, yet we're all so different.

Visit Number Three: Amy is Here!

At the end of the month, Amy came to visit.

That sentence should be followed by an exclamation mark. Let's try that again.

At the end of the month, Amy came to visit!

We were celebrating our upcoming birthdays, and we succeeded in booking a table at the notorious OXO Tower.

The OXO Tower was originally built as a power plant, then it was taken over by the Liebig Extract of Meat Company (producers of the OXO beef stock cubes), and now it's a mixture of housing, restaurants, exhibition space, and shops.

The restaurant is at the top floor, and Amy and I stepped out of the elevator looking like two divas. Amy was fresh off the train from Glasgow, and I arrived straight from work.

Seated outside on the spacious balcony, I put on my sunglasses and Amy lit up a cigarette.

'Can I get you ladies something to drink?' the obliging waiter asked.

'A bottle of prosecco,' we said in unison.

Energetically talking about everything under the sun, the conversation quickly turned to not shopping.

Any new challenges? Any new insights? Anything surprising?

One surprising factor, which neither of us had predicted, was that we were beginning to wear out our clothes.

What you have to understand is that I hadn't worn out my clothes since I was a little girl with braids and glasses, hanging up posters of *The Princess Bride* and Corey Haim on my walls. Wearing out my clothes just didn't happen anymore. With so many outfits to choose from, my clothes had been on a constant rotation, always looking fresh and new.

'The elbows on my brown Zara sweater look like a sieve,' I told Amy.

She told me how her jacket was losing its shape, and all the buttons were falling off.

'Everything is getting ripped, faded, and worn,' she said, shaking her head.

'Oh! My! God! That reminds me! I ripped my jeans the other day,' I said.

'No! Not your skinny jeans!' Amy gasped, looking impressed.

We both knew what this meant: I was down to only one pair of jeans. One!

Far from being distraught by this fact, I felt proud. Proud and victorious. Amy felt the same way about *her* worn clothes. Our clothes showed marks of a life well-lived, just like God intended. How could we not view this as a badge of honour?

Other women might lament and complain that they have nothing to wear, but unlike the rest of the world, Amy and I were *literally* running out of clothes.

But so what? Instead of jeans we would wear dresses, and when we had no dresses left we'd wear our skirts, and when the skirts got worn out, we could bust out our party dresses. Maybe we should *only* wear our party dresses, like all the time? Yes! Let's! That would be amazing!

Too much? Maybe so. I got a bit carried away, but that's only because I was so goddamn pleased with the direction this was going in. The old me would have freaked out over having just one pair of jeans left. Let's be honest, the old me would have freaked out over having only *four* pairs of jeans left.

But now? Running out of clothes was no big deal. No big deal at all.

The weird part was, in three months' time we could start shopping again. I wasn't sure how I felt about that.

In two months' time I'd no longer be living in London.

I wasn't sure how I felt about that either.

Not Shopping in Nepal

Before I end this chapter I want to tell you a story. It's a true story, and it's about a young woman (not me, in case you were wondering) who went to Nepal with her spiritual teacher. (Think female Karate Kid and Mr Myagi.)

Arriving in Kathmandu, the teacher told his student that she wouldn't be allowed to shop during their stay.

Say what?!

You might not know this, but Nepal is really, really cheap. Everything is a bargain. You can pick up almost anything for almost nothing. Silk fabrics, pashmina shawls, jewellery, handmade paper, you name it.

The unexpected shopping curfew hit the student hard. She'd been looking forward to visiting the famous market stalls and bringing home gifts and souvenirs. It was going to be a wonderful part of the journey.

But not one to disobey her teacher, she returned from Nepal empty-handed.

When the other students heard what had happened, their admiration for this student grew like a high-riser. What willpower! What devotion to her teacher! In this little circle, 'not shopping in Nepal' quickly became an inspirational tale of true spiritual power and inner strength.

Were Amy and I of the same calibre? That's not for me to say; it's just an interesting story, that's all.

Chapter Ten
August

Buy, buy, says the sign in the shop window;
Why, why, says the junk in the yard.
— *Paul McCartney*

In three months' time I could go shopping again. As challenging as this journey had been, here are three things I *hadn't* missed about shopping.

1. **The changing room.** This little stall, cell, contraption, torture chamber — call it whatever you want — was clearly invented by a man who hates women. How else would you explain the unflattering lighting and the absence of locks on the doors? And don't get me started on the mirrors. Changing rooms are where self-confidence goes to die.

2. **Trying on new clothes.** Trying on clothes means going to the dreaded changing room, so no thank you.

3. **Buyer's regret.** The past nine months had been blissfully free from questions like, 'I bought what? I thought I could wear this? What was I thinking?! What is happening to my taste? Mayday! Mayday!'

Lessons Learnt

Biggest non-shopping lesson: the fewer clothes I had, the better I looked.

Biggest non-shopping surprise: how complicated the issues around shopping are.

Biggest non-shopping challenge: not listening to the voices in my head that want to go shopping.

Biggest non-shopping motivator: caring for our planet.

I'm aware that I haven't talked about climate change nearly as much as I should have done. I keep avoiding it. It feels too big. It feels like poking a sleeping grizzly bear. (A big brown bear once tried to break into my cabin, so I know *exactly* how scary bears can be.) Also, I didn't want to talk about something as abstract as fracking and oil spills. As horrible as these things are, I wanted to address something that was more in line with the topic of this book, and at the same time was relevant enough for everyone to relate to. More to the point, I wanted to address something that is critical to life as we know it, not just suggest a Pollyanna-ish, 'Shop less!'

In the end I landed on water. I wanted to look at climate change and clothes in relation to water.

Water

Water holds a special place in my heart. I grew up on a small island, and our house was not five feet from the North Sea. Every night I fell asleep to the sounds of the ocean. Lying in my bed I listened to the fishing boats chugging by, I could hear if a storm was brewing, and I was captivated by the gentle *swish swish* of the waves. To this very day it's one of my favourite sounds. In terms of other water related things, I also love rain, puddles, and flushing toilets. I mean, I *really* love flushing toilets.

Until I was about eight years old, we only had an outdoor toilet, the kind with a little heart in the door. When we finally got a proper indoor bathroom with a shower, a sink, and a flushing toilet, I treated that flushing toilet like it was a deity. We might as well have installed a talking Buddha statue in the bathroom. Whenever we went somewhere new, I only had one goal: to check out the toilets and study the flushing mechanisms. 'Where did Inger go? Did she go to the restroom already?' No one could stop me. I took mental notes and made comparisons. *A pulling lever, not a button. Interesting.*

You might not share my adoration for flushing toilets, but to me they perfectly illustrates how nearly everything we do requires water, and how we take that water for granted. Just think about it. Making tea in the morning. Taking a shower. Flushing the toilet. Rinsing an apple. Cooking. Cleaning. Bathing. Growing food. Washing our clothes. You get the picture. A world without water just wouldn't be possible.

- Inconvenient truth number one: every year the world's demand for water is increasing, and at the same time the planet's fresh water supply is shrinking.

- Inconvenient truth number two: ninety-seven percent of the earth's water is salty, and two percent is locked up in snow and ice.

- Inconvenient truth number three: every year almost two million people die from lack of clean drinking water.

So how much water do we need? It depends. In order to live comfortably we need around eighty litres of water per day. In developing countries some people live on as little as two litres of water a day. Londoners consume about one hundred and sixty litres a day, and in the U.S. water consumption is a shocking five hundred litres a day per person. When installing fun things like lawn sprinklers, buying ice cube machines, or turning the back yard into a private swimming pool, no one made provisions for the water crisis we're facing today.

Growing up, I always assumed that stuff like drought and famine only happened in places like Africa and in the Bible, where people were either unfortunate enough to be born in the desert, or being punished by a vengeful God. Now I see that water shortage is a global catastrophe.

I'm not exactly clear on how our water shortage will impact the global community, but what's certain is that we're in no way, shape, or form prepared for it.

But what does water shortage have to do with clothes and shopping? Spoiler alert: everything.

Here's a question for you: how many t-shirts do you have? Go ahead. Count them.

In August 2013 I had twelve t-shirts, fifteen less than the average consumer. To the untrained eye, a cute little t-shirt might look innocent enough, but the amount of water required to grow the cotton for one single t-shirt equals enough drinking water for one person for nine hundred days. Combine that with the fact that cotton is grown in over ninety countries and represents almost half of the fibres used in clothes production worldwide, you start to see why cotton is largely responsible for the ecological freshwater crises we're facing today.

In facts and figures that means, according to WWF's paper on *The Impact of Cotton on Freshwater Resources and Ecosystems*, from 1970 to 1995 we've lost and polluted twenty-five percent of the world's freshwater ecosystems. Twenty-five percent lost in twenty-five years. Imagine what that means for freshwater biodiversity and habitats, not to mention water available for drinking. Imagine what that number looks like today.

Are we paying attention to this? No, of course we're not. The whole thing is like a dull documentary that nobody wants to watch. We know it's happening, sort of, but when we *do* pay attention to it, we act like we're talking in hypotheticals. Or we treat it like it's super surprising, and none of us could see it coming. Like the stock market crash of 1929, or the Lindberg kidnapping.

Only, we *did* see it coming, it's *not* surprising, and yet we've managed to take big steps in the most purposeless directions, we've made inconsequential adjustments, and we've made countless mistakes. We've looked the other way. When it comes to conserving water, we've failed miserably.

And we haven't even talked about the deadly chemicals yet. Thanks to the fast-fashion industry, eight thousand synthetic chemicals are released into freshwater sources worldwide, many of which can never be removed and cause irrevocable damage. The polluted rivers are no longer miracles of nature, but poison in motion. What else to call it?

In China, the villagers who live next to these polluted rivers have a higher cancer rate than the national average. Three hundred and twenty million Chinese don't have access to clean drinking water.

Are we just going to let that go? It's wake-up time, but the way the different industries, including the fast-fashion industry, are handling this leaves much to be desired.

So what can be done about this? First of all: STOP BUYING CLOTHES WE NEVER WEAR. STOP SHOPPING FOR FUN. If I could remember the consequences of water shortage for more than two seconds I'd never go shopping again.

I say that, but I also know how quickly I forget. Also, when it comes to clothes, it's far less disturbing to read about how Coco Chanel embraced tweed (previously considered a cheap and masculine fabric), than to read about people dying of cancer and drought.

When I lived in California, I experienced the damaging consequences of drought first hand. For someone who grew up surrounded by water, this was like being on a different planet. When the rivers ran dry, we took shorter showers and conserved water in every way we could. The signs above the toilets read, 'If it's yellow let it mellow, If it's brown flush it down.'

Poetic, right?

Less poetic were the dying lawns, the wilting flowers, and the mandatory evacuation due to the twenty-thousand-acre forest fire roaring nearby. The smoke was so thick we couldn't see more than two feet in front of us. The flames threatened to burn everything we loved and lived for to the ground. Ten thousand firefighters flew in to the area. They were there to rescue us, but it felt like an invasion. Our little Shangri-La had turned into a horror movie. Without water we were doomed.

Without water we *are* doomed, all of us. When it comes to *conserving* water, it's not just a novel idea, we're talking sink or swim.

Circling back to the strategy of reuse, reduce, and recycle, I hope you see how the simple act of buying one less t-shirt is a significant step toward water conservation. For example, if every person in London bought one less t-shirt a year, the water saved from textile production would mean something like clean drinking water for thirteen million people for over three years.

Wasting less water on clothes production (meaning shopping less), not only makes sense, it's the only sane way forward.

Want and Waste

The planet's shrinking water supply is one thing, but the truly bad news is that our demand for natural resources is exceeding supplies on all fronts. We're running out of staples like food, water, land, and heating oil. What the planet has to deal with is simply not manageable. Think about what this means in terms of war, power struggle, and panic. Think about what this means in terms of the economy. Think about what this means in terms of survival.

I know how insane this sounds. Is it even true? I mean, are we *really* running out of basics like food and water? If so, what are we waiting for? What's the solution?

Should we ban cars? Should air travel become illegal? What about population growth? Should we follow in China's footsteps with only one child per family? And how much time to we have left? And what about chocolate? Are we really running out of *chocolate?* I know I should be more worried about rising sea levels and crop production, but when people talk about the world running out of chocolate, that's when I start to freak out.

Finding the answers to these questions lies way beyond the scope of this book, but I think we all can agree that if it wasn't for our want and waste culture, I wouldn't even be sitting here writing.

Our want and waste culture means that we want more than the planet can supply, and we waste more than Mother Earth can process. The amount of stuff we now have is downright crazy, especially compared to just a few decades ago.

Families used to own one TV; now they own two, or three. Families used to have one phone; now there's one phone per family member, plus a landline that nobody can remember the number to. And don't get me started on electrical appliances. Even our electrical toothbrushes have their own docking stations.

This makes me wonder how we (as a people) became so occupied with stuff. It's a mystery.

How to become *less* enchanted with stuff is also a mystery. The number of people who've made a conscious decision to stop shopping can fit neatly into one small picnic basket, so how do we even begin to break free from our want and waste culture?

On a personal level, in terms of stuff, packing up our London apartment was a nightmare. The amount of stuff we had to deal with was overwhelming. I felt I was drowning in stuff.

But why did I feel so overwhelmed by our belongings, when I was the one who had gone out and bought them all? Had I not willingly brought home decanters, antique teaspoons, and shabby chic candle holders? Was it not Ben and I who had made a habit out of going to a quaint street market in Hampstead on the weekends? When I stumbled upon a box filled with vintage gloves, I believe it was I who said, 'I'll take the whole lot!'

'Why?' asked the saleswomen.

Why indeed.

Part of the shock, part of why packing down our flat was robbing me of the will to live, was tied to the fact that I didn't think we had that much. The way *I* remembered it was that we lived like an austere Zen master. Our home was an oasis of calm. White walls. Empty rooms. A soothing water fountain in the corner.

To have that fantasy shattered by admitting that we owned things like a piano stool (but not a piano), china sets, crystal glasses, fairy lights, giant street signs, wooden statues, incense holders, and a music box in the shape of a red guitar that played 'Stairway to Heaven,' was a mild shock to the system.

Don't get me wrong, having a home filled with stuff is a natural part of life, but in the face of packing, and in the face of the earth running out of natural resources, you begin to question everything (or rather, start to question every *thing*).

What I'm getting to is this: linking consumerism to shrinking natural resources is nothing new, but bringing it up is still like talking about death: nobody wants to deal with it. Besides, death is something that happens to other people.

In writing this book I've come understand that our denial about the current climate change crisis is two-fold.

1.   We don't see the consequences (yet). We read about people dying of starvation, but all of our friends have plenty of food. We hear about the melting icecaps, but our own neighbourhood still looks pretty much the same. We don't see the polluted rivers or the workers in the cotton fields contracting lung diseases from working with all the pesticides, we just see a pair of jeans and think, I bet I would look good in those! We know the earth's core temperature is rising, but our winters are still freezing cold. So what does any of this have to do with us?

2.   We're too busy. Our plate is full. We're stressed out over what to make for dinner, about getting enough sleep, about finding love, then keeping love. We worry about dying

alone. We worry about rising house prices. We wonder about our jobs. Should we move? Should we have another child? What about a ski vacation? Should we read more? We need to drink more water. Exercise more. We have to figure out what to wear. With all of that going on, who has the time to become an eco-warrior?

As a result, we act like we're unwilling participants in a humanitarian and ecological disaster. *Someone else did this to us! Who made that oil spill! Where is my clean water? Who chopped down the forest? Who?*

Unwillingly or not, I just want to go on the record and state that I'm not ready for any doomsday predictions and scary utopian tales. I have no desire to live out some futuristic sci-fi fantasy about moving to another planet. First of all, I would never make the cut. We all know that when the time comes to leave Mother Earth and colonise another planet, only Nobel laureates and Mensa members will be invited to board the spacecraft.

Second of all, I like *this* planet. Especially now that we're moving to the Cotswolds.

House Hunting, Part One

Ever since we resigned, Ben and I split our time between packing and house hunting.

You already know how dreadful the packing process was, but the house hunting was equally off to a rocky start.

Movies have led me to believe that viewing houses is almost like going to a party. The lawn is decorated with an inviting 'To Let' sign, complete with balloons and ribbons. Once inside you're offered a great selection of snacks and drinks, and the groomed estate agent acts like she's your best friend (and a part of you wishes she was).

None of that happened to me. No balloons, no snacks, nothing.

The first house viewing was of a 'quaint and unique country cottage', which turned out to be right next to the noisiest road in the whole wide world. Also, the entire place smelled like old gym socks.

The second house viewing was of a spacious bungalow situated on a horse farm. Or so the brochure in my inbox would have me believe. Instead, the estate agent took me to view a house that can only be described as a doll's house. Barbie and Ken would have loved it.

I've always believed that if I served time in prison, or lived under an oppressive regime, I'd be the kind of person who'd make the most of it and never lose faith. Sort of like a blond Nelson Mandela. But given that I *had* freedom and options, I refused to settle for a *doll's house.*

Why was this so hard? Why was there no good houses out there? We were running out of time.

Preparing for my next viewing, I didn't leave anything to chance. I bombarded the estate agents with questions.

Was the place smelly?

Noisy?

Did I have all the relevant details?

Did I have the *right* details?

Any law-breaking biker gangs nearby?

Any drug dealers? No?

Is it near a Ku Klux Klan gathering spot? (Where did that come from?)

Finally I asked, 'So, you can't think of a single reason I shouldn't come to view this place?'

He couldn't.

I decided to play the viewing from an eye-candy angle. If the place was as great as the pictures indicated — old mansion in a small hamlet, converted into flats, with a spectacular view — I expected some serious competition. That meant I had to give a great first impression. That meant dressing up in clothes I thought an estate agent would like. I even put on nail polish, that's how much I wanted the place.

Sitting on the train on my way to the viewing, the scenery outside shifted from urban, to industrial, to green rolling hills and adorable villages. I stared longingly out of the window. Everything was so pretty. *When faced with so much natural beauty, is it any wonder I find it hard to believe that the world is coming to an end?*

Arriving at Stroud, I looked very fit in my Tiger of Sweden blazer, vintage pussy bow blouse, and leopard print shoes. The estate agent looked like he was about twelve years old. He actually looked like one of the Von Trapp children. *Is this the person I dressed up for?*

My hair was pulled back in a chic bun, which I hoped would give off a playful-slash-serious vibe. Now I wished I'd made pigtails instead.

Her With the Hair

I've always lived by the rule that your hairdo should be the yin to the yang of your clothes. Meaning, you should never have a fancy hairdo when wearing a party outfit, and never have a plain hairdo when wearing everyday clothes.

I say this with authority because hair, my dear friends, happens to be one of my areas of expertise.

For the longest time, the most remarkable thing about me was my long hair. Ever since I was a little girl I've been blessed with thick, lustrous, healthy, and fast-growing hair. This earned me nicknames like Rapunzel, Goldilocks, and *Her with the Hair*.

My hair grew so long I could sit on it. My hair was so thick it took hours to dry. I spent hours in front of the mirror practicing new hairdos, and I perfected every hairstyle from the '60s beehive to the Renaissance look. I also learned how to French braid, fish braid, and Dutch braid with five strands. The most challenging hairdo I ever attempted was the Geisha look, the traditional wareshinobu hairstyle. The hairdo I had the most fun with was the Princess Leia bun.

I became a hairdo master, and every day I received compliments for my hair. Once, when working at a restaurant, a customer called my manager and asked for my phone number. 'I don't know her name,' the customer said, 'but I'm looking for the girl with the amazing hair.'

At the Buddhist centre — where beautiful hair was considered one of the outer signs of spiritual accomplishment — my hair was the source of endless praise and adoration.

Then one day I began to worry that my hair was my only redeeming feature. Did people only notice me because of my hair? What would I look like with shorter hair? Like a she-troll? Like a monster?

Determined to find out, I went to the hairdresser. There I told the stylist, 'I'd like it shorter, please.'

'But you have such long and healthy hair!' she said.

'That's my point,' I said.

I don't think she got it, but nevertheless, she chopped it off. The result was something out of a '50s movie.

With shorter hair, I can't tell you how many elderly men came up to me and said, 'You look just like my mother!' That wasn't *exactly* the kind of attention I was looking for, but OK. At least I wasn't invisible. At least I made people smile.

In any case, I'm talking to you about my hair for two reasons. First of all, being a talented hairdo master (she says modestly) has been a real lifesaver during these shop-stop months. By transforming my hair into bobs, ponytails, twists, and braids, I'm fairly certain no one noticed that I wore the same old outfits for ages.(Of course they didn't. Everyone is too busy with their own clothes, but still...) Also, coming up with new hairdos is both green and creative. By changing our hair and not our clothes, when the world comes to an end, we'll ride into the sunset with a clean conscience and smashing hair. We won't be one of those pathetic people gasping for air, lying on a heap of disposable clothes.

That's why the Emergency Shopping Guide for August must be:

Change your hair, not your clothes.

Secondly, thinking about my hair made me realise how much I'd miss Roy. Roy is my London hairdresser. From the very beginning he's had a unique and inherent understanding of my hair, which means he does everything right. I want my hair long, but not in a flat way. I want highlights, but without making it look like I'm trying too hard. I want it layered, but not in a feathery style. Roy gets this. It's like my hair is an extension of his very soul. With puckered lips and narrowed eyes, he handles his comb, scissors, and clips like a multi-armed deity. He only interrupts his rhythm to shout, 'More tea for my lady here!' On my wedding day, Roy returned from his vacation to do my bridal hairdo. 'I can't have anyone else touch your hair on your special day!'

It's one of the nicest things anyone has ever done for me.

House Hunting, Part Two

But back to my house-viewing.

We were now driving slowly through the narrow country lanes. Everything we drove by — the country pubs, the old stone buildings, the bright green fields — looked quintessentially Cotswold-y. It was like being inside a tourist brochure, or a landscape painting. Even the trees looked Cotswoldian. I instantly felt at home, but that's what I'd felt about London as well.

I remember stepping off the underground and filling my lungs with the polluted stench of the city. My heart raced with excitement, and I wanted to lie down on the ground and lick the tarmac. I longed to drink up the city like a kitten lapping milk; that's how insane I was. Only, at the time, it didn't seem insane at all. It seemed right. I was finally home! *No more country bumpkin for me!* I told myself. When visiting London only a few months earlier, I'd gone straight to Soho and treated myself to a tattoo, in a tattoo parlour above a sex shop no less. Fun! I loved urban living.

But who was I kidding? Nothing beats fresh air and country living. London had been a phase, or like an affair. Like an exciting, crazy, and mind-spinning affair, that over time turned boring, predictable, and stale. Followed by a phase of genuine confusion.

'Here we are!' the boyish estate agent announced.

Bloody hell! Is this place for real? Through the car window I saw a goddess of a house. Arranged over three floors, with tall Gothic windows, and with a stone tiled roof, this house felt more like a mansion to me. It was a unique blend of Fantastic and To Die For. More impressive than the house itself, was the view it presided over. It was the most idyllic landscape scenery I had ever seen. Picture a perfect semicircle filled with acres and acres woodland, lush green fields, and rolling hills. A visual treasure. The sky above was vast and blue.

This view could stop traffic. It certainly stopped me in my tracks.

'Shall we go inside?' the estate agent asked.

'What? Sure! *Sure-sure-sure.*'

There was a kitchen, a drawing room, a hallway, two bedrooms, a bathroom, and a small utility room. *This is too good to be true,* I warned myself. Online there had been no mention of fireplaces and hardwood floors. If this was a dream, I didn't want to wake up. I could already see myself sitting by the window writing, overlooking the gorgeous view. From the kitchen I could hear Ben say, 'Darling, do you want another cup of tea?'

I told the estate, 'I'll take it.'

'Great,' he said. 'I'll get back to you as soon as we've run all the background checks.'

Background checks? I'd forgotten all about that. I was sure it would be fine. I *had* to be.

Consumer Responsibility

On the train back to London, the landscape outside went from adorable villages, to green rolling hills, to industrial scenery, and finally to London. To urban, iconic London.

Have you noticed, by the way, that when people describe London, myself included, they often use the word *iconic?* The iconic red buses, the iconic black cabs, the iconic bobbies, and iconic Piccadilly Circus and Trafalgar Square.

Everything about London is iconic. *London* is iconic. Even

shopping in London is different than shopping in any other parts of the world. You have the iconic Portobello Road market, iconic Camden, and iconic department stores like Fortnum and Mason, Liberty, and Hamleys.

One of my favourite London shops is Berry Bros & Rudd. It's a wine shop dating back to 1698. This incredible wine seller can brag about supplying wine for the *Titanic*, providing wine to smugglers during the American prohibition, and it has no less than two Royal Warrants. I don't care about the wine nearly as much as I enjoy visiting the shop itself. Once inside, I'm treading on historic grounds. Lord Byron used to shop at Berry Bros & Rudd. What more could you possibly want?

That is actually a very good question. *What more could a modern consumer actually want?*

In light of the world coming to an end, I would love for retailers to provide us with more details about their products. I think that's a reasonable request. If we're going to put the burden of creating a sustainable future at the feet of the consumer, we need more facts to go on. As the situation is today, none of us are capable of making an informed decision. A vintage-y looking label with a cool script announcing 'Organic Cotton' is not going to cut it. We need the broad strokes *and* the nuances.

Take Fiji Water for instance. One quick glance at the bottle tells me that the bottle is recyclable, and that the water itself is collected at an artesian aquifer deep within the earth.

I don't know what an *aquifer* is, but at least I'm informed. What kind of information do I have about my clothes?

When you buy a t-shirt, does it say on the label, 'Cotton production is rapidly draining our freshwater resources, so cherish this piece of clothing like it's your only child'?

Of course it doesn't, but it *should* say that. In the spirit of transparency and openness, it should also say, 'The production of this top has contributed to the destruction of rivers and may cause cancer.'

Maybe the labels don't have to be *that* blunt and harsh, but they should say *something*, and preferably printed right next to a picture of a cute baby panda dying of thirst.

And how can we begin to make informed decisions when no one in the fashion world is playing on the same team? Watching the ongoing battle and shifting alliances between style and sustainability, retail owners and factory workers, consumers and style editors, it's like watching a cheap soap opera, or reading a Russian family saga. The priorities and goals of the players involved are all over the place. Is it any wonder we feel confused and get lost?

The New Me

The week following the house viewing, I was playing out my own cheap soap opera. This episode was called 'The One Where Inger is Haunted by the Flat'.

It had already been five days since the viewing. Five long days! How long does a background check take? One week? Two weeks? What were they looking for? How could I speed this up? I tried not to think about it. It only made me nervous. Besides, I had to focus on the new me.

By 'the new me', I mean the woman who would be taking over my job, the women who would replace me. The tedious interview rounds were over, and we had landed on a great new candidate.

I torpedoed her with information.

An efficient secretary has to be a juggler, a mind-reader, and a magician. It's not unusual to prepare for a royal visit, send out dinner invitations, update the Ambassador's schedule, and apply for a landing permission for the PM's private jet, all before lunch. You also have to remember to send out birthday faxes (yes, the Embassy still had a fax machine), go through the mail, reply to emails, and answer the phone. In order to get everything done you have to be at least ten steps ahead, yet fully present.

I told all this to the new secretary, and she scribbled away in her notebook.

Hearing myself talk about everything I do, and showing her *how* to do it, *when* to do it, in what order to do it, *where* to file it, and *whom* to inform, I began to have doubts about leaving.

What am I doing? Why am I quitting this job? Why am I quitting something I'm really good at? For what? For some impossible dream? Since when was THAT a good idea?

I needed air. I rushed to the bathroom and splashed cold water on my face.

Quitting this job felt like leaving a fancy cruise ship and plunging straight into the big dark ocean. I didn't even have a lifeboat, let alone a raft. If only I knew about the flat.

I feared the flat would go to a *normal* couple, someone with proper jobs and predictable incomes. *Why am I putting myself through this? Why this sudden urge to follow my heart? Had I lost my mind? I had a GREAT job! People would kill for this job.*

While drying my face I told myself it would be OK. I was doing the right thing, and not a moment too soon. But, and this is where the knot in the stomach came in, what if the problem wasn't the job; what if the problem was *me*? What if I never found my footing in this world and drifting became my *thing*? And what if my so-called interests and values didn't translate into a career path? What if all that was available to me was a patchwork of eccentric hobbies? I just didn't want to turn into crazy auntie Inger who shows up at family gatherings draped in a colourful shawl and talks about karma and says things like, 'Follow your dreams, dear!'

On the other hand, I was also aware that knowing my way around Outlook and having Scotland Yard on speed-dial was shallow and sad material for a eulogy.

'Inger was very good at setting up meetings and knew all kinds of nifty things about event planning. We shall all miss her very much.'

Over my dead body.

I returned to my desk and showed the new secretary how to work the Outlook calendar. I explained that when it comes to events and appointments, she must put them in *both* the Ambassador's calendar *and* in his driver's. 'And your own calendar, obviously, otherwise you'll just get confused. Like this,' I said, and opened three different calendars simultaneously. They spread across the computer screen like a multi-coloured fan. 'Just copy and paste, and make sure you always include the full address and contact details,' I said.

The new secretary looked confused. I felt relieved. This was all on her now.

The Burberry Coats

In the lunch break I ran into Gigi. She was desperate for another closet clear-out. 'You have to help me,' she said. 'I know you're probably busy with your own packing and everything, but I'd really appreciate it if you could come over one evening.'

She was right. I *was* in the middle of a packing frenzy, but without knowing about the flat the motivation escaped me.

Ben, on the other hand, was working tirelessly on getting his new drone business up and running. There were drone exams (who knew?), registering the company name, creating a website, and updating the equipment. Something inside him had reignited and he was fast-tracking everything.

Being a hyper-organised person, I was supposed to get cracking with the packing, but helping Gigi out was a lot more tempting, so I said yes.

Gigi had developed a new system of organising all her rejects into two neat piles. One pile was reserved for her less-fancy stuff, which she would donate to the local charity shop. The other pile was reserved for her exclusive and expensive stuff, which she would sell to upscale secondhand stores.

Working our way through her coats and jackets, I noticed her putting two beige coats in the 'sell later' pile. I tried not to notice that they were Burberry coats.

Of no fault of my own, I was suddenly lost in a wonderful daydream about wearing Burberry coats in the country. *That's exactly the kind of look I should go for when moving to the Cotswolds,* I told myself. *I would fit right in!*

As if reading my mind, Gigi asked if I'd like to buy them.

Buy them? I thought she was selling them to that fancy store in Kensington.

Yes, she was, she told me, but she felt I should have the first pick.

I felt stunned. Blimey. *What do I do? What do I say?*

'How much?' I asked, hoping the price would be way out of my league. It wasn't. In fact, the price was so shockingly low that my thoughts jumped into lightspeed and began lobbying for the coats.

You have to accept her kind offer, anything else would be totally rude. And how can you be rude to Gigi? She's always so nice to you. I believe it's customary to always treat your friends with kindness and respect. Plus, wearing Burberry in the Cotswolds is the most natural thing in the world. And hello! Do I have to point out that buying clothes from your friends is exactly the kind of thing green consumerism is all about? Buying these coats is sustainability at its best. You know it is.

These thoughts had a point. Wearing Burberry had always been my dream, and this was an incredible deal. I would be stupid not to take it.

Then the reasonable part of my mind shot in. *Slow down! What happened to liking the daydreams more than the clothes themselves? Don't do this. You know you're not allowed to buy anything. I don't care if it's bloody Burberry. Get a grip. Stick with the daydream and let it go.*

End of discussion. *Or was it?*

My head spun in a new direction. *Maybe I can ask Gigi to give them to me? No! No! No! Stop it! Don't be greedy!*

I didn't like feeling this conflicted, but we're talking Burberry here, people, Burberry! How was I supposed to deny myself such loveliness? I wasn't even in a store, I was in Gigi's gorgeous Chelsea flat.

I couldn't help but feel annoyed with myself, but I was also annoyed that I couldn't buy the coats.

I hope you are enjoying this, because I wasn't. I felt like the

Universe was having a go at me. It was one thing to say, 'No thank you, I already have enough,' when it came to shopping at regular stores. But – and this was a **big** BUT – passing up something that could only be described as an opportunity of a lifetime felt foolish and meaningless.

I took another sip of my wine (thank goodness we were drinking alcohol that evening) and tried to will the Burberry urge to go away. I took another sip, praying that the alcohol would guide me to a state of inner peace.

Wait a minute...isn't my niece a Burberry fan? Didn't she tell me that when we went shopping together last month?

I quickly took out my phone and snapped pictures of the coats and texted them to Maya. I wrote, 'Do you think Anna would like these? I can get them for thirty pounds each.'

Within five seconds my phone bleeped. 'Buy now!' she instructed.

My daydream of wearing Burberry coats in the Cotswolds were immediately replaced by feeling like I was at a sophisticated auction house bidding on exclusive oriental art for an anonymous dealer in Barcelona. I was actually having fun. Nothing beats the restorative powers of thinking of others.

Going once! Going twice! Sold to the lady with the blond hair!

And just like that the coats were sold to my sister and would be worn by my niece. This made me happy, but I also felt like screaming into a pillow.

Instant Karma Rocks

The next day I received a call from the estate agent. 'Congratulations, the flat is yours!' he informed me.

I could hardly believe it! The dream flat was ours! This was clearly a reward for being such an altruistic non-shopper. Show me a person who gives Burberry coats to her niece, and I'll show you a saint with a gorgeous flat in the Cotswolds.

Instant karma rocks!

We could move in on September 1, in two weeks, the very same day we had to move out of our London flat. But I had four weeks left at work...Ben could drive down with the moving van, but what about me? Where would I live? No worries. I would figure that part out later.

I told the good news to Gigi, adding that I'd probably spend my last two weeks in London living under a bridge or something. *Ha ha ha*! I honestly didn't care.

'Wait,' Gigi said. 'I leave for Spain on September 1 and I'll be gone exactly two weeks. So you can stay at my place if you like.'

Like? Would I *like* to stay at a bachelorette pad in Chelsea for my last two weeks in London? I gave Gigi a big hug and said, 'Thank you!'

I filed this lucky coincidence under the category: when you jump, the net will follow. The Universe was clearly looking out for me.

Saying Goodbye

Celebrating the house deal, and with our wedding anniversary coming up, Ben and I went on a picnic on Primrose Hill.

Primrose Hill is gorgeous park in North London, and when Ben and I first started dating, he took me there all the time. Nothing is more romantic than watching the sun go down over Primrose Hill, especially if you bring treats and wine, and especially if you go there with the person who loves you the most, and who you happen to love the most in return.

Being there now felt bittersweet. This could very well be the last time we were doing this. All of August had been like that: saying goodbye to old and familiar places, remembering what it was like when I first moved here, and wondering what I would miss and how quickly I would forget.

Feeling a twinge of nostalgia, I busied myself with the picnic basket. We had Sierra Nevada Pale Ale, an old favorite from California. We had truffles, representing our undying love for chocolate. We had macaroons, in honour of Paris. And we had the ultimate comfort food:

sour strawberry straws and tortilla chips. A classic Ben and Inger picnic.

I drained my beer and chewed on a strawberry straw. Ben was in a terrific mood. He only had one more week left at work. 'We should have done this ages ago,' he said, reaching for another truffle.

Roger that. Feeling you should have done something sooner is a sure sign you're doing the right thing.

We were *ready*.

Chapter Eleven
September

> **6** *What I know for sure:*
>
> *Having the best things is no substitute*
> *for having the best life.*
>
> *When you let go of the desire to acquire,*
> *you know you are really on your way.* **9**
> — *Oprah Winfrey*

In the previous chapters you read about the many ways the fashion industry contributes to the destruction of our planet. In this chapter I want to show you the many ways the fashion industry is becoming a beacon of good in this world.

But before doing that, I have to address the silent fear that was keeping me up at night.

Insights?

The Burberry coat episode had left me wondering if I'd graduated from the *Messy Middle* to *I'm Getting Nowhere With This*, only to arrive at the stage called *Total Bewilderment*. Where was the feeling of achievement? Yes, I had walked away from the Burberry coast, but not without a struggle. In a perfect world I would have told Gigi, 'How kind of you, but I'm just not interested in more stuff in my life right now. I have more than enough.'

Which I do, which was true, so why all the drama? The way I saw it, this was a classic case of one step forward and two steps back. Which would have been fine at the beginning of this book, but not toward the end.

The less-is-more strategy, and musing about my random progress and admitting mistakes was one thing, but now I felt it was time for a grand finale. I should be able to write lyrical haikus about my many discoveries. Once again I wanted to be DONE and move on. But how could I move on when I was still stuck in the same old conundrum?

- I could dismiss shopping, but I couldn't dismiss clothes.

- I would always love a good flea market, but I didn't want to be the kind of person whose sole mission in life is to find a good bargain.

- I wanted to be guided by a higher consciousness, but a good coat still brought me to my knees.

When would my consumer personality align itself with my values? When would they meet up, not just by chance like attending the same pool party, but actually form a deep and meaningful connection?

Once again I felt confused. What was my next move? What should I do? What should I *not* do?

Where was my BIG breakthrough?

You have no idea how unfair this felt. Had I not worked hard at this? Had I not had brutally honest conversations with myself? Conversations about my goals, my values, and my place in this world? Was it too much to ask that all this *evaluation* would transform me into a totally different person? At the very least, shouldn't I become an upgraded and improved version of myself? If so, where was she?

This was not the first time I had these kinds of thoughts.

Many years ago, my lama invited me over to talk about my meditation practice.

'How is it going?' he asked.

'It's going well,' I said, 'but when will I change?'

'What do you mean?' he said.

'When will I stop being *me*?' I said.

'Darling, you will always be *you*!' he said.

I looked at him. Had I missed something?

'Listen,' he said, sensing my confusion. 'When you wake up in the morning, do you still want a cup of tea?'

'Yes.'

'If you haven't eaten in a while, do you still get hungry?'

'Yes...'

'If you stay up late, do you get tired?'

'Y-e-e-e-s?'

'There you go.'

And that was the end of *that* conversation.

I saw his point. It's like that mind-bending phrase, 'Things are not as they seem, nor are they otherwise.'

However, this kind of Eastern philosophy works fine one-on-one with your spiritual teacher, and not being able to reach a final conclusion in the privacy in one's own home is *more* than acceptable. It happens. But showing up empty-handed when writing a book? That is a whole new level of disturbing.

Although I had set out to write this book as a personal journey, and not by any means as a self-help book, I now feared I'd done the very opposite of that. Had I unknowingly written a get-worse book? A book that belonged under the category 'Self-Harm'?

That was an unsettling thought. I felt like a fraud. So I asked myself the question that I'd learned from the Defence Attaché back in April, 'What's the worst that can happen?'

Worst Case Scenarios

From a personal standpoint, the following scenarios would be the absolute worst outcomes of this shop-stop challenge:

1. **Eco-bitch:** Still longing after new clothes, but determined not to give in to temptation, I become a recluse. Perched on top of a big grey boulder, like some old crone, I spend my days knitting clothes out of repossessed tobacco leaves. My voice has turned gruff, but that doesn't stop me from shouting profanities at people carrying shopping bags.

2. **Sustainable party pooper:** So caught up in the downsides of consumer culture, I now restrict my diet to nothing but roots, bark, and leaves. *Everything we eat we have to pick ourselves!* I also refuse to travel by any mode of transportation requiring gasoline. This precludes me from visiting my friends and family, but at least my carbon footprint is down to nothing!

3. **Well-meaning ethical police:** I constantly say things like, *'You know that's made by children, right?'* and *'Don't you care about the rainforest? Why is the heater on?'* I mean well, so I feel extremely resentful when people don't compliment me on my efforts. I do go shopping, sometimes, but only because I feel that if people like me don't deserve new clothes, then who does?

Best Case Scenarios

I considered it a testament to my cheerful disposition that I also came up with three dream scenarios. None of them would be of much help to the planet, but they would be great fun for me, personally.

1. **Oprah's new pet:** Oprah reads my book and is so deeply

moved by my story that she invites me to become a regular guest on her Super Soul Sunday show. I gladly accept, and we quickly form a deep and meaningful friendship. I teach her how to shop (or how not to shop), and she introduces me to Martha Beck, Elizabeth Gilbert, and Brené Brown. My life will never be the same again.

2. **Terry Gross's new pet:** Terry Gross reads my book and is so deeply moved by my story that she invites me to be a guest on her radio show, 'Fresh Air'. I gladly accept, and during the interview I dazzle her listeners with insights, humour, and humility. Terry and I form a deep and meaningful friendship, and I become a regular guest on her show. My life will never be the same again.

3. **TED's new pet**: Some high-up person in TED Talks reads my book and is so deeply moved by my story that he instantly invites me to give a TED talk. I gladly accept, and my talk goes viral. This leads to an avalanche of interview requests, a new book contract, and there is talk of a movie deal. My life will never be the same again.

These dream scenarios might seem grandiose to you, but to me they're perfectly normal. Growing up with fictional characters like Annie, Cinderella, and Oliver Twist has led me to believe that anyone can achieve fame and fortune, *especially* those who start out poor and anonymous, like myself.

Follow the Love

They say the truth will set you free, but after reading and writing about deforestation, drought, hunger, and other impending disasters, I didn't feel free, I felt depressed. I walked inside a dark cloud for days. No wonder, then, I failed to conjure up dazzling insights. Who on earth feels wise when in a slump?

Always eager to learn something from my own experiences, I noticed that focusing on the best case scenarios was fun and rejuvenating, while writing about the worst case scenarios bummed me out. That's when I decided to change strategy.

Instead of illuminating only the bad side of this industry, I began to drag the spotlight over to all the positive efforts that were being made. This meant dropping fear and despair, and mobilising love and hope. Which, in all honesty, was a relief. Here's why:

Operating from a place of hopelessness and despair reduces you to a victim. Love, on the other hand, propels you into action. You become a joyful warrior. Love sustains you on your journey.

Yes, it's possible that we've shopped ourselves into a corner.

Yes, it's possible that the world is coming to an end.

And yes, it's possible that all our efforts to reverse the damages are futile.

And yes, it's possible that I will never feel like I have enough coats.

All this might be true, but if you are anything like me (once I calm down), you know that when you are ready to be ruled by the house of love, no challenge is too big or too difficult. It doesn't matter that all the odds are stacked up against you, you still try. That's because an open heart leads to an open mind, and an open mind is solution-oriented and fearless. Strangely enough, this makes you less attached to the outcome. And in case you haven't noticed, solution-oriented people are a lot more fun to be around than downtrodden complainers.

This shift in attitude was a game changer for me. It blew new life into the shop-stop challenge, and a beautiful new path opened up before me. I stayed on this path for the rest of the journey.

The Equal Value Bond

One of the first things I came across on this path was a trend called 'The Equal Value Bond'. Within this trend, stores and brands promote certain values, hoping to capture the attention of customers that share those same values.

Anthon Berg, the Danish world-famous chocolate company, has a branch that lets you pay for chocolate in good deeds. That's right. Anthon Berg lets you walk out of the store with a box of chocolates in exchange for promising to be a good person. The store is called The Generous Store, and the slogan is 'You can never be too generous'.

That's the first example I wanted to share with you. My next example brings us to my old friend H&M. This clothing chain recently launched a garment recycling program where the deal is that we bring our unwanted clothes to one of their stores, and in return they donate to charity. (I've read different versions of this program, but that's more or less the essence of it.) Bravo! Love it!

Then there is TOMS. For every pair of TOMS shoes you buy, they donate a pair to a child in need. Excellent.

I also read that Stella McCartney is fronting clothes and shoes that are eco-friendly, sustainable, and biodegradable. Wonderful!

Finally a shopping culture I could get on board with!

There are two specific things I want to draw attention to here:

1. The equal value bond clearly illustrates that it's possible to run a successful enterprise without being a selfish bastard.

2. The equal value bond also illustrates that embracing a healthier consumer culture doesn't require a weird alternative lifestyle. You can still be you, only with a cleaner conscience.

Eco Fashion

Ruled by the house of love, I also began to seek out people who, like me, wanted to bring an end to the exploitation of people and nature. This lead me to eco-fashion.

Thanks to new regulations and heightened consumer awareness, the eco-fashion movement was gathering strength like never before.

The International Standards Organization (ISO) defines eco-fashion as, 'Identifying the general environmental performance of a product within a product group based on its whole life-cycle in order to contribute to improvements in key environmental measures and to support sustainable consumption patterns.'

In a nutshell: eco-fashion designers create new and improved textiles (using sustainable sources), and improve how the production of clothes impact the environment.

For instance, Patagonia sells clothes made from recycled plastic bottles. Designer Anke Domaske makes an eco-milk fibre called QMilch, designer Suzanne Lee makes faux leather out of Kampuchea, and the designers behind the clothing brand Virus sell clothes made from recycled coffee beans.

Coffee-fabric and Kampuchea-leather? This totally blew my mind.

Did this mean that all eco-fashion clothes had to be made from stuff like carrot peelings and used tea bags? Would our future wedding dresses be made from Tampax strings and eggshells? If so, would that be cool or creepy? Maybe both, but mostly inspiring. As Pete Seeger, American folk singer and activist, once said, 'If it can't be reduced, reused, repaired, rebuilt, refurbished, refinished, resold, recycled or composted, then it should be restricted, redesigned or removed from production.'

I also learned that Colorep, a California-based printing company, has developed a sustainable printing technology called AirDye. The amazing thing about AirDye is that it uses eighty-five percent less energy than traditional dyeing methods. It also uses ninety-five percent less water, and reduces greenhouse gases by eighty-four percent compared to traditional printing and dyeing methods.

I'm incredibly happy to tell you that this eco-friendly printing method is rapidly catching on and is being used by designers like Mary Katrantzou and Alexander McQueen.

Ethical Fashion

Similar to how to the eco-fashion movement was coming up with new and remarkable ways of *producing* clothes, the ethical fashion brands, those who deal with improving the conditions for the people *working* in this industry, the textile workers, were gaining traction as well.

Ethics is a broad and philosophical term, but in this context it means that if a garment is labelled ethical, you know it wasn't made by a modern-day slave. Or to put it another way, it wasn't made in places like Rana Plaza.

I've heard people make snide remarks about the textile workers like, 'At least these people have a job. What are they complaining about?'

Excuse me? *At least they have a job?* I reject that notion. I reject it with my entire being. To talk like that is to invite the argument that once a person goes to work in the morning, he or she is stripped of all fundamental rights and basic decency. It should be dead obvious that regardless of whether you are a white collar worker, a blue collar worker, or a textile worker, the experience of going to work in the morning shouldn't be belittling and dehumanising. Living wages, health care, and safe working conditions are not a privilege for the few, but basic human rights for all workers across the world. To suggest that the textile workers should somehow put up with being exempt from that, is insulting to the entire human race.

Ethical retailers don't exploit underdeveloped countries, they do business *with* them. The ethical business model supports rural communities, works on improving global supply chains, abides by a Code of Conduct, and helps to lessen poverty in countries and communities that need it the most. Furthermore, ethical fashion retailers pay living wages, provide safe working conditions, and produce growth opportunities for local artists and artisans.

The fast-fashion retailers, on the other hand, don't seem to understand any of this.

At any rate, when you see clothes labelled 'Ethical Fashion', this is what you're supporting. This is what your money goes toward.

As I was reading up on this, I realised that it's never been easier to find ethical clothing brands. All I had to do was go online and search for 'ethical clothing brands', or 'up-and-coming ethical fashion houses'.

I must admit, I was a bit nervous that these clothes would be confined to alternative-lifestyle-clothes like the hippie-ish sack dress, the billowy bohemian top (with or without a tie-dye component), and of course the famous hemp sandals. In my mind, ethical clothes were forever linked to Rainbow Gatherings and drum circles.

I had nothing to worry about. Ethical fashion turned out to be far more stylish than it used to be. These clothes actually looked like 'normal' clothes, and they weren't crazy expensive either. Okay, fine, they cost more than £2.99, but that was a good thing. *Why didn't I know about these designers before? These clothes are gorgeous!*

You know how I said we shouldn't just move from one shopping strata to another? That ethical or not, fair trade or fast-fashion, we still had to shop less? I still believed that, but that didn't mean I wasn't moved by the efforts made by these designers. All a girl wants is to wear beautiful clothes without causing harm and destruction along the way, and these designers were on the side of making that happen.

Back in 2008, when I worked as an event coordinator for the United Nations International Children's Conference on the Environment, I had the good fortune to met one of the leading ladies of sustainable and ethical fashion: designer Leila Hafzi. The unique thing about Leila is that she didn't suddenly turn eco-chic just because it happened to be in and trendy. She has embodied the ethos of ethical and sustainable fashion since 1997, long before people even knew what these words meant. She is the real deal. By taking corporate responsibility and sticking to her guns, she's now an expert on fair trade and green practices.

Ideally, this is what all designers should be like: steadfast, moral, courageous, creative, and heroic. Moving forward, I wanted to embody those qualities as well.

Berlin

The next few weeks were super busy. Ben and I moved out of our London flat, Ben moved to the Cotswolds, and I stayed behind in Gigi's luxurious Chelsea flat. On top of everything else, I also managed to squeeze in a girl-trip to Berlin. I was meeting up with two of my childhood friends, Amy and Charis.

The timing of the trip was both good and bad. It was good because it gave me a break from work and moving. It was bad because I had so much to do. But we'd been planning this trip for ages, and I wasn't about to back out now. Also, who knew when I'd be able to meet up with Amy and Charis again?

Friendships don't just happen, you have to invest in them. The people I'm lucky enough to call my friends are all inspiring, brave, daring, alive, fabulous, fun, and loving people. My life would be empty without them.

However, most of my closest friends live far away in countries like Canada, Norway, Scotland, and the U.S. So how do you maintain meaningful connections when you're oceans apart? Romantically I'm attached to the notion of all of us sending each other deep and profound letters, but mostly I'm excited about all the different modes of communication now available to us. Anna and I speak on Skype almost every day. Amy and I speak on the phone constantly. Helene and I used to be prolific letter-writers, but lately we've lapsed into emails and Facebook. It doesn't matter. What's important is that the connection is nourished and that our worlds keep finding new ways of meeting.

Nothing beats seeing your friends in person though, which is why Amy, Charis, and I have made a commitment to meet up once a year. Last year we went to Bath, this year's destination was Berlin.

I'd never been to Berlin before — the only thing I knew about Berlin was that it's the capital of the country that voted for Hitler — but going there appealed to the part of me that is always looking for new experiences.

Maybe we could all get new tattoos? Maybe we should check out the crazy night scene? Maybe I should live a little and get a new haircut?

After checking in at our hotel, unpacking, and buying food at the organic deli across the street, we settled down for a relaxing lunch at our roof terrace.

Amy had booked us in at the ultra-hip Circus Hostel where we splurged on the top-floor penthouse apartment. It was spacious and decorated with trendy furniture, and even thought the place was new to us, it only took us about ten seconds to act like we'd lived there forever. Even the teakettle felt familiar, and the way Amy looked around for snacks was downright predictable.

'Did anyone bring any oats?' she said while rummaging around in the cupboards.

The hot and sultry weather was a wonderful surprise, and with a table filled with treats, and with chilled white wine in our glasses, we didn't feel like going anywhere else.

'To Berlin!' I said and raised my glass.

Charis said, 'Did I tell you guys I forgot my suitcase in the cab at the train station?'

I should mention that while Amy and I were reducing our carbon footprints by not shopping, Charis has always been passionate about green travel. Trains. Bikes. Busses. Boats. Those are her preferred modes of transportation. She's never owed a car. This woman doesn't mess about. She is also fun as hell, a great cook, and an artsy extrovert who happens to be a librarian.

'How could you forget your suitcase?' Amy asked.

Charis explained that she'd been in a hurry and felt rushed, and it wasn't until the train had left the platform she noticed her luggage was gone.

Well, not gone, exactly. She noticed it had never been there in the first place.

'It wasn't so bad,' Charis said. 'I just bought some new clothes when I arrived in Sweden.'

Bought new stuff?

Heh?

Oh, right. That's what you can do when you're not on a shop-stop, which Charis wasn't.

I looked her up and down. Every single garment was brand new. How wild was that? I didn't feel the slightest pang of envy or resentment, only curiosity. *Buying new clothes. What a concept.*

Just like Istanbul, Berlin became all about the food. Trailing up and down the tree-lined streets, we filled our bellies with spicy Russian dumplings, Indian cuisine, heavenly frozen yogurt, berry salads, lattes, Flat Whites, cappuccinos, red wine, white wine, tea, pastry, dark Bavarian bread, cheese, and pancakes. It was both fun and fattening. Even the visit to the Jewish Museum culminated in an eating fest, which, believe you me, felt wrong on so many levels. But it was hardly *my* fault that the museum cafeteria served treats like Tibetan yogurt, tropical fruit, homemade cakes, and sparkling rose water.

These calories were quickly burned off by all the walking. We walked everywhere. This was both time-efficient (no time wasted on figuring out the bus schedule or memorising the U-bahn stations), and energy-efficient (no time wasted on figuring out 'what should we do today, girls?'). We just got out of bed and began to explore our beatnik-y neighbourhood.

We passed a hairdresser, and I decided against getting a new haircut. We passed a lot of fit people and I wondered if I should work out more. We passed a ridiculous amount of trendy coffee houses, each with outdoor seating. I made it my mission to try them all.

On our last evening, back at the roof terrace, after spending hours reading in a park, we uncorked a bottle of wine and settled in for the night. This was more than fine with me. Even though I had been temporarily seduced by the idea of sprucing up my life by finding some groovy nightclub where I could dust off my dance moves, I was incredibly pleased we didn't waste our precious time together by going clubbing. The way I see it, when it comes to hanging out with good friends, it's best done at home while wearing a comfortable pyjamas.

The Yellow Coat

Just like Istanbul, my inaugural trip to Berlin didn't lead to any shopping emergencies. Amy and I both seemed to have forgotten all about shopping. Clothes meant nothing to us. Our full attention was on the frozen yogurt.

'What is *in* this thing? Let me try yours.'

Although not-shopping-in-Berlin hardly made us First Ladies of Not Shopping (after all, not shopping in Berlin is not the same as being the first female bishop, or Amelia Earhart), it still felt like an accomplishment. We'd done well for ourselves.

So no, we didn't go shopping. But I did look at a coat.

Before you roll your eyes at me, let me tell you what happened.

Out walking in Berlin, we came across not one, not two, but three street markets. While standing in front of a table filled with blue tin mugs, vintage posters, industrial desk lamps, and old toys, I spotted a yellow coat. It looked like a '60s coat. The kind Brigitte Bardot would have worn on her way to a photo shoot.

I was *this* close to diving into a frustrated rant about how stupid I was for looking at YET ANOTHER COAT, but then I broadened my field of attention, zoomed way out, and decided to come at it from a different angle. With my eyes fixed on the coat, I called deep on my curiosity and asked myself, 'Why do you love coats so much?'

As a person with a mild coat addiction, it's weird, then, how I've never asked myself that question before. It never even occurred to me.

Many years ago I babysat a clever young girl. She was sharp, observant, and extremely curious. One day while eating ice cream she said, 'I love ice cream!' Two seconds later she turned to me and asked, '*Why* do I love ice cream?'

Questioning our thoughts is a mighty tool, regardless of the situation we find ourselves in. I can't tell you why this girl loved ice cream, but I'll try to explain to you why I love coats so much.

First: coats are magic to me. By putting on a good coat you go from looking like a perpetrator in a lineup to the lawyer arguing for your bail. The transformation takes less than two seconds. It's witchcraft.

Also: the love is mutual. I love coats and coats love me. They actually seek me out. You can ask anybody. When my grandmother's brother-in-law moved house, I was on the receiving end of his brown suede jacket and grey overcoat. When my ex-boyfriend's grandfather died, I inherited his '50s spring coats. When I was fifteen, one of my uncles bought me a white cashmere coat. Then there was the time when my sister gave me her beige safari jacket. More recently, after I repaired the police attaché's vintage suit, she gave me two wool blazers. What can I say? I have coat karma.

Lastly: coats are loyal. From the Mao Tse Tung jacket that my Chinese pen-friend mailed to me all the way from Beijing, to the blue vintage coat I plan to get buried in, coats have always been there for me. They're a part of who I am. Me and my coats bring out the best in each other.

Now, did this insight give me a green light to get yet another coat? No, of course not. Loving something is not an excuse for hoarding. For a brief second I hoped that Amy and Charis would buy the yellow coat for me, as an early Christmas present or something, but as the writer Richard Bach once said, 'If you love something, set it free.'

The Chipping Away Process

Even though the yellow coat incident could easily have escalated into a RED FLAG situation, thanks to switching into question mode I averted the crises and saw the situation in a new light.

Firstly, it helped me understand why I love coats so much.

Secondly, and more importantly, it helped me understand that if I hadn't gone through all the other sticky shopping situations beforehand, arriving at a spacious and curious 'Why?' would have been out of the question. Not in a million years would it have occurred to me to ask, 'Why do I love coats so much?'

The ancient Chinese saying tells us: 'Failure is the mother of success.' Or as Tich Nhat Hanh so poetically put it: 'No mud, no lotus.'

That didn't always feel true to me, but now I realised that if not for all my shopping challenges, if I hadn't experienced so many shop-stop *failures*, I wouldn't have learned anything of value. Transformation happens in the trenches. It was through my darkest non-shopping moments (all those episodes that my younger self would have paid good money for to avoid), that I'd found the greatest clarity. The path I had taken, and everything I'd encountered along the way, had led me exactly to where I needed to be. From the moment I had the meltdown after the closet clear-out, to the moment I found the yellow coat, my old thinking patterns had been carefully cleared away and made room for a new way of being. The way I saw it, the Burberry coat was my darkest-before-dawn moment, and finding the yellow coat felt like being greeted by the sun. I took it as a sign that my biggest challenges were behind me.

Last Week in London

Returning from Berlin I attended not one, not two, but three farewell parties. Gifts were given and good wishes and hugs were exchanged. My colleagues, soon to be ex-colleagues, couldn't have been any nicer.

On my last day at work I was almost as anxious as I'd been on my very first day. Had it really been four years ago? Wearing black trousers and a crisp blue shirt, I had made my way through the bullet proof doors, signed in, and up the stairs I went, followed by a train of ambition and rose coloured aspirations.

That felt like a lifetime ago, yet it felt like no time had passed at all.

Now it was time to tie up loose ends and walk away. I'd pictured one final rounds of goodbyes, one last cup of tea in the staff kitchen, and one final visit to my favourite bathroom.

So much for planning. The phone would not stop ringing. The emails kept pouring in. New assignments. A new event to deal with.

Mail. Messages. Follow-ups. None of this would have been a problem had the new secretary jumped in and taken over the reins, but she acted scared and overwhelmed. Which I suppose she was, but I also knew she was more than capable of handling it all. I wanted to scream, *Just get a grip!* But instead I took a deep breath and said, 'You'll be fine.'

The hours flew by, and before I could catch my breath it was time to leave. I dutifully returned my phone and keys, but I kept my business cards. Those I wanted to keep. They were, after all, the poshest business card I would ever possess.

Inger Dybvig Kenobi - Personal Secretary to the Ambassador.

My New Life

The very next day I boarded the train to the Cotswolds. From the outside it looked like any old train journey, but to me it felt like a NASA space shuttle launch. As for my destination, it was only over an hour away. *Adieu London! Farewell city people! Hello country living!*

By the time the train left the station, my old life was already behind me.

Moving to a new place at the end of a book is a bit of a nuisance. Do I describe the new place in great detail? How do I work it into the story? Do I compare our new home to our home in London? Does it really matter?

Arriving in Stroud, there was a cab waiting for me at the station. 'Do you live here?' the driver asked.

'No, I'm from Lon...' I began, but then I remembered. 'Well, actually! I live here. Yes! I live here now!'

Feeling very pleased with my new life, I couldn't wait to unpack all the boxes and settle in. Not twenty-four hours ago I'd been a cog in a machine, but now I was watching giant cows grazing outside our kitchen window. I felt alive with happiness.

When picking up a particularly heavy box, I felt a sudden sharp pain in my lower back and I fell to the floor. The pain got worse at a furious rate, and on reflex I curled up into a little ball.

Well, I'll be damned.

I tried to move, but I couldn't. *Un-freaking-believable!* So I just laid there. What else could I do? Ben was away for the day, taking another drone exam.

After what seemed like hours, I began to crawl backwards to the bedroom. *This is pathetic!* I heaved myself onto the bed and rolled over like a piece of lumber. Just as I was beginning to relax a little, I realised I'd left the phone in the kitchen. Going back to get it was out of the question. Besides, who would I call? Who could help me?

I'll probably starve to death. I'm thirsty.

I felt incredibly sorry for myself. This was not part of the plan. *Why do bad things happen to good people?*

A faint whimper escaped my lips.

When Ben returned that evening, he did what all Englishmen have been trained to do in times of crises: he made me a strong cup of tea. It actually helped. So did resting, but it was a slow recovery. After three days of lying perfectly still, I was able to walk to the bathroom backwards, with the help of an umbrella. I looked like the Hunchback of Notre Dame, but I felt like Edmund Hillary.

Downton Abbey

Just as I was getting back into the swing of things, I received a phone call from the Embassy. It was one of the admin ladies.

'We were wondering if you would consider coming back to work,' she said. 'Just for a week,' she added hastily.

'What for?' I asked.

The new PA was having problems, she explained, and they would really appreciate it if I could come in and give her some more training.

'You will, of course, get paid your regular salary, and all expenses will be covered,' she said matter-of-factly. Then she added, 'And I've talked with the Ambassador; he says you can stay at the residence.'

Stay at the residence?! That got my attention.

Stay at one of the most prestigious townhouses in all of London? Where the King and Queen of Norway stay? Where the Prime Minister stays? In that house?

I would basically be staying at Downton Abbey.

The following Monday I was back in London.

In case you thought that returning work would be fun for me, let me set the record straight. It was not fun. It was plain weird. The moment I sat down at my old desk, I knew I'd made a huge mistake. It was too soon. I felt homesick. I missed the fresh air. I missed the cows. I missed my view. I missed Ben.

Within five minutes I remembered why I had handed in my notice. Within ten minutes I was bored witless.

I knew these were the wrong kind of feelings. I should have felt pleased they wanted me back. Everything had been arranged for me. People were kind. However, they weren't nearly as interested in my new life as I felt they should be. So much for rehearsing funny anecdotes about country living.

As for new secretary, the lady in distress, she wasn't nearly as disorganised and lost as she thought she was. She was just nervous, and insanely afraid of making mistakes.

I will help here. I wanted to be helpful. *I can get through this. It's only for a week!* I had to remain optimistic. What other choice did I have?

In the evenings, thank goodness, I was free to do whatever I wanted.

As it turned out, I didn't feel like doing anything at all. Nothing and no one could get me out of the house. No museums called my name. No shows or concerts either. I only wanted to hang out at the residence.

But can you blame me? If you were staying at Downton Abbey, would you have gone out?

Although this was the home of the Ambassador, I never ran into him. At work, yes, but never after hours. His flat was on a different floor than mine, and since I happened to be the only guest, I had the entire guest wing to myself. This absence of other people made me feel like I was in a high-class safe house. Or in a deluxe witness protection program. I pretended to be a key witness in a criminal case against the Russian mafia, and this was my home until the trial was over.

I guess I'm saying I felt safe. And a little bit brave.

But I wasn't *totally* alone. Every evening the Embassy driver invited me upstairs to his flat for dinner. Having served in both Iraq wars, and as one of the Queen's Grenadier's Guards (the kind that stands outside Buckingham Palace wearing red jackets and big bearskin hats), he's one of the most alert and attentive people I have ever met.

In the mornings the housekeeper, who lives in the flat in the basement, insisted on making me tea and serving me leftovers from the Queen's visit.

'Here, you eat her grapefruit. It's pre-cut, just how she prefers it.'

If you have never lived in a house with servant before, let me be the first one to tell you that it's just like in the movies. The servants are often, but not always, more laid-back than their masters. They have far more skills and talents than they are credited with, and they sure know how to keep a secret. They are also some of the hardest-working people you will ever meet, and they are big on loyalty. If you befriend any of them, you will have a friend for life.

Time and Shopping

On my last day in London I had to run an errand at Kensington High Street. Approaching the street, coming out of the park, I saw something peculiar. It took me a while to recognise what it was. Not IT, but *they*.

They were shoppers. The street was full of shoppers! There were hundreds of them. Maybe even thousands. Which on the one hand, was perfectly normal. Kensington High Street is, after all, one of London's busiest shopping streets. But, on the other hand, to have a whole street dedicated to nothing but shopping now seemed utterly absurd.

I couldn't stop staring. Perfectly healthy-looking people, grown adults, were milling in and out of the stores. It was like observing the curious antics of some primitive tribe, or witnessing a herd of exotic animals. The whole thing reminded me of watching nature documentaries, and I could almost hear the soothing voice of Sir David Attenborough.

Kensington, London. Home to one of the world's most fascinating shopping breed, the one that is most hostile to any other kind of life form. To discover how and why they shop, you have to enter their world. As you can see, these mammals move quickly from place to place, and they are warm-blooded and focused. Their success will depend on their strength and stamina. The price of all this effort: something new.

Alternatively, *the price of all this effort: a big waste of time.*

Have you ever thought about how much time you spend on shopping? How many hours? How many *years?* Neither had I, not until I came across a shocking study conducted by the British marketing firm OnePoll. According to this study, the average female shopper spends close to four hundred hours a year on shopping.

I agree, that's insane.

One hundred of those hours are deliberately spent on buying clothes. An additional forty hours are spent *looking* for shoes. Over a lifetime, that adds up to almost three solid years spent on nothing but shopping.

I hadn't spent any significant time on shopping this year, but I'd certainly done my fair share of *thinking* about shopping. Now I felt like never thinking about it ever again. *What a waste of time!* The madness had to end. Had there been an official building where you could return your shopping privileges, I would have handed mine over without a fight.

However, at the same time I didn't want to make a bid deal about why this was wrong and what I should be spending my freedom and money on instead. I just wanted be done with the whole thing, once and for all. *No more! I'm shutting this down!*

I also had this overwhelming urge to usher the shoppers home (*there there now, off you go*), acting like a bustling nanny at a boarding school. I wanted to tell them, *Learn a new language instead. Travel! Get a degree! You don't have to do this!*

But I didn't do that. I just crossed the street, went over to Whole Foods, and bought some chocolate for the train ride home.

Chapter Twelve
October

6 *You'll see I wear only gray or blue suits.*

*I don't want to make decisions about
what I'm eating or wearing.* 9
- *Barack Obama*

When my siblings were younger, we used to play a game called 'What if this is a dream?'

'What if this is a dream,' I would ask them, 'and when you wake up you're a cat?' Or, 'What if this is a dream, and when you wake up you're Tarzan?'

This made them smile and squirm in their seats, like golden retriever puppies. But as playful as this game was, it also raised a series of philosophical questions. Questions like: would the person dreaming about us remember the dream when he or she woke up? What happened to *us* while the dreamer was awake? And when night came around again, would we be able to pick up from where we left off in the previous dream?

That's exactly what moving to the Cotswolds felt like to me, like

I was picking up from the last time I was here. I intuitively knew all the ropes and I had no problem settling in. And with a certainty I don't often feel, living there made me feel intact and grounded, like something had been mended. I loved living there. But then again, the Cotswolds isn't exactly a hard place to fall in love with.

The Cotswolds

So what exactly *is* the deal with the Cotswolds? Is it the glorious nature? The cute cottages? The medieval villages? The cosy local pubs? Is it the abundance of historical sites? Is it how being there feels like being introduced to a better part of yourself?

The Cotswolds is a rare blend of all of those things, but it's also so much more. It's not for nothing the Cotswolds is considered to be the largest 'Area of Outstanding Natural Beauty' in all of the UK.

When we first talked about moving here, my mother-in-law said, 'It's a great place to get sick!'

When she saw the puzzled expression on my face, she quickly added that since the Cotswolds is populated with powerful and influential people, the hospitals are 'state of the art.'

By *powerful* she meant members of the royal family, like the Princess Royal and Prince Charles. However, I was far more impressed by the fact that Stella McCartney, Kate Moss, Liz Hurley, and Lily Allen all have houses here. It's also where Jane Austen, William Shakespeare, and Winston Churchill used to live. Learning this made me feel like I'd been invited to a fancy garden party by mistake, yet this was our home now.

During the day I watched Ben set up his new office and workshop. It looked like a space station; it still does. It's filled with flying objects, each with their own set of blinking lights and outer space beeping noises. A wing. A gimbal. Some motor of some kind. It's unbelievably messy and chaotic, which doesn't seem to bother him *at all.*

Like a captain on a spacecraft, Ben hunched over his worktable and methodically mothered his drone. On his breaks he wandered around in the garden with his tea and cigarette, looking just like his grandfather. Same tweed jacket, same dreamy expression in his eyes.

Ben was also getting his drivers licence. Our new car was in the driveway.

I got busy with my writing. I organised all my notebooks by topic. I organised my books by author. I charged my laptop. I placed pens and pencils in the pen holder. I moved the red desk lamp around, determined to get the lighting just right. Obedient to the rules of feng shui, I placed my office chair so that I could see out the window and admire the view. Everything was coming together.

In the afternoons Ben and I took up the age-old tradition of going on country walks. From our doorstep we had direct access to a myriad of pathways and country lanes. Out walking, like generations of ramblers before us, we leaped over brooks, walked across meadows, followed the ancient Public Footpaths, and trudged up the steep hills. We were marching toward the last frontier. That's what it felt like. I had become an explorer. You couldn't find a sluggish drop of blood in my body. *On ahead!*

Back inside, while warming my hands on a hot cup of tea, it always felt like we'd been gone for hours, sometimes even days. But as Margaret Atwood once wrote: 'It can be hard to tell time in nature.'

Talking it all in, I felt ridiculously happy about this new life of ours. Yes, we could fall on our faces. Yes, twelve months could go by and we would have nothing to show for it. And yes, there was a very real chance that this could turn out to be the biggest mistake of our lives. But for now, at least at this moment in time, my life was perfect and amazing.

At night we slept with the windows wide open, and from our comfy new IKEA bed I listened to sounds belonging to nocturnal creatures like owls, badgers, and foxes. The air smelled like apples.

For the longest time, every morning without fail, I looked at the clock precisely at 7.25 a.m. and thought to myself, 'I would be running to the bus right about now.' As far as time went, I was now living in luxury.

But we weren't totally cut off from the real world. The Cotswolds might be like a distant cousin who happens to be a rich Lord who can make his own tweed and will gladly tell you how to stack your firewood, but we still had paved roads. We still had internet access. We had indoor plumbing and a flushing toilet. There were at least six places within walking distance that served a decent latte, or a glass of wine if that's what I felt like having. Our village alone had three pubs; three pubs and one church. Had this been in Norway, it would have been the other way around, minus the pubs.

No Shops?

You've probably noticed that I haven't mentioned clothes or shopping in a while. That's because it's hard to work in stories about clothes and shopping when there are no shops around.

The only 'shop' in our new village, as I found out, was a post office that doubled as a grocery store. Here I could buy things like stamps, locally-grown turnips, and organic ice cream, but no clothes.

I found this a bit ironic, because the Stroud Valley, where we now lived, has a cloth-making legacy dating back to the 14th century. The town of Stroud used to be called 'a sort of capital of the clothing villages.' This entire part of the country used to be dedicated to wool, weaving, textile industry, and design.

The industry is long gone — outsourced, bankrupt, outdated — but the point I'm trying to make is that at the end of the shop-stop I had moved to the very nerve centre of the English textile industry. What were the chances? It seemed fitting somehow.

Not being around clothes made it far easier not to think about them. And of course, not being around shops made it far easier to not think about shopping. And since I was DONE thinking about clothes and shopping, this was like being handed a non-shopping lifeline. *Finally!*

But...it was also kind of weird, because even though I was fed up with thinking about clothes and shopping, I felt I was *supposed* to think about clothes and shopping. Was this not the final month of the shop-stop? In this final act, shouldn't my resolve be tested? Shouldn't I face one last challenge, have one final triumph over consumer culture to write about?

What I *really* wanted, more than anything, was one last grand gesture that would perfectly sum up this journey, and also tie all my experiences into a nice little red bow. Like a present. That would be perfect.

'And then I moved to the country and never shopped again,' just didn't cut it.

If only something dramatic would happen. I had quick images of going to Tokyo and not shop. That would be fun to write about! Or how about winning the lottery and not shop? That would have made an interesting chapter as well.

How Do I Look?

It couldn't be helped. I had to accept the fact that there would be no shopping challenge to deal with, then write about, and finally learn something from. I didn't even have a clothing crisis I could churn into one last funny anecdote.

Did that mean that I no longer cared about what I looked like?

Not at all. I was just as vain as ever. But the reason I didn't fret over finding the perfect outfit was directly related to what I said in one of the earlier chapters: the fewer clothes I had, the better I looked. I'd really come to appreciate the fact that when it comes to clothes, volume is not important. What's important is that you love all your clothes. (You should be writing this down.)

By loving all my clothes, getting dressed in the morning became extraordinarily easy. What a relief! No more time wasted on *Should I give this a try, or what about this old thing?* I no longer had those kinds of clothes; they had been removed during the de-cluttering session, and since I hadn't been shopping for almost a year, my wardrobe was unburdened by clothes bought under the influence of the latest trends or TV shows and movies. This felt like freedom. I wanted every woman on the planet to know what this felt like.

Did that mean I no longer had conflicting voices in my head? Not at all. The voice that one day chirps, 'I love *The Good Wife*. I bet I would look great in those kinds of office suits!' and the next day reconsiders, 'Actually, I'm more Bohemian Belle than Courtroom Goddess. I should wear more kimonos. How about a red one?' And then, after seeing a documentary about drag queens, changes focus again and thinks, 'I obviously need to wear more glitter and sequins!' was still there, but I no longer felt compelled to translate these thoughts into action. Their status had been reduced from a powerful master to a foolish court jester, which meant I could listen to them without being swayed by them.

No longer swayed by these thoughts, I had finally arrived at a point in my life where I knew *exactly* what kind of clothes I liked, *if* I liked wearing them, and *if* they looked good on me. And so, 'How do I look?' became a rhetorical question.

This is the beauty of Fewer Clothes.

But how many clothes constitutes as *fewer*? I keep saying *fewer clothes,* but what does that number look like?

After counting all of my clothes (regretfully I didn't do this at the beginning of the shop-stop), this is what I was left with:

- four pairs of trousers
- five blouses
- eight skirts
- nine cardigans
- twelve sweaters
- eighteen dresses
- four tank-tops
- eight t-shirts

- fifteen jackets

- ten coats

I'm sure some of you would describe this wardrobe as *at-risk,* but I wasn't worried. And in truth, looking over this list made me realise that I still didn't wear all of my clothes. So why did I still have them?

Next question: did this mean I should have another closet clear-out? One last cathartic sweep through of all my clothes?

What a great idea!

By having a final closet clear-out, the book would start and end on the same topic. This appealed to my devotion for symmetry, but as much as I was drawn to the idea, I also knew I didn't have enough clothes for a proper de-cluttering session. And even if I did, I had a feeling it wouldn't have the same dramatic flair as the first one. Besides, I was done with looking back and repeating myself. It was time to look toward the future and nail down what it meant to be a conscious consumer. But before I could do that, I had one last thing to figure out.

A Paradoxical Puzzle

In mathematics there is something called a paradoxical puzzle, or a strange loop. It means that an idea is bounced back and forth in your head like a ping-pong ball, bouncing from one inconceivable truth to another, giving it no place to rest. No matter how you look at it, you always end up exactly where you started.

That's what thinking about the fast-fashion industry felt like to me. Remember what I wrote in the first chapter? I wrote:

Fast-fashion means many conflicting things, and it stands for many different issues, good and bad, all at once. What's more, these conflicting issues happen to be inseparable, like conjoined twins. One twin is all about style, clothes, fashion, image, and trends. It's into fun things like catwalks, dressing up, sexy underwear, and finding the perfect pair of jeans. The other twin is a bit evil, like a screwed-up dare-devil. It's responsible for pollution, greed, and slave labour, and it wants everyone to be a reckless big spender.

The fun twin, the good twin, wins the Best Dressed award, goes to parties, and becomes friends with everyone. The evil twin lurks in the shadows, ends up on Most Wanted posters, and is blacklisted from every respectable school, job, and institution.

How could I even *think* about coming out of the shop-stop when I still hadn't made peace with that fact that something could be *this* good and *this* bad? What should I walk away from? What should I walk toward?

Trying to get my head around these conflicting truths, I began to break it down into smaller chunks. First I looked at the positive side of the fast-fashion industry.

- At best, fashion can enhance your beauty and become a symbol of how great you truly are. When you wear something amazing, people compliment you and treat you better. Everybody just assumes that you're an awesome person. When you're having a bad day, a great outfit can make you escape the real world and let you enter a world of glamour, style, and beauty. Shopping can soothe you, comfort you, and surprise you. To quote Coco Chanel: 'Every day is a fashion show and the world is the runway.'

I agree! Clothes are AMAZING! I love style and beauty.

But wait a minute...what abut Rana Plaza and pollution? What about all the time we waste on shopping? Shopping for clothes we neither like or wear?

Fine, let's look at that.

- At worst, fashion is a selfish hobby fraught with chaos and disasters. Searching for the perfect outfit is like a white whale, and chasing after it is a lonely journey. To quote Vivienne Westwood: 'Shop less, think more.'

*So **true**. Shopping is meaningless and lonely. I hate clothes. Everyone should just stop shopping already and get a life.*

But then another voice weighed in. This voice felt more neutral, but it was still inconclusive. It went like this:

- But here is what no one tells you: Fashion is hard. The stylish people you read about in fashion magazines, and the celebrities you watch gliding down the red carpet, make it look easy and effortless to wear the right kind of clothes. Which it isn't. Wearing the right clothes, for the right occasion, for the right body type, within the right budget, is almost like having a second career. It takes tremendous commitment, time, and energy, especially if you feel you have to do it all over again by next season. And by next season I mean next month. Committing yourself to the latest trends is like loving someone who has a chronic illness, and who also happens to be a serial killer. To quote Gianni Versace: 'When a woman alters her look too much from season to season, she becomes a fashion victim.'

This is spot on. I couldn't agree more. Who wants to be a helpless victim?

One more observation:

- Clothes are fun, but they are not worth half the trouble we (and the planet) go through to get them.

SO WHICH IS IT?! Which one of these statements are true? TELL ME!

These contradictions might not bother you as much as they bothered me, but I desperately wanted to find a place within the fashion world where I could thrive and settle down. This place had to be well-defined and with clear boundaries. I wanted a safe plot of land where my values and priorities could sort themselves out and grow strong roots. I didn't want to run the risk of getting lost and make mistakes. My kingdom, my rules. Keep out.

How to explain why this was so important to me?

Emergency shopping guidelines and shop-stop strategies were fine and dandy while on a shop-stop, but come November 1 I needed something to pledge my allegiance to. I had to be prepared. I had to be realistic. Fashion is tireless and gets in everywhere. We're talking mental, cultural, and financial infiltration. So coming out of the shop-stop, I had to make sure I didn't backslide into mindless shopping. How long would it take before I wanted another pair of jeans? And once that started, how long until my cravings quashed my good intentions? Around clothes my IQ is that of a root vegetable, so how to protect against that?

Right now I was protected by rolling hills and cows, but what would happen when I walked into a store again? What would I think about? How would I act? How soon until the urge for new clothes returned? A great outfit might be lurking in ambush. You never know.

I had thoughts like that, but then I thought, *Am I blowing this out of proportion?* I wasn't like I was planning an exit strategy for the war in Iraq. Exiting a shop-stop pact was hardly a life and death situation. But then again, maybe it was?

An inner debate followed. This year had allowed me to disconnect from my normal routines and seek new answers. *Why do I shop? How do I shop? Why do I love clothes?* That's where I started, and these questions had led me down a path to questions like, *What are my contributions? What is my moral code? Am I living according to my values? What exactly* are *my values?*

And as I was pondering these questions, all other aspects of my life got dragged under the microscope as well, which lead to questions like, *What is my purpose in life? Am I living up to my full potential? Have I lost track of who I really am? How to regain the balance? How long have I felt this way? What's my next move?*

In light of all that, I don't think it's a coincidence that I quit my job and moved to the Cotswolds in a shop-stop year.

I was still me, but my attention, values, and habits had shifted. So on the eve of the shop-stop challenge coming to an end, I wanted to find a shopping strategy that would reflect my current situation. Shopping was no longer an isolated issue of wanting a dress (or not wanting a dress), but about expanding my consciousness to think about my actions in the bigger scheme of things. Women are the fastest growing demographic in the world. We're powerful. If we all changed the way we shopped, we would change the world. So yes, maybe the topic of fashion and shopping *was* a matter of life and death.

Still, I can't tell you how many times being on a shop-stop felt totally and utterly beneath me. I enjoyed it enormously, it was a fun challenge, and I certainly don't regret doing it. However, on the quest of making the world a better place, going a year without shopping is hardly in the same category as rescuing orphans and widows. This made me feel like a stupid spoiled person with typical white-person problems. *Uh! Look at me! I'm not shopping! You're welcome!*

Are you kidding me?

But who's judging? Why make myself miserable by comparing my shop-stop challenge to Mahatma Gandhi's achievements? To quote Theodore Roosevelt: 'Comparison is the thief of joy.'

For the same reasons I don't have monopoly over how to create a better future, no one holds monopoly over what it means to be a force of good in this world. I think it's important to acknowledge that. What I mean to say is, if you want to contribute to the greater good by using less paper, supporting local businesses, and never using plastic bags, I salute you. You're my hero.

The reason I bring up these specific examples is because I know how easy it is to only focus on the big issues. Like the rainforest. Drought. Poverty. Starvation. But these are impossibly big problems. Which means we (often) end up doing nothing about them at all. And since tackling small problems seems pointless and a waste of time, we (often) overlook them completely. But please remember, there is no such thing as a meaningless good cause. If you feel inspired to make a difference, don't worry about your cause being 'big' enough. Make a stand. Just do it. You'll see that even the smallest change will affect every area of your life. This is the law of nature. Start now. Skip a rock across the lake and watch the ripples spread.

But a word of caution. Don't try to impress other people with your good cause. Don't be a bore. Do it for your own sake. And whatever you do, don't make your cause the cornerstone of your conversations.

- 'Plastic bags, thoughts?' - *No!*

- 'I see you drive a car.' - *Stop it!*

- '...about the recent death tolls...' - *Worse! Shut up!*

It's all great stuff, but *oh so* boring for other people to listen to.

But back to my paradoxical puzzle. I hadn't found any satisfying answers, and that truly bugged me. In my final attempt to reach a waterproof conclusion, I made two mistakes:

1. I got stuck in metaphors

2. I argued with reality

Stuck in Metaphors

First I tried to make peace with the contradictions by playing to my love of metaphors. *Maybe all I need is a good metaphor? They are so good at explaining everything. Let's give it a try!*

Like a plucky kindergarten teacher explaining to a group of five-year-olds 'why we don't steal,' I cheerfully invented several metaphors about the fashion industry.

- Is it a maze? I guess in some ways it is, but no. In both places it's easy to get lost, true, but other than that there are no similarities. The fashion industry has no beginning or ends. It's a loop. And there are no high hedges. Pass. Next please.

- It's like a radio! Not bad...! The fast-fashion industry does transmit on many different channels all at once. True, true, true. But does that mean that all we have to do is tune in to the right station, listen to the right voices, and then everything will be fine? Yes –? No –! You have to do better than this. Think!

- OK. OK. How about a river, then? Just hear me out. Let's look at it this way: Clothes might be lovely, but underneath the surface of every outfit runs an undercurrent stream fraught with suffering, pollution, and greed. Happy? No, no, NO! It's not a fucking river. That's the stupidest thing I've ever heard.

Arguing with Reality

When metaphors didn't work, I tried to *will* the fashion industry into submission, similar to how I had *wanted* dreadful outfits to work, simply because I'd once bought them. *Come on, you stupid coat! You can do it!*

To me this meant prying the good and the bad apart. I pictured a wide open gulf between them. The evil fashion twin could live over here, the good twin could go over there (to go back to the old twin metaphor), and in the space between them my clothes and I could live happily ever after.

Inger, you brilliant babe, you've nailed it!

It sounded perfect, don't you think? Only it could never work. In my head, yes, but not in reality.

In real life you can't separate the good from the bad. That had been my biggest mistake all along, thinking that I could.

Once I took a step back and looked at the situation objectively, I saw that the fast-fashion industry is one hundred percent as amazing *and* as awful as I feared it was. Both sets of qualities are interconnected and interdependent of one another. I saw that too. I also saw that not all the horsepower or good intentions in the world could ever change that.

That was a hard pill to swallow. And yet, strangely enough, it felt right.

But what did that *mean*? Was I back at square one? Actually, no. Far from it. I had just stumbled upon something amazing. Something true. I had stumbled upon reality.

The reality of opposite forces coexisting side by side is as old as sin. Yin and Yang, night and day, good and evil, light and shadow. This is the nature of all things. This is how things work.

As well-meaning humans, we find this unsettling. We want things to be *just* good or *just* bad, *thankyouverymuch*. It just makes everything *sooooo* much easier.

I get that. Who wants to deal with the fact that on one hand Hitler was a monster, but he was also an art-loving vegetarian? *He killed the Jews but didn't eat meat? That's the most ridiculous thing I've ever heard!*

It's just easier to live in fairytale land where the witch is evil, the princess is pure to the core, and everything works out in the end.

When it came to the fast-fashion industry, I was so stuck in my habit of being hyper-attached to a mega-positive outcome that I couldn't accept reality for what it was. No wonder I couldn't reach a final conclusion. I was looking in all the wrong places.

Byron Katie tells us, 'I am a lover of what is, not because I'm a spiritual person, but because it hurts when I argue with reality.'

Letting go of separating the good from the bad was a turning point for me. The lens was wiped clean. The gridlock was gone. Everything came into focus. *So this is what the truth looks like!*

Like a proud Voodoo Goddess standing in the garden of good and evil, I saw myself sailing toward the finish line while staring reality square in the face.

Consumer Power

No longer arguing with reality meant I no longer felt the need to section off a corner of the fashion world where I could go into hiding. *Since when did being a conscious consumer become synonymous with being a coward? I thought I had to HIDE?*

I don't know why I had thought that, but this was a good reminder that I had to work on my definitions. Which brought me to my next point: what did it mean to be a conscious consumer? How to define it?

Over this past year I'd spent an unbelievable amount of time and energy thinking about all the things that get in the way of being a conscious consumer — shops in general, consumer culture, peer pressure, the lack of suitable role models, the illusory power of new clothes, the fear of having nothing to wear — that I hadn't really thought about the qualities and characteristics defining a conscious consumer. How could I become something I didn't know how to describe? Words like *ethical, aware, and mindful* had a good ring to them, but those words could just as easily have been used to describe Mother Teresa, or an organic farmer.

If being a mindless consumer had made me feel like a victim, then becoming a mindful consumer would by definition make me feel...powerful? Yes! Conscious consumers are powerful! Damn straight! As consumers we have power, and conscious consumers put that power to good use. *There it is!* I kept going. I wrote things down. I scribbled away. I went on walks. In the end I came up with the following definition:

> *Conscious consumers are creative, curious, and compassionate beings. They are powerful problem solvers who demonstrate independent thinking from mainstream culture. They are ruled by gratitude, not by greed. They choose what's right over what's easy. They choose what's sustainable over what's convenient. Lastly, conscious consumers recognise that experiences trump possessions, always.*

That's what I was striving for. Come November 1, that's what I was pledging my allegiance to.

Gratitude

Composing this definition, I wanted to make sure I included the word *gratitude*. I wanted to give gratitude a seat at the table because so much of our shopping behaviour is driven by focusing on what we *don't* have. This is not entirely our own fault. The game is rigged. There is a trillion-dollar industry feeding us the illusion that unless we get the most current version, the newest upgrade, the latest trends, we'll become lame-ass people who can't keep up with society. This message is especially true if you live in a big city, and it's even more true if you turn on the TV or flick through a magazine. The only way to achieve happiness, we're told, is by getting in the fast lane and never look back. *Shop-shop-shop. Get this! Get that! Buy more! Don't stop!*

It's like a dictatorship of consumerism.

Gratitude, on the other hand, counteracts all that. It may sound simplistic, but don't be fooled. Gratitude is a force to be reckoned with.

Researchers have found that people who actively practice 'an attitude of gratitude' have less stress in their lives, are less fearful, and have fewer negative emotions than the rest of us. When the seed of gratitude within us is watered, we become happier and healthier people. In a weird way, gratitude is like putting on a pair of Happy Trousers. And here is a little known fact: the more we practice gratitude, the more grateful we become, which leads to finding more things to be grateful for, which leads to a deeper sense of gratitude. It's the gift that keeps on giving.

But in order to get to that place, we have to invite gratitude into our lives and make it a habit. I'm talking *actively* practice gratitude, Oprah-style. Like setting aside time to keep a Gratitude Journal, and making daily lists of everything we're grateful for.

Most people start out by being grateful for the big things in life, like 'being alive' and 'having a roof over my head'. That's wonderful, that's fantastic, but it's when we begin to feel grateful for the little things in our lives – the things we take for granted, like our clothes – that we truly start to notice the positive effects of living with gratitude.

For example, how amazing is it to find a bra that fits? Not just fits, but *really fits*. Have you ever thought about that? Or how great it is to put on a soft bathrobe after a hot shower? Especially in the middle of winter. Make it personal. Be grateful for your favourite sweater. Give your coolest dress all the praise it deserves. Make a list of all your favourite outfits and write 'THANK YOU!' next to them. Over time, living with gratitude will shift the focus from feeling like we never have enough to celebrating everything we have.

But how will this change how we shop?

By practicing gratitude you will no longer shop through the filters of Greed, Want, Boredom, or I-Have-Nothing-To-Wear. Instead you start to notice the filters themselves. This doesn't mean these filters go away overnight; dissolving them takes time (*let me tell you!*), but they will start to lose their power. So when the voice in your head demands, 'Get that dress! You need a new black dress!' you will remain as strong as a UN peacekeeper and calmly say, 'Is that so? Have you forgotten that I already have three black dresses at home? I wrote about them in my gratitude journal only yesterday. Let's not fool ourselves.'

Getting in touch with gratitude within ourselves, means getting in touch with the healing energy of mindful transformation. It's a beautiful way of getting calmer, healthier, and more present around the way we shop, think, and structure our lives.

In the spirit of gratitude, I was now ready to salute every style icon, designer, and fashion role model I'd ever had, not to mention all the shops and thrift stores I'd ever been to. Where would I be without them? How could I ever repay them? I didn't think I could, but I could say THANK YOU.

My cherished wardrobe. You have provided me with garments like the baby onesie the nurses dressed me in the day I was born, my knitted Happy Trousers, my maroon chuba skirts, and the black suit I wore the day David Cameron stopped by the Embassy after the Utøya shooting. I've always had more than enough clothes. How could I not feel grateful?

I've had the pleasure and the privilege of being married twice. Two weddings means two wedding dresses. Thank you!

I've been the lucky recipient of many gorgeous hand-me-downs. Growing up, my aunts generously padded my wardrobe with clothes from their own stock. Score! Thank you!

I'm so grateful to have a grandmother who can sew, a mother who can knit, and people in my life who inspire me to improve my own crafts and skills. You're the best!

I'm so grateful to have stylish friends who inspire me to dress better. Claire, everything you wear looks awesome. How dare you? I mean, thank you!

I'm so grateful for my very first fashion icon, my sister Maya. Watching her getting dressed in the morning was dazzling. She killed everything from white leather dresses to colourful Benetton sweaters. Right on!

I'm grateful for Jackie Kennedy, Lorelai Gilmore, and Lady Di. I hope I've done right by you.

I'm grateful for every Freebox, every sale, every vintage store, every mall, and every swapping party I've ever been to. Thank you!

I'm forever grateful for all the coats that have found their way into my life. You rock my world. Thank you!

My cherished wardrobe, you are the direct result of the hard work and sacrifices made by designers, textile workers, retailers, shop owners, and sales personnel. Thank you so, so much!

My cherished wardrobe, you are also the direct results of all the sacrifices made by Mother Nature. I'm so sorry.

My beloved, darling clothes, I salute you. You're awesome.
Yours truly.

One Last Non-Shopping Pow-Wow

How did Amy feel about all of this? What was her exit strategy? I suspected she had her own set of questions and thoughts around this, and I was dying to find out what they were.

Speculations about how we would act once we could go

shopping again had been highly entertaining.

At the very beginning of the shop-stop, I pictured myself racing out the door, running toward the nearest shops, and diving into the clothing racks in an emotional whirlwind of tears and laughter. *Come to Mama! I'm done! The shop-stop is finally over!* I would have moved on from all my shopping mistakes of the past, and I would become the best dressed person in the history of the Embassy. Amen!

Well, that wasn't going to happen.

In more altruistic moments, my imagination pushed me in the direction of, 'I'll never shop again!' Abstaining from shopping was my new way of life. I honestly believed that. For about two seconds.

When I felt truly emotional, I entertained thoughts about our shop-stop sweeping the nation (or the entire planet, why not?), sparking debates and non-violent demonstrations, and thus forcing the fast-fashion industry to change their business model and inspire people to shop less. The pollution would stop, the textile workers would be treated fairly, and Amy and I would end up on the cover of *The Times*, holding hands with the Pope and the Dalai Lama.

In more sober moments I methodically added items to the list of clothes I wanted to buy once the shop-stop was over (the stripy sweater, the boyfriend cardigan, the comfortable blazer...), and congratulated myself on thinking ahead.

Just as I was getting ready to call Amy and talk this over with her, she called me and announced that she was coming for a visit.

Fantastic! What excellent news.

First of all, a visit from Amy meant I could show her my fabulous new Country Girl lifestyle. *Can you believe this! I'm living the dream!* But more importantly, this visit meant we could have one last non-shopping pow-wow before the shop-stop challenge was officially over.

If this was a children's book, or a mommy blog, I would gladly tell you all about how Amy brought her two little girls with her, and describe the wholesome walks we all went on, and give you pointers on how to teach your kids to be less scared of cows, but I'll just skip straight to the part where Amy and I got around to talking about the shop-stop.

It was after dinner. Her girls were in their nighties and watching telly, and Amy and I had kicked off our shoes and propped ourselves up on the king-size hotel bed. We were elegantly sipping wine from the rinsing cups in the bathroom.

Amy looked serious for a second. Then she said, 'Now that the shop-stop is soon over, do you want to start shopping again?'

'No, as a matter of fact, I don't,' I said.

'Neither do I!' she said, almost laughing.

'I'm totally happy with everything I have,' she continued. 'And besides, shopping is *so* overrated.'

This was not even CLOSE to how we thought this would play out. Not for a second. But then again, we used to think of November 1 as the end, not as a new starting point.

Amy twirled her hair, a habit from childhood. It meant she was thinking. I was quiet too. There were so many thoughts flowing through my head.

'So what does this mean?' Amy eventually said. 'Does this mean we *never* shop again? Or do we continue this shop-stop pact for another year?'

Another year of not shopping? No. That didn't feel right. *Been there, done that.* Even though neither of us *wanted* to go shopping again, we agreed it would be more powerful to lift the embargo. We could shop, but we chose not to. That felt right, and totally in keeping with my new Conscious Consumer manifesto.

ME: But you know what? Let's have some rules, or guidelines.

AMY: What for?

ME: Well, I don't know about you, but even though I feel like I never want to go shopping again, I know it's going to happen one day, so when that day comes, we should have some guidelines to go by.

AMY: Like what? Only shop from ethical brands?

ME: Not necessarily. Ideally yes, but I was more thinking that when...if we ever go shopping again, then we have to truly, honestly, cross our hearts and swear to die, love whatever we buy. We need to be freaking insane about it. I mean it! No more weird compromises. No more experimenting. Agree?

AMY: I totally agree! And you know what? We should mostly shop at thrift stores. Thrift stores are green, they are ethical, and the money goes to a good cause. And it's dead cheap!

That was a GREAT guideline. I'm going to interrupt us here and write it down as a one final Emergency Shopping Guideline:

Mostly shop at thrift stores.

We came up with more guidelines. Like, we shouldn't shop for clothes we would never wear, even though we really liked them. (No flask-green dress for me then. Fine.) We still had to wear out our clothes. We still had to mend and make do. We should arrange swapping parties. We should have de-cluttering sessions and donate our unwanted clothes to charity.

AMY: If we get fat, we can't go shopping for new clothes. We have to start exercising.

ME: Agree! That's a great rule! Oh, and how about banning internet shopping?

AMY: Yes please! Do you have any idea how time-consuming shopping online is? I've wasted hours browsing online stores.

ME: Me too! Stupid eBay!

AMY: What else?

This is what being a conscious consumer is all about: acting in a responsible way and limiting our bad choices. I would describe this approach as 'adventurous with a splash of realism'.

The best part of this approach, in my opinion, was the element of flexibility. We were doing this *our* way, and there was nothing forced or fearful about it.

I just couldn't get over the fact that after twelve months of not shopping we couldn't think of a single thing we wanted to buy.

When we were done talking about our new shopping guidelines, we got busy talking about all the new experiences we wanted to have. For starters, next year's Cheltenham Literature Festival was high on our list. I'd heard about it through the Embassy, but I'd never been able to go before. I also wanted to trek the Great Wall of China, and I wanted to try out new recipes. I love cooking. Amy wanted to spend more time in her garden. So would I. Her garden is gorgeous. Amy also wanted to travel more, learn to play an instrument, and spend more quality time with her kids.

I looked over at the girls. Amy and I used to sit in front of the TV just like that, only we didn't watch cartoons, we watched *Hello Dolly, Hair, Annie,* and other musicals. We were nuts about memorising the songs and dancing around in the living room. Amy permed her hair to look more like Annie, and I thought I sounded like Barbara Streisand.

'We also have to figure out where to go on next year's girl-trip,' Amy said.

'Yes we do!' I said. 'But we don't have to think about that right now. A lot can happen in a year.'

Postscript
or
Q & A Session

Cotswolds, 2016

QUESTION:

Did you ever buy new clothes again?

ANSWER:

Yes, I did.

QUESTION:

How long did you wait after the shop-stop ended?

ANSWER:

Funny enough, just a few weeks after the shop-stop ended I got invited to attend a luncheon at a prestigious private club in London. Even thought I didn't believe the voice in my head that said, 'Private club! You need a new outfit!', I did listen to the voice that said, 'Maybe we can visit a few stores while we're in London?' So I did.

QUESTION:

What did you buy on that first shopping trip and did you stick do your new guidelines?

ANSWER:

On my first shopping trip I went to H&M, my old stomping ground. Not so much because I wanted to buy anything, but because I couldn't wait to find out how I would behave. Would I love it? Would I hate it? Would I be mindless? Would I break down and buy every item in the store? Or would I be mindful and act with dignity and grace?

I went into the store, but within ten seconds I was back outside again. The store was too crowded. Too many people. Deafening music. Way too many clothes.

OK...so I'm into regular stores anymore. Good to know. What about thrift shops?

To find out, I went to a Red Cross store right by Buckingham Palace. This store is in an old building with high ceilings and beautiful hardwood floors. It's like being in someone's private walk-in closet. The first thing I saw was a stripy sweater, the kind both Amy and I had written down on our list of things to buy once the shop-stop was over. I looked at the label. All proceeds were going to help victims in Bangladesh. So I bought it. I felt happy buying it. It's still one of my favourite sweaters.

QUESTION:
Overall, what changes have been made permanent? (i.e. do you shop primarily at thrift/vintage shops now, do you only buy things made in certain countries?)

ANSWER:
Permanent changes? That would have to be mostly shopping at thrift shops. I'm sticking to that guideline like white on rice. However, I no longer get roped into buying anything I sort of like, just because it's cheap. I still have to *really* like what I buy. But even with a vigorous screening process in place, I still only wear a fraction of the clothes I buy. That's because I still believe the voice in my head that says, 'I LOVE THIS. I will wear this all the time!' Sometimes that turns out to be true, sometimes not. I'm still learning.

QUESTION:
Have you made any shopping mistakes since the experiment ended?

ANSWER:
Yes! I bought a gorgeous Laura Ashley spring coat, royal blue with a white Peter Pan collar, super adorable. But when I asked my sister if she liked it, she said, 'Maybe if I was going to a mafia funeral.' That's when I saw how horrible the coat was, and out it went. Another mistake was a stiff long skirt. Emphasis on stiff. I looked like a tree-

trunk. I also bought a stupid office skirt that is a million sizes too small, just in case my body suddenly shrinks down to nothing. I'm still waiting for that to happen.

QUESTION:

What has been the hardest thing about being a conscious consumer, and is it still worth it?

ANSWER:

Yes, it's still worth it. Yes, it's still hard, sometimes. But it's getting easier. A few weeks ago Amy and I went back to Bath. There I tried on a gorgeous black lace dress. Totally me. Totally to die for. But...it was from a fast-fashion chain store. And...I knew I didn't need it. I couldn't think of a single time I would wear it. So I didn't buy it. The old me felt betrayed, but the new me was mighty pleased.

If you remember, I used to have this irrational fear that becoming a conscious consumer would render me boring, lame, and unhappy, but in fact I've never been happier. I shop less, but I don't miss anything. I have fewer things, but my life is rich and fulfilling. Experiences still trump possessions, but I still love a good coat. Some things never change.

Living a life that is more aligned with my values has given me the space to make healthier choices (both for me and the planet), step outside my comfort zone, and connect with some truly awesome people. I feel more balanced, connected, and alive. Wholehearted living is the way forward!

All these amazing changes because of a shop-stop challenge.

Go figure.

Acknowledgements
or
People I Would Like to Thank
or
Feeling Grateful

Because this is a work of non-fiction, I would first and foremost like to thank every single character who appears in this book. Knowingly or not, during the twelve months of the shop-stop, your lives interacted with my own personal story, which in turn interacted with the bigger issues, which helps explain how the topics and the chapters evolved along the way.

I have changed the names of some of these characters, but not all of them.

Secondly, not being a scholar, an historian, or in any way an expert on consumer culture or fashion, in writing this book I've humbly relied on the expertise, research, and writings of many fine men and women. I'm not going to provide a list of all the books I've read – or list all the links I've ploughed through on Google – but it's with profound joy and gratitude that I single out some brilliant writers and thank them in turn.

Thank you to the following writers and researchers: Lucy Siegle, Daniel Gilbert, Debra Ollivier, Kiki Feroudi Moutsatsos, Lucy Worsley, Barry Schwartz, Shelly Branch, Sue Callaway, and Mireille Guiliano. A big thank you to Coco Chanel, Elsa Schiaparelli, and Ines de la Fressange. A special thanks to Nora Ephron, Margaret Atwood, and Caitlin Moran.

In writing this book, I'm honoured to join the ranks of every person committed to the creation of a greener future and mindful living. Thank you for leading by example! We need you!

OK. Moving on.

It's a profound understatement to say that without Amy,

this book would never have been written. Thanks to her big heart, boundless humour, childlike curiosity, and deep sense of justice, she's become a lightning rod for positive change.

I would also like to thank my dear friend, editor, and proofreader Candace Palmo. Without her advice, support, and nit-picky accuracy, this book would still be in the folder marked 'Work in Progress' on my laptop. I'd be lost without her.

I'm also grateful for my proofreader Bonny Moseley. You're a life-saver. Thank you!

To my online community, Karen, Amanda, Corrie, Caroline, Margaret, Zee, and Suzanne: connecting with you through Twitter and Google+ has inspired me to do better, and to be braver. May we one day meet in person.

Thank you Glenn Sandvoss for creating such an awesome logo. May you always be happy.

To my uncle Per Dybvig – thank you for making the best book cover a girl could ever hope for. You're the best!

To the rest of my family – what a great clan to belong to. I feel so blessed.

To my darling friends – Claire, Tove, and Tale, thank you for being my cheerleaders and always having my back. I love you guys.

Nicole, I'm so glad I stole you from Ben, but I'm oh so sad you moved to Canada. We will always have Boisdale.

Charlie, you are such an inspiration. Friends for life.

Kristin, out of sight is not out of mind. Never.

Helene, my Vajra sister and guiding light. I'm thrilled to share my karma with you.

Lori, Anna, and Ali, thank you for reminding me of what's important and beautiful. You are all my true north.

To my husband Ben – thank you for being the most authentic and fearless person I know, and for being the love of my life.

To Tara – may we never be apart.

Thank you.

ABOUT THE AUTHOR

Inger D. Kenobi has worn clothes for over three decades. Having worked for two Ambassadors and one CEO, she knows about dressing the part. Having spent most of her twenties living at a Tibetan Buddhist centre, she also knows that kindness never goes out of style.

Inger began writing this book while working at the Norwegian Embassy in London. She currently lives in the Cotswolds where she and her husband run a drone filming company. They have two cats.

This is her first book.